Committees in Congress

Committees
in
Congress

Steven S. Smith and Christopher J. Deering
George Washington University

a division of
Congressional Quarterly Inc.
1414 22nd Street, N.W., Washington, D.C. 20037

Library of Congress Cataloging in Publication Data

Smith, Steven S., 1953-
    Committees in Congress.

    Includes index.
    1. United States. Congresses—Committees. 2. United States. Congress—Reform. 3. United States—Politics and government—1945-   . I. Deering, Christopher J., 1951-   . II. Title.
JK1029.S64   1984   328.73'0765   83-26175
ISBN 0-87187-262-5

To
Barbara
s.s.s.

To
the Mary Deerings
c.j.d.

Preface

Committees long have been the central structural components of Congress. They have been called petty baronies and fiefdoms, the little legislatures, the nerve ends of Congress, and the workshops and laboratories of Congress. They have been the institution's primary source of intelligence and its chief investigators. They have been crucial to the making and unmaking of congressional careers and have provided sources of power within a powerful institution. Their history, in many respects, is a reflection of the history of the nation and of the balance of power within Congress.

Change in committees is constant. Periodically, when considerable external and internal pressures mount, the move toward institutional innovation and change—some call it reform—is accelerated. Quite often these periods of procedural and structural innovation are accompanied and aided by a greater than average turnover among members. Newcomers have less of a stake in the old system and are more willing to adopt revised structures and procedures—particularly those they perceive to be personally beneficial. By the late 1970s, Congress had emerged from just such a period of dramatic change.

This study is a product of that period, although it is not about reform per se. Our interest is in how individual committees change and how they respond to change. Thus we have examined, in addition to formal procedural and structural change, a set of informal changes. In particular, we have assessed the effect that changing personal goals of committee members, shifting agendas, and evolving political environments have on committee decision-making patterns.

There is one stylistic convention that is worth brief mention. Throughout the book, the formal leaders of committees and subcommittees are referred to as "chairs." We fully recognize—and frequently have been reminded—that this term has yet to gain widespread use on Capitol Hill. Nonetheless, we believe that it is neither so grating nor so lacking in usage that it should be avoided here.

Of the many people who have supported this project, Jean L. Woy, formerly of CQ Press, deserves special thanks for her early interest in our research. We are very grateful for her support.

We are indebted to several scholars for their advice and criticism. Roger Davidson, Mary Musca, Bruce Oppenheimer, Robert Peabody, and Bruce Ray each read part or all of the manuscript and made numerous helpful suggestions. Judy Schneider shared her expertise and her treasure-trove of information with us (for which she asked recognition only in footnotes). And numerous other colleagues offered guidance and continuing encouragement during the long gestation of this project. They will see that the manuscript has been improved in many ways because of their efforts and that (as stubborn authors are inclined to do) we have ignored some of their advice. We happily share credit for the improvements.

Joanne Daniels' support kept the project moving ahead and her advice has led to many improvements in the final product. Mary McNeil provided indispensable design and editorial assistance and through her efforts the book now has a look of its own. Everyone at CQ provided the sort of professional support about which we had heard; we can now tell that story from our own personal experience.

The Everett McKinley Dirksen Congressional Leadership Research Center and the University Research Committee of George Washington University provided much needed financial support for several aspects of the research. Lisa Handley, Roger Lukoff, and especially Nathaniel Richmond supplied first-rate research assistance. Marcia Sleight, Margaret Ruffner, Mike Smith, Ann Sweeney, Theresa Volmer, and Matthew Zuliani also provided assistance at various points along the way.

Finally, we thank those current and former members of Congress and staff who patiently answered our questions about congressional committee politics.

Steven S. Smith and Christopher J. Deering

Table of Contents

List of Tables and Figures

Appendix

Committees in Congress

Introduction

Outside of traffic, there is nothing that has held this country back as much as committees.

Will Rogers

Understanding how committees work is vital to understanding legislative decision making in Congress. The vast majority of policy disputes on Capitol Hill are resolved before or during committee consideration of bills, and legislation is seldom considered on the House or Senate floor without a committee's stamp of approval. The careers and reputations of individual members of Congress also are molded in important ways by their committee activities. It is through committees that members most frequently make their contributions to policy, gain media and constituency attention for their involvement with an issue or cause, and develop their closest working relationships with colleagues, executive officials, and lobbyists.

Like their counterparts elsewhere, congressional committees long have been a focal point of frustration about legislative delays, inaction, inefficiency, and ineffectiveness. In the 1950s and 1960s, powerful committee chairs and overlapping committee jurisdictions were the major targets of complaints. By the 1970s dissatisfaction was sufficient enough to stimulate a series of reforms designed to spread control of committee activities more widely and to readjust committee jurisdictions to new issues facing Congress. But frustrations and irritations continue. Some members feel that Congress did not go far enough to renovate its operating structure and procedures, while others argue that reforms have gone too far.

Many observers have argued that the primary effect of changes made in the last 15 years has been to exacerbate the fragmented nature of congressional decision making. The increased number and independence of subcommittees have caused the most stir, leading some observers to describe congressional decision making as "subcommittee government." This description is more accurate for the House than the Senate, but in both chambers junior members' demands to gain a "piece of the

1

Table I-1 Standing Committees of the Senate and Their Counterpart House Committees, 98th Congress

Senate	House
Agriculture	Agriculture
Appropriations	Appropriations
Armed Services	Armed Services
Banking, Housing, and Urban Affairs	Banking, Finance, and Urban Affairs
Budget	Budget
	Energy and Commerce
Commerce, Science, and Technology	Merchant Marine and Fisheries
	Science and Technology
Energy and Natural Resources	Interior
Environment and Public Works	Public Works and Transportation
Finance	Ways and Means
Foreign Relations	Foreign Affairs
	District of Columbia
Governmental Affairs	Government Operations
	Post Office and Civil Service
Judiciary	Judiciary
Labor and Human Resources	Education and Labor
	Rules
Rules and Administration	House Administration
	Standards of Official Conduct
Small Business	Small Business
Veterans' Affairs	Veterans' Affairs

Source: "Committees and Subcommittees of the 98th Congress," *Congressional Quarterly Weekly Report, Special Report*, April 2, 1983.

action" have at times been translated into demands for greater decentralization *within* committees. Through chairing and participating in small subcommittees, junior members can take up issues of their own choosing and craft legislation as they see fit. Increasingly, initial policy decisions have been made within the *subcommittees* of Congress. Rather than complain about dictatorial full committee chairs, members now commonly decry the lack of "responsible leadership" and the presence of "runaway subcommittees." The disintegration and incoherence of congressional decision making is a frequent theme in critiques of Congress.

And yet, past experience indicates that it is unwise to be satisfied with broad generalizations about congressional committees. This is the central lesson of Richard Fenno's *Congressmen in Committees,* a study of six House and six Senate committees in the 1960s.[1] Fenno discovered that committees differ in two vital ways: in the nature of their political environments and in the personal goals of their members. As committee environments differ, so do demands placed on committee members. And members' goals dictate the nature of legislative products that committees seek to create. Together, environments and members' goals shape relations among committee members, especially the formal and informal mechanisms they devise for making committee decisions.

Just as Fenno observed that committees *differ* in important ways, it also must be noted that committees *change* in a variety of ways. Changes, in particular policy agendas, membership composition, and committee members' attitudes and goals, may enhance, moderate, or even counter the effects of formal alterations in committee structure and procedure. Thus, among other things, decentralization patterns among House and Senate committees may be quite varied. Committee-specific changes must be understood before broad interpretations of trends in committee politics can be made. The focus of this study, therefore, is the *variety in the patterns of change* among congressional committees since the late 1960s. This attention to variety requires that we take advantage of previous scholarship, especially that of Fenno, who identifies fundamental ways in which committees and their members differ.[2] It also requires that the study's central components be defined to capture the dynamic quality of political relationships. A model of change in individual committees is diagrammed in Figure 1.

We seek to explain the significance of environmental change and changes in formal structures and procedures for committee members' personal political goals and the decision-making processes of their committees. Special care should be taken not to confuse the model of change in individual committees with a theory of change in Congress as a whole. If we were attempting to explain change in Congress, we certainly would treat environmental and member goal changes as major determinants of structural and procedural change. This subject, which is beyond the scope of the model, is treated briefly in Chapters 1 and 2. The individual committee is the unit of analysis specified in the model. Thus, for this study, changes in statute, chamber rules, or party rules are external to a committee and are properly viewed as exogenous to other variables in the model.

Organizational and procedural changes are specified in the model as having three major potential effects. First, they may reshape commit-

Figure I-1   Model of Change in Individual Committees

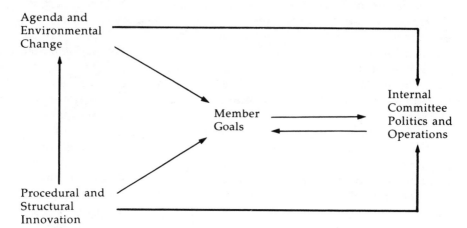

tee jurisdictions, thus redefining committees' agendas and changing the identities of interested outsiders. Second, reform may affect committee sizes and member assignment limitations, thereby encouraging or discouraging change in the membership of particular committees. And, of course, reform may directly modify the formal decision-making procedures and internal operations of committees. Chapter 2 describes the nature of the 1970s reforms; we consider their effects throughout the rest of the book.

Issue agendas, and the identities of individuals and groups placing demands on committees are very closely related and therefore are treated together throughout this study. These factors are shaped primarily by events outside members' immediate control, although jurisdictional reform and members' actions can play a critical role at times. Changes in issues and pressures can affect the attractiveness of committees by influencing the mix of political objectives members can pursue in them. In addition, the nature of issues and political coalitions can directly affect relations among committee members, including relations between full and subcommittee chairs, staff, and other persons involved in decision making. Chapter 3 explores the different types of agenda and external-actor changes that occurred between the late 1960s and early 1980s.

As Fenno demonstrated so convincingly in his study of committees in the 1960s, committees differ in the degree to which their members emphasize reelection, which we have broadened to constituency-related concerns, good public policy, and influence in the chamber.[3] Membership turnover can shift the balance among committee members' goals. Chapter 4 outlines the nature of committee members' personal political goals and considers how those goals have changed as the membership, operating procedures, and committee agendas have changed.

Along with reform and agenda change, shifting member goals can be a major determinant of patterns of change in committee decision-making processes. At any one time, a committee's procedures and agenda offer its members a set of opportunities to pursue their particular mix of political objectives. Those objectives lead to varying demands for participation in committee decisions, varying tolerances of strong leadership from committee chairs, varying staffing requirements, and varying levels and forms of political conflict. As the mix of objectives shifts, the character of these demands, tolerances, and conflicts can be expected to change as well. Chapters 5, 6, and 7 examine the patterns of change in committee decision making, leadership, and staff utilization, focusing especially on the degree of committee decentralization.

The research strategy employed here differs from previous research on congressional committees in several ways. Rather than suggesting that we train a microscope on each of just a handful of committees, our interest in variety and broader judgments about recent changes in Congress dictated that we include all standing committees of the House and Senate in our study. A comparison of House and Senate committees is especially important, permitting a review of those with similar agendas yet different memberships and chamber rules for committee procedure. The breadth of the analysis necessitates an inability to examine each committee in as much detail as it deserves. Our approach requires that the choice of committee characteristics be selective and that the use of quotations from committee participants be limited. Nevertheless, we believe that our observations are sufficiently well focused to permit valid conclusions.

Unlike previous studies with a cross-sectional focus, our post hoc examination of committee change risks falling into what methodologists call a "post-test only" study. While we have interviewed 187 committee members and staff, the restriction of those interviews to 1981-1983 may result in rather poor descriptions of committee politics during the late 1960s, providing a weak basis for assessing change since that time. We have attempted to avoid this pitfall by (1) utilizing primary documentary sources that provide comparable data on committee activities and decisions for the entire period, (2) drawing upon written descriptions of committee politics by contemporary political scientists, journalists, and participants, and (3) interviewing experienced members and committee staff who have observed their committees through most of the 1967-1983 period.

Like previous studies of congressional committees, this study primarily reflects the experiences and perceptions of the committee members and staff we have interviewed.[4] In nearly all cases, we guaranteed the interviewees anonymity to encourage candid responses to our questions. Throughout the book, we have sought to use the documentary record creatively to reinforce participants' observations and to provide a basis for the broad comparisons of central concern.

NOTES

1. Richard F. Fenno, *Congressmen in Committees* (Boston: Little, Brown & Co., 1973). Also see George Goodwin, Jr., *The Little Legislatures* (Amherst: University of Massachusetts Press, 1970).
2. Fenno, ibid.
3. Fenno, ibid., Chap. 1.
4. Fenno, *Congressmen in Committees*, and *The Power of the Purse* (Boston: Little, Brown & Co., 1966); Goodwin, *The Little Legislatures*; John F. Manley, *The Politics of Finance* (Boston: Little, Brown & Co., 1970); David Price, *Who Makes the Laws* (Cambridge, Mass.: Schenkman Publishing Co., 1972).

Development of the Congressional Committee Systems | 1

Congressional reorganization is a continuous political process. Not only do congressional rules, procedures, and structures change, but a constant interplay exists between these formal, highly visible aspects of organization and the ongoing interactions among participants in the policy process. A particular organizational arrangement can either enhance or inhibit the ability of individuals and groups to achieve their political goals. As a result, interpretations of congressional organization fluctuate with the shifting political strengths and strategies of participants.

Committees, as central components of the congressional infrastructure, have played a wide variety of roles in the legislative process, roles that differ from committee to committee and that change as various members' goals, powers, and strategies evolve. This book describes and explains the dynamics of committee politics during the last 15 years. This chapter outlines the development of the committee systems of the House of Representatives and the Senate, providing a context in which to view changes made during the 1970s and 1980s.

Participation and Structure

Congress's development frequently has been characterized as varying along a continuum running from highly centralized to highly decentalized. In highly centralized institutions, decisions are made by a single individual or, at least, by a very few individuals acting in concert. The individual is given the formal and informal tools to shape important decisions. In contrast, successive decisions within highly decentralized bodies are made by separate individuals or small groups of individuals. No single person or group dominates decision making.

For the purpose of placing recent Congresses in their developmental context a somewhat more complex view is required, although the centralization/decentralization continuum occasionally will serve as a useful summary perspective. Two interrelated dimensions of congressional decision-making patterns, participation and structure, must be considered.[1]

The participation dimension describes the number of individuals with an effective voice in decision making. Participation is greatest when all members are permitted to contribute substantially to decisions. Movement away from such perfect participation—that is, movement toward proportionately fewer potential participants—may take one of two general forms: (1) the same small group of individuals controlling most decisions or (2) distinctions being drawn between types of decisions, with different subgroups controlling separate sets of decisions. These forms are recognizable as centralizing or decentralizing changes, respectively. The important feature to note is that the perfect participation situation does not fall neatly on the centralization/decentralization continuum. Rather, both centralization and decentralization imply restricted participation, with the difference lying in the manner of restriction.

The structural dimension concerns the number of sub-organizational units (or degree of "pluralization") within which significant decisions are made.[2] Of course, a close but imperfect relationship exists between participation and the number of such units, as the centralization/decentralization continuum suggests. At the centralized end of the continuum, a single unit, for example the office of a party leader, would control the decisions of the chamber. At the decentralized end, many units, each with a separate jurisdictional sphere, would control decisions; members' participation is limited to shaping decisions of these separate units. In addition to these two plausible alternatives, other forms are possible. A single unit, a committee of the whole, so to speak, may be composed of all of the members of the body, and that unit may be the focus of the body's decision-making activities. Moreover, a handful of individuals may make most decisions for the full body through their membership in various other units of the formal decision-making structure. This subgroup therefore forms an effective, informal decision-making body with a variety of formal identities.

Throughout the nearly 200-year history of Congress, various participatory and structural forms have been played out. Most of them, however, do not fit the popular conception of decision-making patterns as simply centralized or decentralized. To examine the development of congressional organization, we have somewhat arbitrarily identified six periods that parallel changes in the number of standing committees in the two chambers. The six periods are illustrated in Figure 1-1.

Standing committees were used infrequently during the period of the earliest Congresses. The standing committee systems grew and acquired most of their essential functions during the second period, prior to the Civil War. In the latter half of the nineteenth century, standing committees proliferated in both houses but eventually were brought under the control of majority party leaders. Following the revolt against Speaker Joseph Cannon of Illinois in 1909-1910, a process of consolidation occurred. Party leaders had less of a hold on the policy process. By the late 1940s the legislative process was dominated by powerful committee chairs in newly reorganized committee systems, setting the stage for the reform movement of the late 1960s and 1970s (see Chapter 2).

Figure 1-1 Number of Congressional Standing Committees, 1789-1983

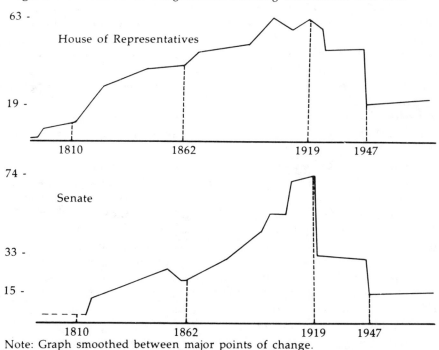

Note: Graph smoothed between major points of change.

Source: *The Congressional Directory*; Lauris G. McConachie, *Congressional Committees*, (New York: Thomas Y. Crowell, 1898); *Annals of Congress; Register of Debates in Congress; Congressional Globe; Journal of the House; Journal of the Senate; The Congressional Record.*

The Early Congresses: 1789-1809

Many members of the first Congresses, influenced by the experiences of the Continental Congress, their colonial and state legislatures, and the British House of Commons, held strong views about how their new legislative process should operate. The desire to devise mechanisms allowing the full expression of the will of congressional majorities while maintaining the equality of all legislators inspired attitudes about the legislative process that would be quite alien to modern legislators.[3] The fundamental assumption was that all legislators were capable of ascertaining and evaluating the relevant facts for each issue facing Congress. As a result, members of the first Congresses preferred that each chamber, as a whole, determine general policy by "majority decisions through rational discussion and mutual enlightenment" prior to entrusting a subgroup of the membership with the responsibility to devise detailed legislation.[4]

The House of Representatives, which shouldered the greatest legislative burden in the early Congresses by acting first on most matters, led the way in creating legislative procedures. One of the most important was a parliamentary creature called the "committee of the whole," designed to maximize members' participation by minimizing structural constraints. A committee of the whole operates as a committee but is composed of all members of the House. Most significant policy questions, and many less significant ones, were considered first by the entire House membership in the flexible procedural setting of this committee, where a relatively free exchange among members was permitted.

Thus, for the first eight or nine Congresses, House committees usually took the form of special or select committees that devised legislation on particular topics in concurrence with policy principles established by the House. Several hundred of these small ad hoc committees were created in the House (and the Senate) during this early period. Because legislators feared that committees with substantial policy discretion and permanence might distort the will of the majority, the select committees were dissolved upon the completion of their tasks. This approach retained original debate and policy determination for the full membership, yet turned over the drafting of details to more manageable select committees.

The House, nevertheless, began to develop the foundations of a standing committee system at an early point, establishing a few permanent committees in routine policy areas and in other recurrent, complex policy areas requiring regular investigation.[5] The House had created 10 standing committees by the end of this first period. For example, the Interstate and Foreign Commerce Committee, which became the Energy and Commerce Committee in 1981, was created in 1795, and the Committee on Ways and Means, which still retains that title, was established as a standing committee in 1802. These committees ranged in size from three to seventeen members at the time of their creation, while membership in the House grew from 64 members in the First Congress to 142 members in the 10th. Gradually, the practice of first referral to a committee of the whole began to lose its signifi- cance, and the committees began to assume more discretion in writing legislation. As early as the Fourth Congress, parts of presidential messages to Congress routinely were sent, without directives, to committees. On other legislative matters, discussion of principles in a committee of the whole had less influence on the final legislative product, depending upon the nature of the issue and the willingness of the House to struggle with the policy principles involved.[6]

In its formative years, the Senate used select committees exclusively on legislative matters, creating only four standing committees to deal with internal housekeeping matters: the Joint Committee on Enrolled Bills, the Committee on Engrossed Bills, the Committee on the Library, and the Committee to Audit and Control the Contingent Expenses of the Senate. While senators shared with their House colleagues a distrust of permanent committees, the Senate used its select committees with greater flexibility than did the House.[7]

> Select committees were limited to the technical job of legislative drafting; others were directed to make policy recommendations; still others were told to do both. These tasks were assigned either before or after, or both before and after, initial floor consideration. The Senate treated its select committees as convenient tools to be employed in any manner most appropriate to the matter at hand.[8]

A smaller membership, greater flexibility in floor procedure, and a much lighter workload—with the Senate always waiting for the House to act first on legislation—permitted the Senate to use select committees in a wider variety of ways than did the House, while still maintaining full chamber control over legislation. Debate by the entire Senate prior to referral of legislation to a select committee was the norm. But in 1806 the Senate adopted the practice of referring to a committee all matters relating to the subject for which the committee had been created. For example, the committees created to consider the various parts of the president's annual message to Congress continued to receive all related matters throughout the session. These "sessional" committees exhibited some continuity of jurisdiction from Congress to Congress, providing a rationale for creating permanent standing committees.

In the early Congresses, the chamber majority created select committees composed of individuals in agreement with the majority's views. As Thomas Jefferson's *Manual of Parliamentary Practice* put it, "the child is not to be put to a nurse that cares not for it." [9] Beginning in 1790, each House committee was appointed by the Speaker, with the primary sponsor of a legislative proposal typically appointed as chair. The House retained the authority to make committee assignments by other means if it should decide, by majority vote, to do so—such as when there was some suspicion that the Speaker could not be trusted to appoint proponents of the legislation under consideration. The Senate chose its committees by ballot, and the chair usually was given to whomever received the most votes in the balloting. Committee assignments in both houses also were made with some concern for geographical balance, knowledge, and expertise. Indeed, attempts were made to provide representation for each state on important House committees until the increasing number of states made it impractical to continue the practice. In both chambers, partisanship, which often was related to policy views, quickly became the primary criterion for assignment.

Initially, committee chairs were conceived merely as agents or moderators of the committees. [10] By the beginning of the nineteenth century, however, several House and Senate committee chairs dominated their committees' activities, determining when and where the committees would meet and controlling their proceedings while in session. In fact, a committee chair's ability to delay committee action became a widely recognized problem in the second term of Thomas Jefferson's administration. Acting on behalf of Jefferson, John Randolph, chairman of the House Ways and Means Committee, was responsible for long delays in moving his committee to action on matters the president wanted to stall or kill. As a result of such abuses, the House adopted a rule in the Eighth Congress that permitted committees to elect their own chairs if they so desired. The House adopted a further rule in the Ninth Congress that allowed any two members of a committee to call a meeting of their committee. [11]

In both the House and the Senate, then, the use of committees was dictated by the desire to maximize the participation of the full membership in decision making. Full participation, in turn, required that each chamber depend as little as possible on a permanent structure of committees and, where committees were necessary, to carefully limit their authority and tenure. Even in this early period, movement away from this ideal could be seen. Practical and political considerations hastened that movement in the following years.

Institutionalization
of the Committee Systems: 1810-1865 _____

In the 50-year period prior to the Civil War, the standing committee systems of both chambers became institutional fixtures. Both houses of Congress shifted from using select committees to using standing committees, regularly adding to the number of standing committees while eliminating or combining few of them. In the House, the number of standing committees increased from 10 to 28 between 1810 and 1825 and to 39 by the beginning of the Civil War. The Senate established its first significant standing committees in 1816, when it created 12. Of these 12, Foreign Relations, Finance, and Judiciary have retained their names up to the present, although their jurisdictions have been altered several times. The Senate standing committee system had grown to 22 committees by the time of the Civil War. In both houses the standing committees remained small in size. House standing committees ranged from three to nine members, although three committees reached 15 or 16 members for short periods of time. Senate committees typically had only three members in the early 1800s but had grown to six members by 1860.[12]

Several factors played important roles in the expansion and institutionalization of the committee systems.[13] For the House, the most immediate consideration was the growth of its workload, which made it increasingly difficult for members to meet demands without some division of labor. Issues and events such as western expansion, the development of interstate and international trade, and the War of 1812 placed increasing demands on the federal government and stimulated committee growth in Congress. The dramatic growth in the size of the House—an increase from 64 members in the First Congress to 241 in the 29th (1833-1835)—complicated matters. The size of the House alone made rational discussions of principles, originally envisioned to take place in a committee of the whole, impractical.

The importance of committees to members of Congress also increased with the rising political significance of direct congressional interaction with the executive departments.[14] Following the Jefferson administration, the antifederalist coalition continued to disintegrate, and relatively weak Republican presidents were unable to control factionalism within Congress and the executive branch. Joseph Cooper argues that

> what occured once presidential power declined was intensification of the long-run process of mutual reinforcement on the part of departments and smaller committees. In this continuing process departments provided committees with expert information and advice, detailed plans, and prestige in exchange for political support. This in turn made smaller committees more influential on the floor and increased the need for departments to work through them. Moreover, in the case of select committees it had the additional effect of generating pressure for regular appointment and stable, general jurisdiction, for conversion into standing committees.[15]

Committee-department interaction increased the value of committee activity for rank-and-file members seeking special influence in a particular policy area.

Finally, the Speaker of the House began to forcefully exercise the committee appointment power to gain control over committee consideration of major pieces of legislation. Henry Clay of Kentucky, who assumed the speakership in 1811 and served as Speaker for six nonconsecutive terms over the next 15 years, transformed the role of Speaker into one of policy leadership and increased the partisan significance of committee activity.[16] Rather than allowing the full House first to determine the nature of the legislation to be written, Clay preferred to have a somewhat stable group of members supportive of his policy views write the legislation and shape a winning coalition before bringing it to the floor. Standing committees served this function very well for Clay, and he encouraged their creation during his speakership.

These developments were accompanied by two procedural changes that further transformed the role of House committees. First, the practice of referring legislation to a committee of the whole prior to referral to a select or standing committee was completely discontinued by the end of the 1820s.[17] Instead, first referral to a standing or select committee became the norm. Second, the original procedure requiring the House to grant a leave before a committee could report a bill to the floor was discontinued. The new procedure of allowing committees to report at their own discretion was codified into the rules of the House in 1822.[18] With these two changes, House standing committees gained a routinized role in the consideration of virtually all legislation.

The changes in the operation of the House committee system coincided with a fundamental and lasting shift in members' views toward the proper relationship between participation and structure.[19] While policy control by the House majority continued to be a dominant principle, a division of labor through standing committees came to be seen as a necessity. Preliminary debate by the full House came to be viewed as a useless procedure, and full membership participation soon was reserved solely for individual committee decisions. Restricted participation in a committee setting gradually was perceived as the appropriate approach to determining both general policy principles and the details of legislation. And, in contrast to the select committee practice, the House came to recognize that the minority should receive representation on standing committees.

By degrees, then, the standing committees became much more than mere agents of the House. Tough policy decisions increasingly were made at the committee stage and internal committee politics became vital to the proponents and opponents of legislation. Moreover, committee members increasingly were expected to become specialists in committee affairs. This required that some apprenticeship period be served prior to active participation in committee decision making. After all, if committees were to play a central role within their policy spheres, their members should be particularly well qualified to be entrusted with that role. This was a major shift from the earlier assumption that all members could collect and digest the information required to arrive at rational decisions on the floor of the House. Of course, the power of committees was tempered by the right of the House to discharge legislation from committees when they were slow to act and to review committee decisions on the floor. But along with committee expertise came a sense of deference to that expertise that limited the use of the discharge authority and the comprehensiveness of floor review. It should not be forgotten that such behavioral norms worked to the advantage of the majority party, which controlled the committees through the use of the Speaker's appointment power.

Pressures for change in the Senate's committee system were not so great as they were in the House of Representatives. The Senate mainly depended on House-passed bills for its legislative agenda. As a result, the Senate could manage its legislative agenda in serial fashion, depending less on the simultaneous consideration of a broad range of legislation in committees. Moreover, the Senate did not grow in size so quickly as did the House. In 1835, for example, the Senate had only 48 members—fewer members than the House had during the First Congress. Finally, the development of party activity in the Senate had the effect of deemphasizing committee decisions, in sharp contrast to the House. There were no party leaders in the Senate who could control standing committees during most of the antebellum period. In fact, factional rivalries motivated at least a dozen changes in the method of appointing committees during this period, as senators sought to devise mechanisms to suit their political advantage. Committees and their chairs often opposed the majority party leaders' policy positions. Consequently, Senate party leaders assumed the personal responsibility of managing most of the important legislation on the floor. They often did not seek to have legislation referred to committee in the first place.[20] Ironically, it was Henry Clay, as Senate Whig leader during the 1830s, who was particularly careful to avoid unfriendly committees.

As a result, the Senate's standing committees, with one or two important exceptions, played a relatively insignificant role in the legislative process prior to the Civil War.[21] Committees were given the authority to report bills at their own discretion on all subjects referred to them in 1817, but they seldom made important revisions, and often their reported legislation was not considered on the floor. In fact, the debates on Senate committee reform in 1856 indicated that 15 Senate committees simply had nothing to do.[22] Nonetheless, assignments to such committees retained political value because membership, and particularly the chairmanship, on some of them, was prestigious and allowed members ready access to executive officials. Committee chairs also could hire clerks who were commonly used as personal secretaries, and a committee usually could be maintained on the grounds that future legislative business was foreseen. Nearly all important decisions were made when the legislation was before the full Senate. This, indeed, was the heyday of great floor debate led by several of the most renowned orators in Senate history: John C. Calhoun, Henry Clay, and Daniel Webster.

The House and Senate also continued to differ in their development of committee assignment procedures. The Speaker of the House continued to appoint committee members throughout this early period. But committee assignments were not a simple responsibility that the Speaker managed routinely. To the contrary, assignment decisions often were part of the bargaining process for the speakership itself and, as has been noted, they were a central component of an elected Speaker's efforts to control the House on behalf of his party or faction. Prior service and the developing norm of giving minority party members some representation on committees in proportion to their representation in the full House tempered the Speaker's discretion in making assignments. Yet Speakers seldom permitted placement of minority and senior members on committees that might subvert partisan policy goals. The earlier rule giving committees the option to elect their own chairs was allowed to expire as the Speaker's control over the process increased.

In contrast, although political parties eventually gained control over committee assignments, the procedures for making those assignments never stabilized in the Senate.[23] The Senate experimented with committee appointment by ballot, by the vice president, by the president pro tempore, and by combinations of these procedures. In the mid-1840s the Senate used a procedure of suspending Senate rules and adopting committee lists drawn by the leaders of the two major parties. The majority party allocated fewer seats on each committee to the minority party than their proportion in the chamber might dictate, but minority leaders were given the discretion to make minority assignments as they saw fit, a procedure that later would become routine. But when the Democrats assumed control of the Senate in 1849, they returned to the practice of having the president pro tempore, who the majority party controlled, make committee appointments.

While many congressional committee chairs gained public notoriety during this period, party leaders in both chambers prevented them from becoming the dominant political powers within the spheres of their committees' jurisdictions. Speakers of the House appointed chairs, like other committee members, with an eye toward retaining control over major policy decisions. There was a tendency to reappoint chairs to their former posts, but that practice was subservient to the Speaker's political preferences.[24] Senate committee chairs showed greater stability during this period, generally changing only with turnover in membership and changes in party control of the Senate (with the exception of a brief period when chairs were rotated among committee members of the majority party). As in the House, chairs normally cooperated with party leaders and, when there was conflict between the two, the leaders were able to keep legislation on the floor without referral or to have it referred to a select committee.[25] Both House and Senate committee chairs often assumed nearly dictatorial powers within their committees, occasionally presenting them with completely drafted legislation if the issue was even discussed, completing the majority party leaders' chain of command.[26]

By the 1860s the practice of hiring committee clerks at public expense had become routine in both the House and the Senate. Also, committees regularly were assigned rooms in the Capitol to conduct their business. Because many committees had no business to conduct, the rooms and clerks simply became perquisites of office for committee chairs. Senate committees usually could obtain approval to hire a clerk for one session or Congress at a time.[27] The House kept a tighter rein on the hiring of committee clerks, adopting a rule in 1838 that required committees to receive special approval from the full House before hiring a clerk. Approval routinely was given to most committees, however.[28]

17

By the Civil War, standing committees had assumed a central role in the legislative process. Although committees still played a limited role by today's standards, questions about the fundamental functions of congressional committees had disappeared. The House floor and, especially, the Senate floor continued to be critical decision-making centers, but increasingly the participation of rank-and-file members was constrained by the committee systems.

Expanding the Committee Systems: 1866-1918

In the half-century following the Civil War, the role of committees was strongly influenced by three factors. First, the country's dramatic economic, geographic, and population growth placed new and greater demands on the Congress, which responded with more legislation and new committees. Second, further development of American political parties and the increasing strength of congressional party leaders, especially in the late nineteenth century, led to an even greater integration of congressional parties and committee systems. Third, members of Congress, first in the Senate and then in the House, increasingly viewed service in Congress as a desirable long-term career, which in turn increased the personal significance of congressional organization, particularly the committee systems, for rank-and-file members. By the end of this period, these often-conflicting pressures resulted in bloated standing committee systems that needed reform.

Both House and Senate committee systems continued to expand during the late 1800s. A strong tendency existed to create new committees to meet new policy demands rather than to enlarge or reorganize old committees' jurisdictions. Quite often, leaders and other members were unwilling to entrust certain types of legislation to the senior members of old committees. Majority party leaders also found useful the flexibility in making committee assignments allowed by a large number of committees. And the perquisites of chairs and the political value of claiming membership on some committees continued to make it difficult to eliminate committees. By 1918 the House had acquired nearly 60 committees and the Senate, thanks to a blanket grant of standing committee status to many select committees in 1913, had 74 committees. Nearly half of these probably had no legislative or investigative business; in the early 1900s, junior members regularly complained about receiving assignments to committees that never met.[29]

Further structural complexity developed in Congress's committee systems with the creation of subcommittees, a development that would come to have much greater significance later in the twentieth century. Although the historical record does not identify when subcommittees were first used or give a precise count of their number, a member of Congress reported in 1915 that about 35 House committees and 27 Senate committees were using formal subcommittees on a regular basis. About half of those committees had permanent or standing subcommittees.[30] Even in the early 1900s, active committees' workloads, especially those with appropriations authority, made further division of labor desirable, if only to make it easier for them to establish quorums to conduct business. The standing subcommittee structure within committees further reduced the number of members participating in the initial development of legislation.

The most important jurisdictional changes during this period concerned money matters. The House Ways and Means and Senate Finance committees' expenditure and revenue-raising responsibilities increased dramatically during the Civil War. Their increased burdens and power stimulated successful efforts in both houses to create separate appropriations committees in the mid-1860s.[31] Personal, factional, and intercommittee antagonisms later led to a further distribution of appropriations authority to several other committees of the House and the Senate. By 1900 the unified control over government financial matters originally invested in the Ways and Means and Finance committees had been distributed among nearly 20 committees.

These structural developments did not lead automatically to a more "decentralized" Congress. To the contrary, majority party leaders of both chambers used the restricted participation imposed by the committee systems as an integral part of maintaining control over decision making. In the House, the period between the Civil War and 1910 brought a series of activist Speakers—Samuel J. Randall, John G. Carlisle, Thomas B. Reed, and Joseph G. "Uncle Joe" Cannon—who substantially expanded their control over the flow of legislation.[32] These Speakers aggressively used the committee appointment power to stack important committees with friendly members and to take advantage of a new bill-referral power to send legislation to friendly committees. In addition, these Speakers asserted that a petition to discharge a bill from a committee was not a privileged motion; assumed the discretion, without appeal, to recognize members seeking to speak on the floor; transformed the Rules Committee into a standing committee chaired by the Speaker; and gave the Rules Committee the authority to report special orders that set the floor agenda for the consideration of legislation. Special orders were particularly important because they could set the length of debate and the number and type of amendments allowed. These powers gave

19

the Speaker the ability to grant a right-of-way to certain legislation. They also allowed him to block legislation by selectively recognizing members on the floor or by clogging the floor agenda with preferred legislation. Through the appointment process and the Speaker's control over the flow of legislation on the floor, committees often served as the Speaker's extended arms.

Senate organization in the years following the Civil War was dictated by Republicans who controlled that chamber for all but two Congresses between 1860 and 1913. The Republicans emerged from the war with no party leader or faction capable of controlling the Senate. Relatively independent committees and committee chairs became the dominant force in Senate deliberations.[33] By the late 1890s, however, elections had made the Senate Republican party a smaller and more homogeneous group, and a coterie of like-minded Republicans had ascended to leadership positions. This group controlled the party's Committee on Committees, which made committee assignments, and the Steering Committee, which controlled the legislative schedule of the Senate.[34] These developments made all Senate committees handling important legislation the instruments of an interlocking directorate of party leaders.

Despite party leaders' control over committee assignments in the House and Senate in the late nineteenth century, their discretion increasingly was constrained by the emerging norm of seniority. The seniority principle gave committee chairs to members with the longest service on each committee and allowed members to remain on a committee as long as they wished. This seldom constrained party leaders because senior members of their party generally held political views similar to their own. Seniority gained importance earlier in the Senate than in the House. This was due, at least in part, to the fact that the House had developed a regular appointment procedure at an early date, while the Senate had struggled with conflict-ridden assignments in nearly every Congress up to the Civil War. Seniority provided a routinized process that minimized conflict among most senators. It also was consistent with the developing careerism prevalent in the Senate, which made rank-and-file members more concerned about their long-range committee responsibilities and power and less willing to depend upon the whims of party leaders.[35] Thus, even by the 1870s, seniority had become the standard guide for making Senate committee assignments and chair selections. By the turn of the century it had become an "iron-clad formula." [36]

Committee assignments continued to play a part in politicking for the speakership in the House, frequently causing Speakers to violate the seniority system by rewarding supporters and ostracizing opponents. By the late nineteenth century intraparty speakership contests had diminished in intensity, and more House members were aspiring to long careers in the chamber. In fact, during the last 20 years of the nineteenth century, the number of violations of the seniority rule had dropped from well over half of all appointments to approximately a third of the cases. Nevertheless, violations of seniority continued in approximately a quarter of the House committee chair appointments during the early 1900s, and violations of the principle also were common in rank-and-file appointments.[37] By the turn of the century, real discretion in committee assignments for both House and Senate party leaders was limited primarily to new members.

The increasing use of seniority as a guide to committee assignments in the House was reversed, albeit temporarily, in the first decade of the twentieth century. Republican Speaker Joseph Cannon from Illinois employed his appointment and recognition powers to block the legislative efforts of progressives within his own party. In 1907, for example, Cannon failed to reappoint four progressive incumbent committee chairs and passed over three other senior members in line for chairs. The removal of the incumbent chairs after a Speaker's first term—in ways unrelated to building a coalition in the speakership contest—was unprecedented.[38] It also bucked the trend toward a more routine application of the seniority principle at a time when members were seeking longer, more secure careers in the House. These nearly dictatorial actions, combined with the ideological differences underlying them, stimulated a revolt against Cannon by Republican insurgents and opposition Democrats.

The most important lasting product of the revolt was in the composition of the Rules Committee. New House rules prohibited the Speaker from membership on the committee, expanded the size of the committee, and stripped away the Speaker's power to appoint the committee's members. It was hoped that an elected Rules Committee would be more representative of House opinion in its consideration of special orders and changes in House rules.[39]

When the Democrats gained control of the House after the 1910 elections, major changes were instituted in their committee assignment procedures. The Democrats transferred assignment authority for their caucus from the Speaker to the Democratic members of the Committee on Ways and Means. Because the majority leader typically chaired Ways and Means, the power remained in the leadership's hands, although not in the hands of the Speaker. Democratic leaders also used the temporarily cohesive party caucus, the so-called "King Caucus," to bind party members to policy positions. The caucus's cohesiveness began to wane in 1916, reducing the effectiveness of Majority Leader Oscar Underwood's centralized control and resulting in a decline in the use of the caucus and in violations of seniority in committee assignments. House Republicans continued to allow their party leaders to make committee assignments for them until they created a separate Committee on Committees within the party in 1917.

Committee chairs rose to even greater importance during this period. Indeed, Woodrow Wilson concluded in 1885 that American government was best characterized as "government by the chairmen of the Standing Committees of Congress."[40] They often delayed, and sometimes refused to report to the floor, legislation that their committees had approved. They also managed the floor debate on all legislation that originated in their committees. As noted, though, committee chairs soon were constrained by majority party leaders. Consider the following complaint by progressive Representative George Norris:

> At the very first meeting of one of the important committees of the House, to which a new member had been assigned, Norris was astounded to hear one of the older members of the committee inquire of the chairman if he had seen the Speaker in regard to a particular bill that was then under consideration. He was still more astounded when, at that meeting, a motion actually was made and passed instructing the chairman to have a conference with the Speaker and to ascertain whether he would permit the passage of the bill in question.[41]

This kind of relationship between the central party leaders and committee chairs continued until about 1916 in the House and nearly as long in the Senate.

From 1915 to 1920, majority party Democrats began to fractionalize, undercutting the power of their leaders and leading to a greater disenchantment with the structure and operation of the congressional committee systems. The fact that the bloated, incoherent committee systems had not created complete chaos much earlier is testimony to the strength of previous party leaders. With declining leadership power, however, the fragmented, overlapping jurisdictional structure of committee systems was less tolerable and by 1918 demands for reform had become loud and frequent.

Consolidating the Committee Systems: 1919-1946

The most striking feature of the 1919-1946 period was a decline in the number of standing committees. Unlike the previous 130 years, this period saw few new standing committees added. And in 1920 the Republican Senate eliminated 41 inactive standing committees, a move tolerated by senators because of the greater availability of personal staff assistance and office space. The most important jurisdictional change prior to the 1940s involved the reconcentration of appropriations authority in the Appropriations committees. In anticipation of an improved executive budgeting system ordered by the Budget and Accounting Act of 1921, the House restored its Appropriations Committee's jurisdiction in June 1920. The Senate followed suit in 1922. The new Appropriations committees restructured their subcommittees so that each would have jurisdiction over one of the appropriations bills within the full committees' jurisdiction.

House Republicans attempted to retain strong party control of the House when they gained the majority after the 1918 elections,[42] but the Republican years of the 1920s had resulted in a substantial weakening of the links between party leaders and committees.[43] The majority leader no longer chaired a major committee, chairs of major committees could not serve on the party's Steering Committee, and no committee chair could sit on the Rules Committee. Democrats adopted similar practices. Both House parties earmarked certain major committees, such as Appropriations, Rules, and Ways and Means, as exclusive by preventing their members from gaining membership on other committees (although Republicans occasionally granted exemptions). Finally, both parties rigorously began to apply the seniority rule in committee appointments. These changes formally divorced the leadership from the committee system, allowing committee chairs to become independent powers within the jurisdiction of their committees. Party leadership became a somewhat more fluid group of elected leaders and selected lieutenants, who were now more dependent upon personal skills than formal powers to shape House decision making.

The House Rules Committee benefited greatly from the changes of the 1920s. The Rules Committee retained all of its vital functions in setting the floor agenda and gained even greater independence with the complete institutionalization of the seniority rule. The committee often refused to report a special order allowing important legislation to be considered on the floor and held legislation hostage until a legislative committee made changes demanded by the Rules Committee. The Rules Committee chair even refused to report special orders adopted by the committee.[44] During most of the 1920s and 1930s, the Rules Committee cooperated with the majority party leadership so that its decisions were not so arbitrary and self-serving as they sometimes appeared. Beginning in late 1937, however, a coalition of conservative, majority party Democrats and minority Republicans used the committee to block President Franklin D. Roosevelt's programs and to pave the way for conservative legislation.

Senate committees operated relatively independently of majority party leaders in the 1920s, but their success on the Senate floor declined because of deep cleavages within the ranks of the majority party Republicans. Progressive Republicans and Democrats had effective control of the Senate on several issues and were able to reject or simply neglect the actions of committees controlled by regular Republicans. Senate Republican insurgents and Democrats were aided by their ability to filibuster legislation they opposed.

As a result of Republican ability to win nonsouthern seats during the 1920s, southern Democrats made up a large proportion of all Democrats in Congress and were able to gain seniority and access to prestigious committees in large numbers. When the Democrats took control of the House in 1931 and of the Senate in 1933, southerners acquired far more than half of the committee chairs, much more than their proportion of the party.[45] President Roosevelt and party leaders were able to keep the chairs in line during his first term, but conservative chairs, especially the southerners, began to challenge Roosevelt's program in his second term. This factional split within the Democratic party marked not only the origin of the conservative coalition in Congress, but also the beginning of a long period of strong, independent committee chairs willing to oppose a president and congressional leaders of their own party.[46]

By the 1940s a confluence of pressures for committee system reform had developed. The power of committee chairs, the seniority system (which brought chairs into power through longevity), and the Rules Committee's power all came under attack from liberals wary of the long-term domination by conservatives then in power. Nonetheless, the increasing size and power of the executive branch during the New Deal and World War II led many members to recognize the ineffectiveness of congressional organization and operation. With the help of reports prepared by a committee of the American Political Science Association and others, attention was drawn to weaknesses in the committee systems. The large number of committees and their overlapping jurisdictions were responsible for unequal distributions of work and participation among members. They caused difficulties in coordination between the House and the Senate and made oversight of executive branch activities difficult. Numerous committee assignments made it difficult for members to concentrate on any one committee's work or to develop the expertise necessary for an effective review of legislative proposals and executive operations. Committees also lacked staff assistance to conduct studies of policy problems and executive branch activities.

The reform effort resulted in the Legislative Reorganization Act of 1946. Because of their purported inability to reach a consensus, the joint committee studying reform recommended no changes affecting the seniority system or the powers of the House Rules Committee, and none were included in the act. Even so, the act featured a series of important innovations. Sweeping changes were enacted in the number and jurisdictions of standing committees, with the number of standing committees reduced to 19 in the House and 15 in the Senate. This reduction in number primarily resulted from consolidating several groups of committees into single committees.[47] The standing committees in each house were made nearly equal in size, and the number of committee assignments was reduced to one for most House members and two for most senators. The act authorized committees to hire up to four professional and six clerical staff members on a nonpartisan, merit basis; the House and Senate Appropriations committees were permitted to appoint as many staff members as they deemed necessary. The staff of the Legislative Reference Service was strengthened by the act; many of these new staffers would be detailed to committees for special projects. Finally, the act directed the standing committees to exercise "continuous watchfulness" over the implementation of laws by the executive branch. The reorganized and well-staffed committees would be in a better position to perform this function.

The Legislative Reorganization Act of 1946 had the effect of further increasing the power of standing committee chairs. Provisions of the act dealing with regular committee meetings, proxy voting, and committee reports constrained chairs in some ways, but most benefited from greatly expanded jurisdictions and the new committee staff, which they would control. The act helped guarantee that committee chairs would dominate congressional policy making for the forseeable future and that the participation of rank-and-file members, especially in the larger House of Representatives, would be centered in their assigned committees. The act had consolidated the structure of the standing committee systems, and the power of independent committee chairs as well.

The Era of Strong
Committee Chairs: 1947-1964

The central features of congressional politics remained relatively stable during the 1947-1964 period. Democrats controlled both houses in all but two Congresses and during most of the period were led by two skillful Texans, Lyndon B. Johnson in the Senate and Sam Rayburn in the House. The House and Senate's standing committee systems exhibited their greatest structural stability in the history of Congress during this period, adding only an aeronautics and space committee to each chamber in 1958. House and Senate membership also was exceptionally stable. Usually more than 80 percent of the members were reelected from one Congress to the next and a marked increase occurred in the number of House members serving 10 or more terms.[48] Committee chairs also exhibited great longevity. More than 60 percent of committee chairs serving during this period held their positions for more than five years, including approximately two dozen who served more than a decade in their positions, despite the fact that it took longer than ever before to gain a chair.

Students of Congress during this period noted the presence of a set of strong, informal norms governing individual behavior. Donald Matthews discovered in the late 1950s that the Senate

> has its unwritten rules of the game, its norms of conduct, its approved manner of behavior. Some things are just not done; others are met with widespread approval. "There is great pressure for conformity," one of its influential members said. "It's just like living in a small town."[49]

Matthews noted two norms directly affecting committees. The first was specialization: a member "ought to specialize, to focus his energy on the relatively few matters that come before his committees or that directly and immediately affect his state."[50] The second norm expected new members to serve an apprenticeship period during which they listened and learned from senior members and refrained from active participation in committee or floor deliberations. These norms, also found to be important in the House,[51] emphasized the development of expertise in one's own committee's affairs and deference to the assumed expertise of other committees. The collective justification for these norms was that such expertise and deference produce better legislation and promote more efficient decision making. The individual's tolerance of these constraints was based upon the belief that one's own expertise would eventually serve as an important base of power as seniority accrued.

The powers of committee chairs during this period were succinctly summarized by George Galloway in 1953:

> Just as the standing committees control legislative action, so the chairmen are masters of their committees. . . . They arrange the agenda of the committees, appoint the subcommittees, and refer bills to them. They decide what pending measures shall be considered and when, call committee meetings, and decide whether or not to hold hearings and

when. They approve lists of scheduled witnesses and authorize staff studies, and preside at committee meetings. They handle reported bills on the floor and participate as principal managers in conference committees. They are in a position to expedite measures they favor and to retard or pigeon-hole those they dislike.[52]

The power of Senate chairs was bolstered by membership on major committees other than the ones they chaired, placing them in an excellent bargaining position with most rank-and-file members.[53] In short, chairs were in an excellent position to enforce the norms of proper conduct and to pursue their own policy objectives.

Despite maintaining tight control over committee activities, most chairs were not tyrants within their committees. Rank-and-file members were well aware of their power, of course, but most chairs were effective because they were among the most knowledgeable and active members of their committees.[54] Typically, committee chairs held political views similar to their committee majorities, which often were composed of conservative Democrats and minority party Republicans. Consequently, they seldom needed to resort to strong-arm tactics.[55] The aura of great power surrounding many chairs often stemmed as much from personal skill and flexibility in molding successful coalitions as from their formal authority.

Nevertheless, conservative chairs, particularly southerners, proved to be a major obstacle to Democratic liberals even when a clear majority of the party supported the liberal view. For example, Graham Barden of North Carolina, chairman of the House Committee on Education and Labor, and A. Willis Robertson of Virginia, chairman of the Senate Committee on Banking and Currency, used their offices' powers to thwart federal aid to education and to block challenges against conservative banking policies.[56] The disproportionate number of conservatives serving as committee chairs by virtue of their seniority was especially irritating to liberals. The seniority system had allowed members from electorally stable areas of the country to rise up through the ranks without interruption, while members from more competitive areas were less likely to remain in Congress long enough to gain committee chairs. Committee transfers among northern members also contributed to southern overrepresentation among chairs. And although southern strength declined during this period, anxious liberals perceived only bleak prospects for replacing conservative chairs in the near future.[57]

House liberals organized the Democratic Study Group in 1959 to combat the conservative power structure. Their immediate target was a conservative coalition on the Rules Committee, led by Chairman Howard Smith of Virginia, that held a stranglehold on committee actions.

The liberals recommended reinstatement of the 21-day rule that permitted the reporting legislative committee to demand floor consideration of legislation on which the Rules Committee had refused to act for at least 21 days. A similar rule, adopted in 1949, had been repealed in 1951. The liberals also sought to expand the Rules Committee to permit liberals to be appointed. Speaker Rayburn talked them out of pursuing their proposals after assuring them that the Rules Committee would cease its blockage of legislation. But Rayburn was unable to deliver on his promise, and, after the Democrats regained control of the White House in 1961, House liberals renewed their efforts to curb the committees' obstructionism. This time, with the help of Rayburn and the new Democratic administration, they successfully expanded the Rules Committee and new, more party-oriented Democrats were added.

The reduction in the number of standing committees as a result of the 1946 reforms stimulated the creation of new subcommittees. An estimated 97 House subcommittees and 34 Senate subcommittees existed prior to the 1946 reforms.[58] After the reorganization, the number of subcommittees initially dropped to a little more than 60 in the House but rose to about 60 in the Senate (Figure 1-2). Most of the newly created Senate subcommittees mirrored previous standing committees' jurisdictions, which had been folded into new committees by the 1946 act. The number of subcommittees gradually grew throughout this period, reaching more than 100 in the House and more than 80 in the Senate by 1964. A majority of the committees in both houses exhibited increases in the number of subcommittees.[59]

The growth in the number of subcommittees had roots in the practical problems involved in managing larger and more complex workloads, in the desire of larger numbers of senior members for a "piece of the action," and in isolated efforts on individual committees to loosen the grip of chairs on committee activity.[60] Chairs of less important committees, especially in the Senate where members held at least two full committee assignments, occasionally discovered that it was necessary to give subcommittee chairs to certain members as an incentive to get them interested in the committee's work and to help shoulder the committee's workload. Generally, however, subcommittees served as important political tools of the full committee chairs. The committee chair determined the subcommittee structure and membership. In some cases, chairs merely numbered subcommittees and gave them no standing policy jurisdiction in order to maintain freedom to refer legislation to a subcommittee that would act on the legislation in accordance with the chair's views. By directing a subcommittee as well, the full committee chair and a small group of friendly colleagues

Figure 1-2 Number of Standing Subcommittees on House and Senate Standing Committees

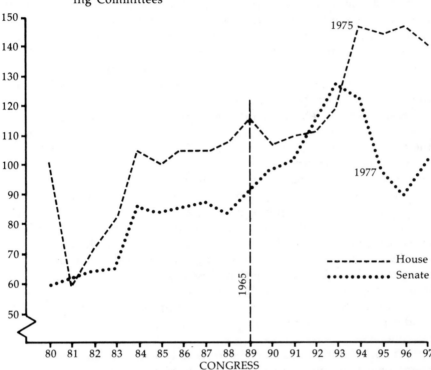

Source: Sula P. Richardson and Susan Schjelderup, "Standing Committee Structure and Assignments: House and Senate" (Washington, D.C.: Congressional Research Service, 1982), Report No. 82-42 GOV., 76-77.

frequently dominated the committee's consideration of such legislation. A few chairs, most notably those of the House Ways and Means and Senate Finance committees, refused to establish subcommittees in order to retain personal control of all legislation at the full committee level. Effective participation often became limited to two or three people in each chamber, as structured by the committee and subcommittee systems.

Congressional committee staffs blossomed during this period, further augmenting the resources of committee chairs. Chairs took advantage of the Legislative Reorganization Act of 1946 to bolster their staffs, and they acquired additional authorizations to move well beyond the levels set by the act. Total standing committee staff more than doubled between 1947 and 1964: from 182 to 489 in the House and from 232 to 492 in the Senate.[61] Committee staff continued to be appointed and

29

managed by the full committee chairs, although a few committees permitted the minority party to appoint a small number of staff members. While many committee staff members were highly professional, nearly all were loyal to the chair and his or her political goals. Even when a staff was highly competent, additional staff gave the chairs better access to policy and legislative drafting expertise.

Formal committee assignment procedures did not change during the 1947-1964 period. Ways and Means Chairman Wilbur Mills of Arkansas and his fellow committee Democrats developed power well beyond the scope of their substantive policy jurisdiction by continuing their role in the assignment process.[62] In the Senate, Majority Leader Lyndon Johnson instituted the so-called "Johnson rule," which gave all Democrats, even the most junior members, the opportunity for a seat on one of the major committees: Appropriations, Armed Services, Finance, and Foreign Relations. Johnson, as chairman of his party's Steering Committee, nevertheless retained centralized control over majority party assignments. Senate Republicans later followed the Democratic lead by adopting the practice of sharing top committee slots among all party members. With the exception provided by the Johnson rule and its Republican counterpart, Senate committee assignments were made according to the seniority of senators seeking particular assignments.[63] Leadership discretion, therefore, was greatest in making assignments for new members.

Chairs of this period have been described as "barons" and "lords" ruling over fiefdoms of broad jurisdiction. More accurately, they served as the chief brokers of many competing interests in their committees' broad jurisdictions.[64] Chairs were effective brokers because of their committees' preeminence in the decision-making process and the control they exercised over the staffing and activities of their committees. For the rank-and-file member, the role of committees and their chairs meant that virtually all participation was restricted to their assigned committees, especially in the House. Moreover, in most committees, participation was limited or structured by the chair. In many respects, House and Senate leadership resembled confederations of committee chairs, each acting as the sovereign over a committee's jurisdiction.

Conclusion: House-Senate Differences

The role of Congress's changing political environment and membership in shaping its internal structure and operations is illustrated in the remarkably similar development of the House and Senate committee systems. In both chambers, a large number of committees and sub-committees had been created by the mid-1960s, and members' primary contributions to congressional decision making were made within their separate committees. The end product of the first 175 years of evolution was a more decentralized decision-making process, with the larger House more fragmented than the Senate.

The centralization/decentralization continuum does not capture fully, however, the differences between the two chambers. Simply put, the continuum cannot be applied to the Senate as well as it can be to the House. In general, the Senate has allowed greater participation of rank-and-file members in floor deliberation by making it easier for them to be recognized, to amend legislation, or even to filibuster. And it has had relatively simple, flexible rules for discharging legislation from commit-tees. As a result of its individualist orientation, the Senate has been embroiled less frequently in controversy over its committee system's formal structure and has felt less pressure than the House to engage in structural change.[65] The House's decision-making processes have changed more in accordance with the centralization/decentralization continuum, from the centralized process of the late 1800s to the decentralized process of the 1950s and 1960s. There, structure and procedure have played a more important role in shaping the level and mode of rank-and-file participation than in the Senate.

NOTES

1. See Joseph Cooper, "The Origins of the Standing Committees and the Development of the Modern House," *Rice University Studies,* vol. 56, no. 3: 116, for a similar interpretation.
2. David E. Price, *Who Makes the Laws* (Cambridge, Mass.: Schenkman Publishing Co., 1972), 14.
3. Cooper, "Origins," 8-17.
4. Ibid., 17-22.
5. Ibid., 11.
6. Ibid., 14.
7. Walter Kravitz, "Evolution of the Senate's Committee System," *Annals of the American Academy of Political and Social Science* 411 (January 1974): 28; Lee Robinson, "The Development of the Senate Committee System," (Ph.D. diss., New York University, 1954), 20-21.
8. Kravitz, "Evolution," 28-29.
9. Thomas Jefferson, *Manual of Parliamentary Practice,* House Doc. 95-403, 95th Cong., 2d Sess., 1979, Sect. XXVI.
10. Cooper, "Origins," 26.

11. An important function delegated to committees from the earliest Congresses, particularly in the more active House, was investigations of executive branch activity. See Cooper, "Origins," 29-40. These investigations focused primarily on the use of funds and misconduct in office. The scope of the investigations was carefully limited by the parent body to ensure that investigations did not impinge upon the president's authority to administer the law and to supervise executive officials. Nonetheless, committees frequently delegated authority to send for persons and papers necessary for obtaining pertinent information. Investigations were nearly always delegated to select committees, and only committee chairs were allowed to question witnesses.

12. Lauros G. McConachie, *Congressional Committees: A Study of the Origins and Development of Our National and Local Legislative Methods* (New York: Thomas Y. Crowell Co., 1898), 349-355; Robinson, "The Development of the Committee System," 149.

13. Cooper, "Origins," 41-50.

14. Ralph V. Harlow, *The History of Legislative Methods in the Period Before 1825* (New Haven: Yale University Press, 1917), 238 ff.

15. Cooper, "Origins," 45.

16. Cooper, "Origins," 56; Harlow, *The History of Legislative Methods*, 216-219.

17. Cooper, "Origins," 50.

18. Cooper, "Origins," 56; Harlow, *The History of Legislative Methods*, 226; George B. Galloway, *The History of the House of Representatives*, 2d ed. (New York: Thomas Y. Crowell Co., 1976), 86.

19. Harlow, *The History of Legislative Methods*, 227; Cooper, "Origins," 58, 70.

20. Robinson, "The Development of the Senate Committee System," 74-75.

21. Ibid., Chaps. 3 and 4.

22. Ibid., 151-154.

23. Ibid., 121-140.

24. Cooper, "Origins," 67-68.

25. Robinson, "The Development of the Senate Committee System," 195 ff.

26. Ibid., 72.

27. Ibid., 151-153.

28. Cooper, "Origins," 61; Galloway, *History*, 79. It should also be noted that committee oversight activity became more vigorous during this period. The previous House practice of limiting the scope of investigations gave way to broad investigations as early as the 1820s. The Senate did not actively pursue investigations until the early 1830s. Even Senate committees regularly sought to inform themselves about administrative matters in cases where no particular legislative response was contemplated until the 1850s. See Cooper, "Origins," 78, and Robinson, "The Development of the Senate Committee System," 88, 232.

29. Chang-Wei Chiu, *The Speaker of the House of Representatives Since 1896* (New York: Columbia University Press, 1928), 311; Robinson, "The Development of the Senate Committee System," 302-305.

30. Burton K. French, "Subcommittees of Congress," *American Political Science Review* (February 1915): 68-92.

31. DeAlva Stanwood Alexander, *History and Procedure of the House of Representatives* (Boston: Houghton Mifflin Co., 1916), 235; Robinson, "The Development of the Senate Committee System," 369.

32. See Mary P. Follett, *The Speaker of the House of Representatives* (New York: Burt Franklin & Co., 1974).
33. David J. Rothman, *Politics and Power: The United States Senate 1869-1901* (New York: Atheneum Publishers, 1969), Chap. 1.
34. Ibid., Chap. 2.
35. Randall B. Ripley, *Congress: Process and Policy*, 2d ed. (New York: W. W. Norton & Co., 1978), 73-74.
36. Rothman, *Politics and Power*, 51.
37. Nelson W. Polsby, "The Institutionalization of the U.S. House of Representatives," *American Political Science Review* 62 (1968): 160-161.
38. See Nelson W. Polsby, Miriam Gallaher, and Barry Spencer Rundquist, "The Growth of the Seniority System in the U.S. House of Representatives," *American Political Science Review* 63 (1969): 787-807.
39. Two other products of the revolt were Calendar Wednesday and the committee discharge procedure. Calendar Wednesday permitted committees to call legislation off a House calendar, bypassing the Rules Committee. It soon fell into disuse because majority party leaders could still block legislation by having friendly committee chairs call up their legislation, preventing other legislation from being considered. The discharge procedure was designed to make it easier for members to bring to the floor legislation that was bottled up in obstructionist committees. The requirement that a constitutional majority support a discharge motion and obstructionists' ability to clog the discharge machinery with bogus motions made the rule unworkable.
40. Woodrow Wilson, *Congressional Government* (Boston: Houghton Mifflin Co., 1885), 102.
41. Quoted in Chiu, *The Speaker of the House of Representatives*, 90.
42. Ibid., 331.
43. Paul D. Hasbrouck, *Party Government in the House of Representatives* (New York: Macmillan, 1927), 92.
44. See Chiu, *The Speaker of the House of Representatives*, 146-151; Joseph Cooper, "Congress and Its Committees" (Ph.D. diss., Harvard University, 1960), 161-162.
45. Barbara Hinckley, *The Seniority System in Congress* (Bloomington: Indiana University Press, 1971), 75.
46. Roger H. Davidson and Walter J. Oleszek, *Congress against Itself* (Bloomington: Indiana University Press, 1977), 37-43.
47. George B. Galloway, *The Legislative Process in Congress* (New York: Thomas Y. Crowell Co., 1953), 276-278.
48. Charles S. Bullock III, "House Careerists; Changing Patterns of Longevity and Attrition," *American Political Science Review* 66 (1969): 1295-1305.
49. Donald R. Matthews, *U.S. Senators and Their World* (New York: Vintage Books, 1960), 92.
50. Ibid., 95.
51. Herbert B. Asher, "The Learning of Legislative Norms," *American Political Science Review* 67 (1973): 499-513.
52. Galloway, *The Legislative Process in Congress*, 289.
53. Matthews, *U.S. Senators and Their World*, 151.
54. Ibid., 160-161; John F. Manley, "Wilbur D. Mills: A Study in Congressional Leadership," *American Political Science Review* 63 (1969): 442-464.

55. Lewis A. Froman, *The Congressional Process: Strategies, Rules and Procedures* (Boston: Little, Brown & Co., 1967), 180-181; Hinckley, *The Seniority System*, 86-88.
56. John F. Bibby, "The Senate Committee on Banking and Currency," in *On Capitol Hill*, ed. John F. Bibby and Roger H. Davidson (New York: Holt, Rinehart & Winston, 1967); Richard F. Fenno, Jr., "The House of Representatives and Federal Aid to Education," in *New Perspectives on the House of Representatives*, 2d ed., ed. Robert L. Peabody and Nelson W. Polsby (Chicago: Rand McNally & Co., 1963), 283-323.
57. Hinckley, *The Seniority System*, 36-43.
58. Galloway, *The Legislative Process in Congress*, 594.
59. Sula P. Richardson and Susan Schjelderup, "Standing Committee Structure and Assignments: House and Senate," Congressional Research Service, March 12, 1982.
60. Lawrence C. Dodd and Bruce I. Oppenheimer, "The House in Transition," in *Congress Reconsidered*, ed. Lawrence C. Dodd and Bruce I. Oppenheimer (New York: Praeger Publishers, 1977), 33-34.
61. "The Senate Committee System," First Staff Report to the Temporary Select Committee to Study the Senate Committee System (Washington, D.C.: Government Printing Office, 1976), 198-201.
62. John F. Manley, *The Politics of Finance: The House Committee on Ways and Means* (Boston: Little, Brown & Co., 1970), 77-78, 244-245.
63. Matthews, *U.S. Senators and Their World*, 127-128.
64. Lawrence C. Dodd and Bruce I. Oppenheimer, "The House in Transition: Change and Consolidation," in *Congress Reconsidered*, 2d ed., ed. Lawrence C. Dodd and Bruce I. Oppenheimer (Washington, D.C.: CQ Press, 1981), 40.
65. On Senate individualism see Randall B. Ripley, *Power In The Senate* (New York: St. Martin's Press, 1969), 3-19.

Committee Reform in the 1970s | 2

By the late 1960s, members of Congress who until then only had grumbled about the power of committee chairs and the seniority system began to make concerted demands for major congressional reform. These demands were especially strong among junior members and some longstanding liberal Democrats, who found their efforts to shape public policy stymied by their more conservative senior colleagues. These members, and the outsiders whose causes they supported, were concerned about issues that were not receiving active committee consideration and that did not fall easily into existing committee jurisdictions. A nascent environmental movement, opposition to the Vietnam War, and a continuing interest in civil rights legislation placed new challenges before congressional committees. These Democrats, with the occasional support of their party leaders and minority Republicans, sought to improve their participation in Congress's decision-making processes by restructuring congressional organization and procedures. The results, which comprise the first variable in the committee change model outlined on p. 4, are described here.

Pressures for Change

At the beginning of every Congress, and sometimes more often, the House and Senate consider changes in their formal rules. In most cases, these changes represent only incremental alterations in the chambers' structures and procedures. Occasionally, major reform efforts are mounted. Two prominent examples are the revolt against Speaker Joseph Cannon in 1910 and the legislative reorganization efforts of 1921 and 1946.

Typically, major reform efforts are a product of the combination of abnormally high levels of external and internal pressures. Roger H. Davidson and Walter J. Oleszek have argued that, like most organizations, Congress seeks to maintain vitality by adapting to external demands and by making consolidative adjustments to various internal stresses.[1] Because Congress continually faces external demands and internal stresses, it is hardly surprising that the institution is in a constant state of flux. It should be clear that major reform efforts result from unusually intense external and internal pressures, pressures similar to those faced by the House and Senate in the late 1960s and early 1970s.

External Demands

As Chapter 1 illustrated, changes in Congress often reflect the ebb and flow of events in its political environment. Throughout the mid- to late 1960s, a period of uncommon sociocultural change in the United States, Congress faced a series of new and heightened challenges in its political environment:

- While Congress perennially receives relatively low performance ratings from the American public, opinion polls during this period sank to new depths. By 1973 only a third of the electorate gave Congress a favorable job rating.[2]
- After nearly a quarter century of post-World War II recovery, the United States found itself in an increasingly complex, interdependent world.[3] As a result of this and continued economic and technological growth, Congress faced an array of issues that cut across House and Senate committees' existing jurisdictional alignments. Energy policy, environmental policy, and the economy proved to be especially problematic in this regard. Thus Congress found itself with the same old problems, but it also found that new demands were being placed upon it by the evolving international system.
- The federal government's role grew during the 1960s. Closely associated with this expansion was the president's greater dominance in governmental affairs—the so-called "imperial presidency."[4] Activist presidents with ambitious legislative agendas, presidential access to a growing bureaucracy, increased media attention, and executive dominance in international issues led to the development of an "inferiority complex" on Capitol Hill. The Democratic and Republican administrations' conduct of the undeclared Vietnam War was an especially sensitive area for liberal Democrats, as were battles over federal spending and President Nixon's impoundment of funds appropriated by Congress for social programs.
- Lobbying activities directed at Congress, and especially at its committees, expanded in scope, became increasingly sophisticated, and added new, countervailing voices to the traditional collection of lobbying organizations. In part, the expansion of lobbying was a response to the federal government's broader scope of activity. In addition, new interest groups emerged to fight against what were perceived as the entrenched traditional interests of business, labor, and agriculture. New public interest, environmental, consumer, and other

groups were of particular interest in the late 1960s because they stimulated new legislative activity and represented (on balance) a young, newly activist portion of the electorate with relatively weak partisan ties.[5]

The new issues, an expanded executive branch, an increasingly demanding electorate, and more numerous and sophisticated interest groups created a fifth external pressure on Congress and its committees—a dramatically increased workload. Members of Congress were asked, and many felt inclined, to do more work. But they were asked to work within a structure and with resources that had remained fairly constant since the early 1950s and now seemed inadequate. Many observers felt that Congress was losing its grip on public policy decisions because of the sheer number of decisions to be made.

Internal Stress

Independent of external pressures, several internal stresses also existed in the late 1960s. These internal stresses were shaped, in part, by changes in Congress's political environment, but they also made a distinctive contribution to the reform movement:

● Factional evolution in Congress created stress within the House and Senate. The number of southern Democrats dropped in the House, and both chambers became more liberal in composition.[6] Nonetheless, liberal Democrats in the House continued to complain that southern Democrats held a disproportionate share of important committee positions by virtue of their seniority. Thus, despite their growing numbers, northern liberals found many of their policy proposals stymied in committee.

● An array of new, complex, and cross-cutting issues caused more frequent jurisdictional battles in the House and Senate. In part, this resulted from maneuvers by liberal members to direct legislation to friendly committees. But it also resulted from new issues that did not fit readily into existing committee jurisdictions. Again, environmental and energy issues were prominent examples.

● As external demands increased Congress's workload, the quickened pace of congressional activities created internal stresses. By all accounts—hours and days in session, number of bills introduced, number of votes, number of committee assignments—the legislative workload was increasing. New, more active members were creating part of this workload as the old apprenticeship norm declined.

● Spending battles with the Nixon administration were accompanied by internal disputes between the authorizing, appropriations, and tax writing committees of Congress.[7] In large part, the problems were caused by deficits generated by the lack of tax increases to cover costs of the Vietnam War. These deficits forced tax committees to consider politically unpopular increases in the debt ceiling and, eventually, to increase taxes. At the same time tax committees pointed the finger at Appropriations committees to cut spending. A series of expenditure ceilings from 1967 to 1972 failed to solve the problem. Appropriations committees, on the other hand, complained that federal spending was escaping their control because more funds were being allocated as the result of laws, under authorization committees' jurisdictions, committing the federal government to certain spending. Simply put, Congress had no mechanism through which these components of fiscal policy could be integrated.

● As always, new members created and reflected a certain amount of stress until they became acclimated to their new surroundings. Congress traditionally has coped with such stress via apprenticeship, which encouraged new members to enter an unassertive learning phase while members of greater seniority managed most business.

This last form of stress was of particular importance. Individuals entering the House and Senate in the late 1960s and early 1970s differed from their predecessors. They brought a different set of experiences and expectations to Congress. Unlike most members of the 1950s and early 1960s, this new generation of legislators had little firsthand experience with the partisanship created during the Great Depression, the New Deal, or World War II. Rather, the civil rights movement, urban riots, the Vietnam War, and Watergate were their common political experiences. These more recent events caused a questioning of the legitimacy of authority, an intolerance of seniority norms, and a cynicism about the purposes and values of those in power. Writing in the mid-1970s, former House Republican floor leader John Rhodes of Arizona described the change:

> The average Congressman of yesteryear was congenial, polite and willing to work with his colleagues whenever possible. Most important, his main concern was attending to his congressional duties. Today, a large number of Congressmen are cynical, abrasive, frequently uncommunicative and ambitious to an inordinate degree.[8]

The differing perspectives of generations may account for some of Rhodes' interpretation, but his is a widely shared view.

New members also were individualistic. Increasingly, candidates for congressional seats were forced to operate as independent political entrepreneurs, each creating his or her own campaign organization, base of financial support, and electoral coalition. New members brought their electoral independence with them to the House and the Senate. Advice about how to manage time, resources, and even committee responsibilities increasingly came from sources emphasizing the importance of individual decisions rather than the role of committee team player. Congressional newcomers were less likely to perceive committee chairs as sources of information about what would be expected from them. Coupled with their individualism was an intolerance of apprenticeship and the seniority system it reinforced. In fact, the lack of deference to senior members in positions of authority was by far the most common response of long-term members and staff to our questions about changes that occurred in the late 1960s and early 1970s.

In aggregate, these internal stresses began to build up pressures for change—first in the House and, because of greater individual resources and a tradition of more equal participation, later in the Senate. Quite naturally, committees became a primary target of disgruntled members: workloads had to be better managed, more staff was needed, and jurisdictions had to be rationalized. The power of committee chairs needed to be reduced and committee assignment processes had to be changed. Reform-oriented members quickly asked: How do we do this?

Mechanisms for Structural and Procedural Change

Article I, Section 5 of the Constitution states that ". . . each house may determine the rules of its proceedings." As a result, Congress's two chambers have distinct sets of rules that, while roughly parallel, differ in the number, size, jurisdiction, and procedures specified for their committees. Moreover, the two chambers' rules are not the only source of guidance for committee structure and procedures.[9] Statutes, rules of the two party caucuses in each chamber, individual committees' written rules, and informal norms and folkways all help to define the House and Senate committee systems.

Statutes, such as the the Legislative Reorganization Acts of 1946 and 1970, help to shape the committee systems by creating new panels. The old Joint Committee on Atomic Energy, the Joint Economic Committee, the two Small Business committees, and the two Budget committees all were created by statute. In most situations the statutory approach, which involves passage of a bill by both chambers, is needlessly complicated and time consuming, leading reformers to seek changes in chamber or even party rules. Party rules may establish processes for assigning members to committees, dictate the selection of committee leaders, limit the powers of full committee chairs, or, as in the case of House Democrats, even set rules for the use of subcommittees. Individual committees also adopt their own rules. These rules must be consistent with chamber rules, but often go into greater detail about the chair's privileges and committee procedures. Finally, each chamber has evolved a set of recognizable, yet unwritten, norms or folkways that constrain individual members' behavior and, as a result, committees' performances.[10] The best known, and most criticized, of these was the traditional seniority-apprenticeship system prescribing that newer members be "seen but not heard" (see Chapter 1).

These five sets of "rules" define the two committee systems in Congress. To change the committee systems to suit their needs, members frequently alter one or more of these sets. The set targeted depends on the balance of power within the House and Senate, within congressional parties, and within particular committees. If committees cease to reflect the balance of legislative power, pressures for reform increase. Occasionally, when serious imbalances coexist with external pressures, rapid change is likely to occur.

Bicameral Legislative Reform Efforts

Since the mid-1960s, more than half-a-dozen formal reform efforts have occurred in the House and Senate (Table 2-1). Five of these—two in bicameral committees, two in bipartisan intrachamber committees, and one in a party caucus committee—are worth more complete examination because they produced most of the committee reforms.

The Legislative Reorganization Act of 1970

The first major reform effort of the 1960s was designed to emulate the endeavors that resulted in the Legislative Reorganization Act of 1946.[11] The reformers' first strategy was to make a broad, direct assault on congressional organization and procedure. On March 11, 1965, the Joint Committee on the Organization of Congress was created to take a wide-ranging look at organizational reform. Among the major topics for study were committee procedures and organization, committee staff, legislative research support, floor procedures, lobbying regulations, fiscal controls and procedures, and the role of political parties.

In its final report, based on lengthy hearings during the 1965 session, the second Joint Committee made reform recommendations in every area except that of the role of political parties. Despite quick Senate action on the report, the Joint Committee's final recommendations took five years to be signed into law. The objections of powerful House interests to several proposed reforms were responsible for the delay. When finally enacted into law, the Legislative Reorganization Act

Table 2-1 Major Reform and Study Efforts, House and Senate

House
- Joint Committee on the Organization of Congress
  March 11, 1965-July 21, 1966
- Committee on Organization, Study, and Review
  "Hansen Committee"
  March 1970-October 8, 1974
- Joint Study Committee on Budget Control
  October 27, 1972-April 18, 1973
- Select Committee on Committees
  "Bolling Committee"
  January 31, 1973-October 8, 1974
- Committee on Administrative Review
  "Obey Commission"
  July 1, 1976-October 12, 1977
- Select Committee on Committees
  "Patterson Committee"
  March 20, 1979-April 30, 1980

Senate
- Joint Committee on the Organization of Congress
  March 11, 1965-July 21, 1966*
- Joint Study Committee on Budget Control
  October 27, 1972-April 18, 1973
- Temporary Select Committee to Study the Senate Committee System
  "Stevenson Committee"
  March 31, 1976-February 4, 1977
- Commission on the Operation of the Senate
  "Culver Commission"
  July 29, 1975-December 31, 1976

---

* Senate members of the Joint Committee continued their work as an intrachamber committee and filed an additional report on September 21, 1966.

of 1970 contained none of the provisions recommended by the Joint Committee regarding seniority, electronic voting, or lobby reform, but it did include a series of procedural reforms. Among other things, the act required committees to make public all recorded votes and limited proxy votes, allowed a majority of members to call meetings, and encouraged committees to hold open hearings and meetings. Floor procedure was affected also—primarily by permitting recorded teller votes during the amending process and by authorizing (rather than requiring) the use of electronic voting.[12]

The Legislative Reorganization Act, despite its somewhat limited effects, remains an important milestone in legislative reformers' efforts. It marks the end of an era when powerful committee chairs and other senior members could forestall structural and procedural changes that appeared to undermine their authority. And it marked the beginning of nearly a decade of continuous and fairly dramatic change in Congress. The act provided the opening wedge for further committee changes and taught important strategy lessons to reformers.

The Congressional Budget and Impoundment Control Act of 1974

In 1972, after nearly a decade of inter- and intrabranch wrangling over budget formulation, fiscal policy making, and executive impoundment of funds, Congress created a joint committee to study new budget mechanisms and procedures. Members of the Joint Study Committee on Budget Control were drawn almost entirely (28 of 32 members) from the House and Senate Appropriations committees, the House Ways and Means Committee, and the Senate Finance Committee.[13] Budget reform legislation was referred to the House Rules Committee and (sequentially) to the Senate Government Operations and Rules and Administration committees. These committees approved budget reform measures in late 1973 and early 1974 that subsequently were passed by both chambers. After further changes were made in the House/Senate conference, the bill was signed into law on July 12, 1974, less than two years after the first serious calls for reform.

The budget process created by the 1974 act was added to the existing committee structure, providing new mechanisms for integrating appropriations, revenue, and authorization committees' work and producing a congressional budget for each fiscal year. House and Senate Budget committees were created, an analytical staff (the Congressional Budget Office) was established, and a timetable was fixed for constructing a budget for each fiscal year. Each year two budget resolutions, required by the act, would set spending targets in broad programmatic categories, set total revenues, and stipulate the deficit (or surplus) and total federal debt. The first resolution, to be adopted in May, was intended to provide guidelines for money committees during the summer months. The second resolution, to be adopted in September, would be binding. A "reconciliation" process was created to settle any differences between the fiscal decisions of the summer months and the second budget resolution before the start of the fiscal year on October 1. In addition, the reform included a procedure for congressional review and a veto of presidential delays (deferrals) or cancellations (rescissions) of appropriated funds—making presidential impoundments or funds more difficult.

By virtually all accounts, the Budget Act was found to be one of the most important congressional initiatives of the post-World War II period. Not the least of its effects has been on the relations among the budget, authorizations, revenue, and appropriations committees. The appropriations committees' decade-long shift from "guardians" of the federal purse to "claimants" of the purse had been cemented. Budget constraints and the new time limits had partially reoriented authorizing committees toward greater oversight. And economic conditions and changes in the budget process had forced the revenue committees into a much more active role in tax policy. Needless to say, such changes often have strained relations among committees. Properly managed, the new budget process held out the possibility of much more coherent and centralized fiscal policy making. But this would be achieved only through significant alterations in committee relationships.

Structural and Procedural Changes in the House

Unlike bicameral efforts at structural and procedural change, which came to a head in debates preceding passage of legislation, House intrachamber reforms were achieved gradually. Two groups, the Hansen Committee on Organization, Study, and Review and the Bolling Select Committee on Committees, were responsible for these efforts.

The Hansen Committee

After the Legislative Reorganization Act of 1970 was completed, a major reform group in the House, the Democratic Study Group (DSG), an organization of liberal and reform-oriented Democrats, altered its strategy for achieving reform. House rules, which outline the committees' broad structure, became less important. The DSG, with prodding from its executive director, Richard Conlon, focused on the power of committee chairs and unwritten seniority rules. Because use of seniority as a method of allocating committee chairs was an intraparty practice, the party caucus became a natural forum for this effort. As groundwork, a core of DSG liberals sought to revitalize the Democratic Caucus and shape it into an engine of reform. At first, monthly caucus meetings, called for by a 1969 change in caucus rules, failed to stimulate interest because a quorum of 50 members seldom appeared.[14] In March 1970, however, reformers succeeded in gaining from the caucus authorization for a Committee on Organization, Study, and Review to study the seniority system. Members of the 11-member committee, chaired by Julia Butler Hansen of Washington, were diverse. The Hansen Committee, as it came to be called, was balanced geographically, ideologically, and in terms of seniority. Virtually all observers since have agreed that this balance helped ensure the appeal of the committee's recommendations to a broad cross section of Democrats.

The Hansen Committee's first set of recommendations was adopted by the Democratic Caucus on January 20, 1971. The Hansen reform provisions limited the full committee chairs' ability to dominate their committees. First, and most importantly, Democrats limited their members to holding one legislative subcommittee chair. As a result, full committee chairs no longer could chair several subcommittees. Second, subcommittee chairs were allowed to select one professional staff member for their respective subcommittees—subject to approval by their full committee caucus. This gave resources to subcommittee chairs that were beyond the direct control of full committee chairs. And third, the system for electing full committee chairs and committee members, who traditionally had been presented as a slate, was altered so that nominations would be presented one committee at a time. This third change also allowed—on the request of 10 or more members—debate, a separate vote, and, in the event of a defeat, a new nomination by the Committee on Committees for each chair nominated.

Encouraged by these successes, DSG Director Conlon and Common Cause Director David Cohen helped to draft and lobby for another round of reforms at the end of 1972. With the caucus's revitalization, the strategists planned to go directly to their party colleagues with this new round of reforms. In a surprise move, however, the newly elected chairman of the Democratic Caucus, Olin E. Teague of Texas, summarily reconvened the Hansen Committee and asked it to review the new suggestions. Although the Hansen group dropped some DSG proposals, in 1973 they recommended, and the caucus ultimately ratified, another significant set of reforms:[15]

> ● Automatic votes on committee chairs (with a secret ballot to be provided on the demand of 20 percent of the caucus) were required to make chairs more accountable to the caucus's rank-and-file members. (A similar rule had been implemented by the House Republican Caucus in January 1971.)

● The Democratic Committee on Committees (formerly comprised solely of Democratic members of the Ways and Means Committee) was expanded to include the Speaker, who would now chair the group, the majority leader, and the caucus chair. This would reduce the control of conservative Ways and Means Democrats over other Democrats' committee assignments.

● A new, 23-member, Steering and Policy Committee was created within the caucus to serve as a leadership forum for considering and pushing party policy positions.

● The caucus approved a procedure allowing the caucus to demand more open rules for floor deliberations—a reform aimed chiefly at the Ways and Means Committee.

● Though hardly noticed at the time, the caucus also approved a collection of subcommittee reforms—since dubbed the Subcommittee Bill of Rights—that included guaranteed referral of legislation to subcommittee, stripped full committee chairs of their power to single-handedly appoint subcommittees, and guaranteed fixed jurisdictions for subcommittees.[16]

Collectively, these reforms rivaled anything yet attempted in the House of Representatives. Spurred by the DSG, aided by outside lobbying efforts (the AFL-CIO, Common Cause, the UAW, Ralph Nader's Public Citizen, and the Americans for Democratic Action), and backed by Democratic party leaders, the reformists' new party-oriented strategy had paid handsome dividends.

The Bolling Committee

Although the Hansen panel appeared to have finished its work, reformers were not yet satisfied. About this time, a renewed, leadership-sponsored effort to continue a bipartisan study of the committee system was being pushed in the House. This effort resulted in the creation of the House Select Committee on Committees in early 1973.[17] The committee was dubbed the Bolling Committee after its chief sponsor and chairman, Democrat Richard Bolling from Missouri.

From a reformer's standpoint, the Bolling Committee had major disadvantages. At a time when reform efforts within the Democratic Caucus were meeting with considerable success, the Bolling panel broadened the forum by shifting mechanisms to the whole House. This meant that the Bolling group's reform proposals would have to appeal to a larger, more diverse body than had the Hansen proposals. Unlike the Hansen group, which had won praise for its political balance, the Bolling Committee was a distinctly reformist, albeit bipartisan, panel, and its decisions were less likely to be viewed as evenhanded. Moreover, the Bolling Committee, which had an apparently limited life span, did not enjoy the option of proposing its changes incrementally, a pattern into which the Hansen Committee had fallen.

Although the Bolling Committee's mandate was broad, the two major tasks it adopted were untangling the jurisdictions of the House committee system and balancing unequal committee workloads. On December 7, 1973, after 10 weeks of hearings, 4 weeks of committee deliberations, and countless hours of staff research, the committee floated a preliminary proposal. This proposal, a compromise among committee members, featured 15 exclusive and 7 nonexclusive committees. According to the plan, most members would serve on a single, "exclusive" committee, and a few members would serve on an additional nonexclusive committee. The plan called for major jurisdictional shifts that would have cut into the broad jurisdictions of Ways and Means, Commerce, and Education and Labor, while adding to the jurisdictions of Foreign Affairs, Public Works, Science and Astronautics.[18] Post Office and Civil Service and the Internal Security committees were to be disbanded, and their jurisdictions given to other committees. Beyond these jurisdictional changes, the Bolling proposal also suggested improved scheduling procedures, an early organizational start for each new Congress, better oversight of executive activities by House committees, and a mechanism for referral of bills to multiple committees (multiple-referral).

To no one's surprise, the proposal, released March 21, 1974, as House Resolution 988, began to draw immediate fire from members. As Bolling put it at the time: "It took a while to get everyone's attention, but I think now we've got it." [19] The plan threatened to undermine years of accumulated seniority and the political connections of members serving on committees targeted for dissolution or jurisdictional reduction. Many staff members, equally threatened, rallied to protect their committees from dismemberment. Outside Congress, reform advocates split on the plan, some viewing it as insufficient, while others, such as the AFL-CIO, feared a loss of access to sympathetic committees. The most telling blow, however, may have been the silence of House Democratic party leaders.

Despite Republican endorsement of the plan, a badly split Democratic Caucus once again revived the Hansen Committee and, by a narrow 16-vote margin, referred the Bolling plan to the Hansen Committee for review. The Hansen Committee drafted a substitute proposal that replaced the Bolling plan's controversial jurisdictional alterations with a series of relatively minor adjustments. The new plan did not jettison any committees and upgraded Small Business from select to standing committee status. Provisions for referring legislation to multiple committees and for early organization of each Congress, both from the Bolling plan, were retained. The plan also directed committees with 15 or more members to establish at least four subcommittees (a rule aimed at Ways and Means), increased committee staff sizes, guaranteed one-third of House committee staffs to the minority, and banned proxy voting in committee. Without a significant leadership effort to back Bolling, the Hansen plan gathered enough Republicans and dissatisfied Democrats to win approval on a 203-to-165 vote.[20]

Despite defeat of the ambitious Bolling plan, reform Democrats (spurred by the DSG) focused once again on the caucus and its first early organizational meeting at the beginning of the 94th Congress. With support from most of their new party colleagues (75 Democratic members dubbed "Watergate Babies" in the aftermath of the November 1974 election) the Democrats topped off the two previous Congresses' reforms by adopting a final series of major alterations. Ways and Means Democrats were stripped of their longstanding role as the party's Committee on Committees (with responsibility for committee assignments) and their function was transferred to the leadership-dominated Steering and Policy Committee. The Ways and Means Committee was expanded from 25 to 37 members to give more junior and liberal members access to this powerful committee.

The Appropriations Committee's subcommittee chairs henceforth would be required to gain election to their positions through the same party caucus mechanism as full committee chairs, a move that recognized their status as tantamount to full committee chairs. Finally, the caucus approved a procedure that would allow the Speaker to nominate Democratic members of the Rules Committee. Then, as if to add emphasis to these strikes at the power of full committee chairs, the new caucus, bolstered by the 75 "Watergate Babies," deposed the senior chairs of the Agriculture, Banking, and Armed Services committees (W. R. Poage of Texas, Wright Patman of Texas, and F. Edward Hebert of Louisiana, respectively).

By 1975 the House committee system and the means by which the ruling Democrats organized and operated that system had been altered dramatically. Although reform efforts did not cease, a watershed period for reform had drawn to a close. In 1977 the House Commission on Administrative Review (the Obey Commission, named after David R. Obey of Wisconsin) produced a report recommending a wide range of procedural innovations and further investigation of the committee system. The report was rejected by the House on a procedural vote. And in 1979 a new Select Committee on Committees (the Patterson Committee, named after California Democrat Jerry Patterson) was formed and given a year to renew the study of the committee system.

The House was clearly in no mood for more reform. It rejected the Patterson Committee's proposal to consolidate energy jurisdiction into a single House committee and opted instead simply to rename the powerful Interstate and Foreign Commerce Committee the Energy and Commerce Committee. No jurisdiction was taken from other House committees that considered energy issues, but the House rules were changed to give the "new" Energy Committee a general oversight jurisdictional grant over energy problems.

Structural and Procedural Changes in the Senate

For most of this period, the Senate committee structure had remained remarkably unchanged, although pressures for reform had continued to build. By 1976 the Senate was ready to create its own reform committee. The Senate's major committee reform effort originated within a bipartisan group of relatively junior members. Their concerns, which were similar to those of House reformers, stimulated several changes during the first half of the 1970s: open markup sessions, some committee staff assistance for junior members, and secret-ballot elections for committee chair nominees. Nonetheless, most members still saw the need for improvement. As in the House, these early reforms failed to deal with overlapping jurisdictions, poor committee scheduling, multiple committee and subcommittee assignments, and unequal committee workloads. These problems were especially acute in the Senate because of the greater number of committee assignments held by senators (about 17 committees and subcommittees per senator) and the added burdens senators held by being national figures. These differences account for the dissimilar emphases of House and Senate reforms.

The Stevenson Committee

Following several unsuccessful attempts to stir member interest, a resolution was adopted on March 31, 1976, creating a 12-member, bipartisan Temporary Select Committee to Study the Senate Committee System.[21] The committee, chaired by Democrat Adlai Stevenson of Illinois and co-chaired by Republican William Brock of Tennessee, was given just 11 months to make its recommendations. Like the Bolling Committee in the House, it was composed largely of reform-oriented members. After several months of study and brief hearings in July and September, the Stevenson panel sketched three alternative committee plans: a minimal-change plan, a 12-committee plan organized along functional lines, and a 5-committee scheme containing 60 standing subcommittees. These proposals drew the attention of chamber colleagues and outsiders. At a second set of hearings in September 1976, 24 senators and a large number of interest groups commented on various aspects of the proposed changes. Realizing the Senate was not yet ready for a radical restructuring of its committees, the Stevenson Committee quickly settled on the 12-committee plan and reported its recommendations to the Senate.[22] Stevenson introduced a resolution (S. Res. 586) embodying those recommendations on October 15, 1976.

At this point, prospects for substantial reform looked bright. Both parties' leaders, Democrat Mike Mansfield of Montana and Republican Hugh Scott of Pennsylvania, were slated to retire at the end of the 94th Congress, and their prospective replacements were in favor of reform. In the November 1976 elections, the chairs of three standing committees designated to be abolished were defeated.[23] And in December, Stevenson and Oregon's Bob Packwood (the new co-chairman replacing the defeated Brock) won an agreement from key members of the Rules and Administration Committee facilitating prompt consideration of the reform resolution. The parties delayed making new committee assignments until deliberation on the resolution was completed. When Stevenson reintroduced the reform resolution (now S. Res. 4) at the beginning of the next Congress, it was referred to the Rules and Administration Committee, which immediately held well-attended hearings. Not only did 39 senators appear, but a committee-spanning spectrum of interest groups also testified. Most participants praised the reforms in general while damning changes that affected their self-interest. S. Res. 4 was approved unanimously by the committee and passed the Senate on a vote of 89-1. Only Quentin Burdick, the North Dakota Democrat in line to chair the abolished Post Office Committee, voted against the resolution.

Evaluating the Stevenson Committee

By the time the Senate had finished its work, the committee reorganization plan had evolved from an innovative restructuring to a moderate, yet significant, realignment of the old committee system. Nearly all of the Senate's select and special committees had been abolished along with the Post Office and District of Columbia commit-tees. Wholesale jurisdictional changes involving energy, the environ-ment, science and technology, human resources, and government af-fairs, had been achieved. Limits were placed on the number of assignments (three committees and eight subcommittees) and the num-ber of chairs (four committees and subcommittees in the 95th and three in the 96th Congress) senators could hold. The reforms also expanded minority staffing and computerized scheduling in a further effort to relieve overburdened senators.

At each successive phase, plans of the Stevenson Committee had been weakened by members fearful of losing jurisdiction. Despite this, a substantial alteration remained that in structural terms far exceeded the House's achievements. The reverse was true where procedural matters were involved. On these matters, the House Democratic Caucus had made more substantial progress. The question on most people's minds was what effects these reforms would have on Congress and its two committee systems.

A Preliminary Look at the Organizational Effects of House and Senate Reform

The most obvious effects of reform can be seen by looking at the patterns of change in four structural features of the House and Senate. These are: the total number of committees and subcommittees; the number of committee and subcommittee chairs; the staff distribution between committees and subcommittees; and member workload.

Committees and Subcommittees

As noted earlier, the number of standing committees in the House and Senate has remained stable for the last 35 years. In contrast, the number of subcommittees in the two chambers climbed steadily from the early 1950s to the mid-1970s. (See Figure 1-1 in Chapter 1.) After passage of the Stevenson Committee recommendations, however, an immediate retrenchment in the number of Senate subcommittees oc-curred. The number of Senate subcommittees declined from 122 in the 94th Congress to 90 in the 96th and then increased marginally in the 97th—primarily due to the elevation of Small Business to standing committee status.

The growth in House subcommittees also has leveled off. The number of House subcommittees increased fairly dramatically during the reform period in the House—from 109 in the 92d Congress, to 119 in the 93d, and 139 in the 94th—but has been fairly stable from the 95th through the 98th. House Democrats established a cap on the number of subcommittees each committee could form at the beginning of the 97th Congress (see Chapter 5). The cap essentially froze the number of subcommittees at the level present in the 96th Congress, with a couple of exceptions. The constant change in subcommittee structure has been as important as the growth in the number of committees. As Table A-1 (Appendix), makes clear, both House and Senate committees engage in a fairly constant restructuring of their subcommittees—a restructuring not accounted for solely by reforms. The data also indicate that growth in the number of subcommittees is a long-term phenomenon and not uniquely tied to reform movements in the House and Senate. (See Chapters 5, 6, and 7 for greater detail.)

Chair and Subcommittee Chair Positions

Not surprisingly, as the number of formal power positions expanded, so did the number of members holding such positions. From the 84th to the 90th Congress (1955-1968) the proportion of House majority party members chairing at least one committee or subcommittee increased from 27.2 percent to 44.9 percent.[24] (Table 2-2) By the 96th Congress (1979-1980), more than half the majority members (52.1 percent) chaired at least one committee or subcommittee. As with the increase in total subcommittees, positions of power in the House had

Table 2-2 Number of Committee and Subcommittee Chairs: Selected Congresses*

Congress	House Chairs	Senate Chairs
80 (1955-57)	63 (27.2)**	42 (87.5)
90 (1967-69)	111 (44.9)	55 (85.9)
92 (1971-73)	120 (47.2)	51 (92.7)
94 (1975-77)	140 (49.1)	57 (91.9)
96 (1979-81)	144 (52.2)	58 (98.3)
97 (1981-83)	132 (49.8)	51 (96.2)

* Standing committees and subcommittees
** Percentage of majority members with chairs

Source: Norman J. Ornstein, Thomas E. Mann, Michael J. Malbin, John F. Bibby, *Vital Statistics On Congress 1982* (Washington, D.C.: American Enterprise Institute for Public Policy Research, 1982), 101-102.

been widely distributed by the 90th Congress. Thus the reforms served as an additional impetus to further decentralizion of the committee system by increasing the number of effective participants and the number of decision-making units in which they served.

In the Senate, small numbers of majority members and large numbers of available positions combined to create widespread member participation. Even so, the proportion of majority party members holding at least one chair increased from 85.9 percent in the 90th Congress to 98.3 percent in the 96th Congress. Thus, even with the cutback in subcommittees forced by the 1977 reforms, Senate committee leadership positions were widely distributed among majority party members. Similar effects can be seen within House and Senate minority parties. In the 96th Congress, all Republican senators and 80 percent of Republican representatives were ranking minority members of committees or sub-committees.[25]

Staff Distributions

Both House and Senate committee staffs have increased steadily during the last decade, contributing to an overall increase in support staff for Congress. House committee and subcommittee staff tripled between the 91st and 97th Congresses. (Table 2-3) Senate committee and subcommittee staffs increased approximately 80 percent during this

Table 2-3 Distribution of Senate and House Standing Committee and Subcommittee Staff: 91st-97th Congresses (*in percent*)*

	91st	*92d*	*93d*	*94th*	*95th*	*96th*	*97th*
Senate							
Full committee	57.9**	55.4	59.5	67.9	72.3	65.4	67.5
Subcommittee	42.1	44.6	40.5	32.1	27.7	34.5	32.5
Total Staff	504	635	775	859	869	902	906
House							
Full committee	76.8	72.3	63.6	67.2	61.2	57.0	60.2
Subcommittee	23.2	27.7	36.4	32.8	38.8	43.0	39.8
Total Staff	461	575	664	1,083	1,250	1,608	1,507

* Excludes select and special committees.
** Without the Senate Judiciary Committee, the figures for full and subcommittee staff are, respectively, 78.2 and 21.8. Judiciary similarly affects the figures throughout the period.
Source: *Congressional Staff Directory.*

period. The different rates of increase can be attributed to the fact that most Senate committee staffs remained centralized under the control of full committee chairs and their staff directors. While House subcommittees steadily increased their share of committee staff from the 91st through the 96th Congress, Senate full committee staffs had increased in absolute and relative terms since the 91st Congress. Also important to note is that half of all Senate subcommittee staff in the 91st Congress belonged to a single committee—Judiciary. By the 96th Congress, Judiciary and Governmental Affairs (which had grown steadily during the period) employed 228 of 312 subcommittee staff in the Senate. In the aggregate, Senate committee staff—except on a couple of committees such as Governmental Affairs and Judiciary—have been and remain highly centralized in comparison with the House. The number of House and Senate committee staff seem to have leveled off in recent years. Senate committee staff peaked in the mid-1970s, as did House staff at the beginning of the 1980s. In part, this leveling was caused by pressures to reduce spending, but it also may reflect a satisfaction of committee appetites and a capacity to absorb new staff members.[26] (Committee-specific patterns of staffing change are examined in Chapter 6.)

Workload

With some variations, the average number of committee and subcommittee assignments for each member of Congress has increased steadily since the Legislative Reorganization Act of 1946 (Table 2-4). In the 80th Congress the average senator held roughly 5.5 seats on standing committees and subcommittees, and the average House member held almost 3 seats. By the 91st Congress the respective figures were 10.5 for the average senator and a little more than 4 for the average representative. In 1983 the average senator had 9.75 assignments and the average representative 5.25.

Beyond the sheer number of assignments, other indicators demonstrate that, with few exceptions, such as total legislation introduced and the number of roll calls, Congress still faces a burgeoning workload. And, as with committee assignments, the trend is long-term. The number of committee and subcommittee meetings has increased steadily for nearly three decades, as has the total number of hours in session. In each case increases occurred after reforms made in the 92d Congress. From the 92d Congress to the 94th Congress the total number of House committee and subcommittee meetings increased from a little more than 5,000 to nearly 7,500.[27] During the same period the total number of

Table 2-4   Average Number of Standing Committee and Subcommittee Assignments Per Member: Selected Congresses 1947 to 1982

Congress (Years)	Senate		House	
	Committee Assignments	Subcommittee Assignments	Committee Assignments	Subcommittee Assignments
80th (1947-49)	2.10	3.36	1.19	1.70
84th (1955-57)	2.20	5.53	1.25	2.08
88th (1963-65)	2.56	6.60	1.36	2.50
91st (1969-71)	2.45	7.97	1.46	2.73
92d (1971-73)	2.47	8.95	1.54	3.08
93rd (1973-75)	2.58	9.46	1.64	3.43
94th (1975-77)	2.30	8.27	1.71	4.04
95th (1977-79)	2.43	6.58	1.78	3.89
96th (1979-81)	2.52	6.68	1.75	3.73
97th (1981-83)	2.82	6.93	1.71	3.54

Source: Sula P. Richardson and Susan Schjelderup, "Standing Committee Structure and Assignments: House and Senate" (Washington, D.C.: Congressional Research Service, 1982), Report No. 82-42 GOV., 76-77.

hours in session increased from a little more than 1,400 hours to nearly 1,800 hours.

Conclusion: Reform in House and Senate Committees

In several respects, the House reforms of the 1970s made the chamber more similar to the Senate by reducing the structural and procedural constraints on rank-and-file participation in decision making. Democratizing majority party operations within committees and electing full committee chairs put the finishing touches on the elimination of the apprenticeship norm. The creation of more subcommittees and the broader distribution of subcommittee chairs and staff gave more members the resources to pursue their own interests and to bargain with other members. House Democratic Caucus rules changes, which made it easier to demand opportunities to amend legislation on the floor, considerably weakened the protective shields that closed rules had provided some committees, especially Ways and Means.

Yet reform efforts in the House and Senate reflected longstanding differences between the chambers outlined in Chapter 1. The House, which had been more decentralized than the Senate prior to the 1970s, became even more decentralized in formal organization as a result of the reforms. Indeed, House reformers' focus on distributing formal authority among party leaders and committee members, in contrast to the Senate's lack of attention to procedural changes, reflected the House's characteristic attention to organization and procedure. The Senate, despite its larger percentage of junior members when reforms were adopted, rejected proposals that would have guaranteed junior members more access to subcommittee chairs and staff. Even after the House democratizing reforms, representatives remained far more dependent than senators on their committee assignments to determine policy areas in which they would actively participate in chamber decision making.

For individual committees, externally imposed procedural or jurisdictional reforms could dramatically affect their internal politics. But reforms were not the only, nor always the most important, source of change. Shifting agendas, even with stable formal jurisdictions, and changes in membership and members' motivations could enhance or reduce the affects of reform. The next two chapters illustrate these sources of change in committee politics.

NOTES

1. Roger H. Davidson and Walter J. Oleszek, "Adaptation and Consolidation: Structural Innovation in the U.S. House of Representatives," *Legislative Studies Quarterly* 1 (February 1976): 37-65. As noted in the Introduction, we are stepping back from the model to describe the general effects of structural and procedural change. These "reforms" are conditioned by a variety of external factors (environmental or agenda changes) and internal factors (especially member goals). If reform was the dependent variable in this analysis, our model would show these relationships reversed. Our interest here is on the effects of reforms on individual committees. In this chapter, the broad outlines of the reform movement are offered as a preliminary step to examining change within committees.
2. Davidson and Oleszek, "Adaptation and Consolidation," 45.
3. See, for example, Seyom Brown, *New Forces in World Politics* (Washington, D.C.: The Brookings Institution, 1974).
4. Arthur Schlesinger, *The Imperial Presidency* (Boston: Houghton Mifflin, 1973). On the modern struggle between the branches, see James L. Sundquist, *The Decline and Resurgence of Congress* (Washington, D.C.: The Brookings Institution, 1981).
5. Jeffrey M. Berry, *Lobbying For The People* (Princeton, N.J.: Princeton University Press, 1977). See also Robert H. Salisbury, "Interest Groups: Toward a

New Understanding," in *Interest Group Politics*, ed. Allan J. Cigler and Burdett A. Loomis (Washington, D.C.: CQ Press, 1983), 354-369.

6. See Lawrence C. Dodd and Bruce I. Oppenheimer, "The House in Transition: Change and Consolidation," and Norman J. Ornstein, Robert L. Peabody, and David W. Rohde, "The Contemporary Senate: Into the 1980s," in *Congress Reconsidered*, 2d ed., ed. Lawrence C. Dodd and Bruce I. Oppenheimer (Washington, D.C.: CQ Press, 1981).

7. See Allen Schick, *Congress and Money: Budgeting, Spending and Taxing* (Washington, D.C.: The Urban Institute Press, 1980).

8. John J. Rhodes, *The Futile System* (McLean, Va.: EPM Publications, 1976), 7.

9. In the House, Rules 10 and 11 define the number, size, and jurisdictions of the standing committees. In the Senate, Rules XXIV and XXV fulfill the same function. And, interestingly, committees are important enough in the House and Senate to be the subject of roughly one-third and two-thirds (respectively) of the total language in each chambers' standing rules.

10. On the development of legislative norms in the Senate and House, respectively, see Donald R. Matthews, *U.S. Senators and Their World* (Chapel Hill: The University of North Carolina Press, 1960); and Herbert B. Asher, "The Learning of Legislative Norms," *American Political Science Review* (June 1973): 499-513.

11. While the Legislative Reorganization Act was the first major set of reforms, the earlier expansion of the Rules Committee in the 1960s was perhaps the first notable reform during this decade. See the description of these events in Chapter 1. It also should be noted that in early 1965, after Republican Gerald R. Ford of Michigan had been elected minority leader, a series of reforms were implemented within the Republican Conference.

12. "Legislative Reorganization Act: First Year's Record," *Congressional Quarterly Weekly Report*, March 4, 1972, 485-491.

13. Schick, *Congress and Money*, 53-71.

14. Norman J. Ornstein, "Causes and Consequences of Congressional Change: Subcommittee Reforms in the House of Representatives, 1970-73," in *Congress in Change: Evolution and Reform*, ed. Norman J. Ornstein (New York: Praeger Publishers, 1975), 88-114.

15. "House Reform: Easy To Advocate, Hard To Define," *Congressional Quarterly Weekly Report*, January 20, 1973, 69-72.

16. For a summary of subcommittee reforms during this period see Christopher J. Deering and Steven S. Smith, "Majority Party Leadership and the New House Subcommittee System," in *Understanding Congressional Leadership*, ed. Frank H. Mackaman (Washington, D.C.: CQ Press, 1981), 264.

17. An in-depth history of the Bolling Committee is provided by Roger H. Davidson and Walter J. Oleszek, *Congress against Itself*, (Bloomington: Indiana University Press, 1977).

18. See "Jurisdiction Overhaul Recommended For House," *Congressional Quarterly Weekly Report*, December 22, 1973, 3358-3366, and U.S., Congress, House, Select Committee on Committees, "Committee Reform Amendments of 1974," 93d Congress, 2d sess., March 1973, House Rept. 916.

19. Roger H. Davidson, "Two Avenues of Change: House and Senate Committee Reorganization," in *Congress Reconsidered*, ed. Dodd and Oppenheimer, 114.

20. Davidson and Oleszek, *Congress against Itself*, 250.

21. This account of the Stevenson Committee is drawn from Judith H. Parris, "The Senate Reorganizes Its Committees, 1977," *Political Science Quarterly* 95 (Summer 1979): 319-337, and Roger H. Davidson, "Two Avenues of Change: House and Senate Committee Reorganization," in *Congress Reconsidered*, ed. Dodd and Oppenheimer, 120-128.
22. The Select Committee had no legislative authority—it could not report legislation to the floor. Therefore, upon completion of a report, a bill or resolution embracing suggestions of the committee had to be formally introduced.
23. The members were Frank Moss of Utah, Vance Hartke of Indiana, and Gale McGee of Wyoming.
24. John F. Bibby, Thomas E. Mann, and Norman J. Ornstein, *Vital Statistics on Congress, 1980* (Washington, D.C.: American Enterprise Institute for Public Policy Research, 1980), 61-62.
25. The reader is cautioned to treat data on staff with some care. A variety of sources, including the *Congressional Staff Directory* (Mount Vernon, Va.: Congressional Staff Directory, Ltd.) are available, and each has different results or totals. Thus these figures will not match those of other sources. Nonetheless, the substantive conclusions offered here remain regardless of source.
26. Roger H. Davidson, "Subcommittee Government: New Channels For Policy Making," in *The New Congress*, ed. Thomas E. Mann and Norman J. Ornstein (Washington, D.C.: American Enterprise Institute for Public Policy Research, 1981), 109.
27. Davidson, "Subcommittee Government," 116.

Agenda and Environmental Influences | 3

"They deal with different issues and face different pressures," retorted a senator to a question about the differences between two committees. Members of Congress often refer to the variety of subject matter and political environments they face when explaining how their committees differ. And rightly so. Consider these extremes. The Judiciary committees handle such highly salient and divisive issues as abortion, school prayer, and the Equal Rights Amendment. As a result, their members receive national media attention, are inundated with contradictory demands from dozens of well-organized groups and the general public, and are forced to take positions on proposed legislation that alienate large numbers of constituents. In contrast, the veterans committees typically handle issues of genuine interest only to veterans. These issues usually spark active lobbying by a comparatively small number of veterans organizations that frequently are in agreement with the basic thrust of public policy. Clearly, the substantive issues handled by committees vary widely, and outsiders concerned about the issues differ greatly.

Issues and interested outsiders also change over time. These changes sometimes are due to adjustments in committees' jurisdictions, but more often they are the result of events largely outside of members' control. A war, an industrial accident, increasing incidents of a disease, or rising expectations for government services may quickly or gradually redirect a committee's attention and change the kind of outsiders interested in it. Thus shifting issues and environments are the second major impetus for change in committee politics.

Issues and outsiders create both opportunities and constraints for committee members. Popular causes, for example, provide opportunities for strategically placed committee members to gain publicity back home or even across the nation. The attention of interest groups, constituents, and others gives committee members an opportunity to serve them—

59

and gain political credits for doing so. But the same outsiders also can act in certain ways to put constraints on committee members. For example, they can help define political issues to be considered and limit the range of politically acceptable options available to a committee or to individual members. These opportunities and constraints play an important role in defining the attractiveness of committees to members. The changing variety of issue agendas and political environments is explored in this chapter.[1]

Examining Environmental Factors

Committee environments can be divided into three components. First, each committee operates within a public environment comprised of the general public and representatives of organized interests. Second, most committees deal with an interbranch environment that includes some part or parts of the federal establishment: the administration, bureaucracy, and the courts. Finally, all committees function within a congressional environment. Party leaders, chamber colleagues, and the other chamber make up this immediate environment. The character and significance of these components vary from committee to committee.

Three properties of these committee environments, each closely related to policy properties, are especially useful for understanding the differences among and changes within committees. The first is *fragmentation*. Fragmentation concerns the degree to which a committee attracts the attention of outsiders who perceive their interests as unrelated to each other. Fragmentation in a committee's political environment is rooted in the committee's jurisdiction: the larger the number of topics falling under its jurisdiction, the more fragmented the committee's political environment is likely to be. Major changes in environmental fragmentation are stimulated by changes in a committee's formal jurisdiction. But because all possible topics are not always on a committee's active agenda, most changes in environmental fragmentation reflect the number of separate issues under active consideration. Jurisdictional and environmental fragmentation, as will be seen in later chapters, helps to structure committees' decision-making processes by defining the number of political problems presented to them.

The second and third properties are *salience* and *environmental conflict*. Each distinguishable agenda item can vary in salience and environmental conflict, as David Price has indicated.[2] Salience can be judged in the public at large, as it usually is,[3] within the Congress,[4] or even within particular constituencies. An issue's salience stems, at least in part, from inherent policy characteristics, such as the pattern of costs and benefits involved in policy alternatives being considered. The greater the number of people affected by a potential policy decision, the greater the issue's salience is likely to be. Not surprisingly, members of Congress are sensitive to the number of people who care about an issue.

Conflict refers to the degree to which interested outsiders see their interests as competing or compatible with each other. This distinction has been called the level of controversy, zero-sum versus positive-sum, and competitive versus noncompetitive.[5] Conflict also is grounded in a policy decision's perceived distribution of costs and benefits. Conflict among interested outsiders often forces members to pick and choose among competing interests, favoring some and perhaps alienating others. Thus the level of conflict in a committee's environment helps to shape the incentives and disincentives for members to participate in various committee activities.

An accounting of a committee's environmental salience and conflict requires an aggregation over all issues within its jurisdiction. In the case of salience, the total number of interested outsiders is the most important descriptive feature. Committees with a large number of topics under their jurisdictions, and thus fragmented environments, are likely to have environments of great scope. In the case of conflict, we will refer to the modal conflict situation. A committee's environment is likely to be conflictual when its jurisdiction and the number of interested outsiders are large. While it is not possible to detail each committee's environment here, it is important to recognize the variety in committee environments and to spot extreme cases for each of these properties. We begin by noting the differences and changes in committee jurisdictions that underlie many of the differences and changes in committee environments.

Jurisdictional Fragmentation

Members of Congress have disagreed vehemently at times about the best division of labor in their committee systems, but most have agreed that related policy areas should be placed under the same committee's jurisdiction.[6] Such coherent jurisdictions permit an efficient development and application of legislative expertise and encourage simultaneous consideration of interrelated issues. Unfortunately, coherent but distinct jurisdictions are difficult to create, even in principle. Jurisdictional lines inevitably are somewhat overlapping and arbitrary because of the great interdependence of governmental policies affecting economic, political, and social life. Even if mutually exclusive and coherent jurisdictions could be devised, events outside Congress's control would gradually undermine the alignment's rationale. For individual committees, such events may create new relationships among subjects under their jurisdictions, perhaps increasing or decreasing the fragmentation of their political environments and producing new jurisdictional conflicts with other committees.

Despite efforts to mold coherent jurisdictions, to eliminate committees with small jurisdictions, and to equalize legislative burdens among standing committees, most congressional committees have jurisdictions that include subjects that have no real relationship to each other. In some cases, this jurisdictional fragmentation is by design. For example, the 1977 Senate reforms added space and transportation issues to the Commerce Committee's large jurisdiction, which already included such disparate subjects as sports, consumer protection, and the merchant marine. In other cases, jurisdictions grew in a more gradual fashion—the result of an accumulation of new policy areas conceptually linked to existing jurisdictions. To one degree or another, nearly all standing committees are holding companies for disconnected policy areas.

Jurisdictional fragmentation varies widely among committees. Table 3-1 groups House and Senate committees according to their average rank on two indicators of jurisdictional fragmentation: (1) the number of separate executive departments and independent agencies that fall under each committee's jurisdiction and (2) the number of subjects listed in each committee's jurisdiction under its chamber's rules. While it cannot be assumed that each department or subject is politically independent of others that fall within a committee's jurisdiction, the resulting rankings yield a fairly accurate view of the spectrum of jurisdictional fragmentation.

House committees are ranked similarly to their Senate counterparts. In both chambers, the appropriations, commerce, labor, and foreign policy committees have large, highly fragmented jurisdictions.[7] The House Interior and Insular Affairs Committee and its closest Senate counterpart, Energy and Natural Resources, are important exceptions. The jurisdictional fragmentation of these committees is similar in absolute terms, but the broader, more fragmented jurisdictions of several Senate committees result in a relatively lower standing for Energy and Natural Resources. The House rankings reflect modest increases in five House committees' fragmentation that resulted from the 1975 Bolling-Hansen reforms. The clear loser in these jurisdictional shifts was Ways and Means, which lost jurisdiction over general revenue sharing, nontax

Table 3-1 Jurisdictional Fragmentation Among
Congressional Committees

Jurisdictional Fragmentation	House	Senate
High	Appropriations Energy and Commerce Interior Education & Labor Public Works Foreign Affairs Judiciary	Appropriations Labor Commerce Foreign Relations Governmental Affairs Judiciary Environment & Public Works
Medium	Agriculture Science & Technology Government Operations Merchant Marine Banking Armed Services	Banking Energy & Natural Resources Agriculture Finance Armed Services
Low	House Administration Small Business District of Columbia Veterans' Affairs Rules Standards of Official Conduct	Rules & Administration Veterans' Affairs Small Business

Note: Committees listed in rank order. Budget committees are excluded.
Source: See Tables A-2 and A-3, Appendix.

aspects of health policy, and other areas. The Senate rankings also reflect that chamber's 1977 jurisdictional realignment (see box, p. 64).

The Public Environment

Data on the three properties are most complete for the public environment, and each of the properties is detailed here for that category. Fortunately, the interbranch and chamber environments, where less systematic data are available, run closely parallel to the public environment. Thus a more complete discussion here will provide a backdrop for the discussion of the other environments below.

Fragmentation

For most committees, jurisdictional fragmentation is closely related to the fragmentation of their public environments. That is, committees with highly fragmented jurisdictions also have many separate sets of groups and individuals making unrelated demands on committee members. In both chambers, the Appropriations committees attract dozens of groups' attention each year as they consider funding bills for federal programs. These committees, by far, have the most fragmented public environments. At the other extreme, the House and Senate Veterans' Affairs committees regularly face a handful of national veterans groups with overlapping concerns. Both Veterans' Affairs committees have routinized their interaction with veterans groups by holding separate

---

1977 Senate Jurisdictional Changes

The following standing committees gained major new areas of jurisdiction from S Res 4, adopted by the Senate on February 4, 1977:

Agriculture, Nutrition, and Forestry	Previously Agriculture and Forestry, this committee gained nutrition jurisdiction from the abolished Select Nutrition Committee and gained school lunch program jurisdiction from the Labor Committee.
Banking, Housing, and Urban Affairs	Banking gained foreign commerce and veterans' housing jurisdiction from Commerce and Veterans' Affairs.
Commerce, Science, and Transportation	Commerce gained the jurisdiction of the abolished Aeronautical and Space Sciences Committee.
Energy and Natural Resources	Previously Interior and Insular Affairs, Energy gained most of the jurisdiction of the old committee plus nonmilitary atomic energy, water power, naval petroleum reserves, and other energy areas.
Environment and Public Works	Previously Public Works, Environment and Public Works gained fisheries and wildlife jurisdiction from Commerce.
Governmental Affairs	Previously Government Operations, this committee gained the jurisdiction of the abolished District of Columbia Committee and the abolished Post Office and Civil Service Committee.

---

hearings on the groups' legislative recommendations each year. No other committee interacts with outside clientele groups in this way.

Jurisdictional fragmentation is a misleading indicator of fragmentation in the public environments of two sets of committees. First, the House Government Operations and Senate Governmental Affairs committees have broad oversight jurisdictions that make their public environments highly variable from year to year. These committees have been given authority to examine the "economy and efficiency" of any government program or agency. This authority enables them to call before their committees the full gamut of outsiders with interests spanning all policy areas. Government Operations' and Governmental Affairs' environments are thus more dependent on their members' temporary policy interests than other committees and are difficult to characterize in any straightforward manner. In absolute terms, Senate Governmental Affairs has a more complex environment than does House Government Operations because of its jurisdiction's greater diversity. The Senate committee gained jurisidiction over the Postal Service, the District of Columbia, and other areas in 1977.

Second, the two tax committees, House Ways and Means and Senate Finance, have jurisdictions that appear relatively unfragmented when judged by the number of subjects listed in chamber rules and the number of agencies explicitly under their purview. Nevertheless, they attract scores of separate private sector interests that typically treat their concerns as unrelated. Businesses, industries, individuals, and organizations of all kinds regularly seek preferential treatment in the tax code. The committees' focus on one topic (taxation) and one agency (Treasury) obscures the vast number of separate interests affected by the tax code. While claims for favorable tax treatment all affect the government's revenues, the involved groups usually make independent appeals to the committees. The appeals are related only in that the committees usually deal with them in the same large piece of legislation.

The public environment of Senate Finance was more complex than Ways and Means' environment during the 1950s and 1960s.[8] This reflected two factors. First, according to the Constitution, tax bills must originate in the House, which in practice means that House Ways and Means takes action before Senate Finance formally begins to consider legislation.[9] Second, Ways and Means traditionally has been able to insulate itself from some lobbying pressure by closing to the public its markups and hearings with administration officials. As a result, groups generally had less access to the House committee; those that were dissatisfied with House decisions would turn to the Senate committee. But between the mid-1970s and 1983, Ways and Means lacked the protective cover of closed meetings and, as would be expected, its environment became more similar to Finance's.[10] Ways and Means members regularly engaged in the bargaining and logrolling that have long characterized Finance members' interaction with their environment.

Beginning in July 1983, however, Ways and Means members closed many of the meetings in which tax bills were written. Committee members found it difficult to close tax loopholes with lobbyists scrutinizing their every action. Even members opposed to closed meetings recognized the pitfalls of open meetings. Democratic opponent Don J. Pease of Ohio admitted that members are "unable to agree to controversial provisions that they would be more reluctant to agree to if lobbyists were sitting out there watching."[11] The committee's top staffer noted: "Members are much more willing to feel free to say things they would never say in public—a particular problem they might have because of a constituent for instance."[12] It is too early to determine if a new pattern is being established that again will reshape Ways and Means' relations with interest groups.

Salience

High fragmentation in jurisdictions or environments does not translate directly into high public salience. Ideally, this proposition could be demonstrated by using survey data on the scope of interest in issues falling under each committee's jurisdiction. Unfortunately, no such survey data are available. Examining the content of television network news broadcasts is a convenient alternative. Given the preeminent status of network television as an information source for the American public, it is reasonable to assume that the amount of time devoted to a topic in network news broadcasts is indicative of public interest in that topic.[13] For each committee, the amount of television time devoted to topics falling within its legislative jurisdiction was determined from a systematic sample of CBS Evening News broadcasts during the 1969-1980 period.[14] The results, a summation of the first and second halves of the period, are presented in Table 3-2.[15]

Table 3-2 shows how consistently topics under the jurisdictions of the foreign policy, judiciary, and commerce committees dominate national attention. The difference between the first and second periods for the foreign policy committees is due to the absence of Vietnam-related stories in the tallies, but it does reflect the shift in national attention from Vietnam to the Mideast. Crime and, on a less regular basis, civil rights, are the dominating subjects for the judiciary committees, al-

Table 3-2 Minutes of CBS Evening News Devoted to Topics Falling Within Committee Jurisdictions (From a 50 Percent Sample of Newscasts), Ranked by the 1975-1980 Standing*

House	1969-1974	1975-1980	Senate	1969-1974	1975-1980
Foreign Affairs	2109	4879	Foreign Relations	2109	4879
Judiciary**	1216	1299	Judiciary	1518	1299
Commerce	823	882	Commerce	698	835
Armed Services	467	524	Labor	569	808
Education & Labor	333	462	Energy (Int.)	243	772
Ways & Means	268	347	Armed Services	467	623
Public Works	180	339	Envir. (Pub. Wks.)	335	399
Interior	249	275	Finance	268	347
Merchant Marine	200	216	Banking	280	166
Science & Technology	423	211	Agriculture	101	156
Agriculture	97	155	Governmental Affairs	22	90
Banking	280	153	Veterans' Affairs	42	44
Government Operations	22	52	Rules & Administration	75	35
Post Office	52	48	Small Business	—	10
Veterans' Affairs	42	44			
House Administration	54	35	Committees abolished in 1977:		
Small Business	5	10	Aeronautics	387	55
District of Columbia	1	6	Post Office	52	14
Rules	10	5	District of Columbia	1	0

Cross-cutting issues excluded from the above tallies:

	1969-1974	1975-1980
Vietnam/Indochina	2606	608
Economy	733	748
Energy	343	614

* The Appropriations committees are excluded.
** Excludes Watergate-related stories, which totaled nearly 1,300 minutes in 1973-74.

Source: Television News Index and Abstracts.

though including the coverage of Watergate and the House Judiciary impeachment proceedings would add a substantial amount of time to the tally for that committee. The commerce committees' salience is drawn from more than half-a-dozen subjects, reflecting the committees' great jurisdictional fragmentation. The House Commerce Committee has a somewhat more salient jurisdiction than its Senate counterpart because of its jurisdiction over health and air pollution issues. The difference would be even greater, especially for the 1975-1980 period, if energy stories were added to the House committee's total. Health and air pollution fall under the Senate's Labor and Environment committees' jurisdictions, respectively. Because of these differences, both committees' jurisdictions are more salient than their House counterparts'.

Equally important to note is that eight or nine House committees and four or five Senate committees have jurisdictions of consistently low national salience. Except for the government operations committees, these committees have narrow, relatively unfragmented jurisdictions. They include three committees—House Rules, House Administration, and Senate Rules and Administration—that deal primarily with the chambers' internal matters.

Significant changes in the salience of several issues on the national agenda, other than energy and Vietnam, are hidden within the aggregate totals of Table 3-2. Most importantly, pollution control issues, which topped the nation's agenda in the late 1960s and early 1970s, received less attention in the late 1970s and thereafter. Several committees were affected by this change, especially Commerce, Interior, Merchant Marine, and Public Works in the House and Environment and Public Works in the Senate. Most of the increase in the House Public Works' tally is due to the transfer of aviation to the committee's jurisdiction and the great attention paid to aviation safety during the late 1970s and early 1980s. Other important changes included:

●Issues under House Science and Technology and Senate Aeronautics and Space lost salience as attention to the space program faded with the demise of the manned space program in the 1970s.

●National attention to issues associated with the labor committees shifted away from equal employment opportunities and occupational safety and health questions.

●Civil rights issues, such as school busing, which fall under the Judiciary committees, faded during the 1970s and were replaced by abortion and school prayer after the Supreme Court issued decisions on those matters.

●Issues under the government operations committees' jurisdiction showed slight increases in salience as government waste and fraud gained more attention in the mid- and late 1970s.

●Urban problems before the Banking committees declined in salience after a period of increased attention to price controls during the Nixon administration.

Thus agendas change constantly—and sometimes rapidly—altering the salience of otherwise static committee jurisidictions.

The news broadcast tallies also suggest why, in addition to their smaller number and larger constituencies, senators typically are more visible than House members. Senate committee jurisdictions are more salient, on the average, than House committee jurisdictions, reflecting the distribution of Senate jurisdictions among fewer committees. A more even distribution of highly salient jurisdictions also exists among the top six or seven Senate committees. Thus senators, with their larger number of committee assignments, are more likely to belong to a committee with very salient jurisdiction: 77 percent of senators were assigned to at least one of the six most highly ranked committees in the 97th Congress, while only 47 percent of House members sat on one or more of that chamber's six most highly ranked committees.

Conflict

As David Price correctly points out, salience is closely related to conflict in committee environments.[16] The presence of conflict means that an issue is salient to at least someone. Intense conflict, moreover, may stimulate media and public interest in an issue. But committees with jurisdiction over equally salient subjects often experience quite different levels of conflict in their environments. Members and staff recognize these differences, and they are sensitive to changes in the level of conflict within their committees' environments. As the senator quoted at the beginning of the chapter explained about "pressure," "I don't just mean pressure to do something, I mean pressure to choose between two very polarized sides to an issue—that's pressure." Based on the comments of committee members and staff, we have placed committees into three categories. The results are provided in Table 3-3, where the relative salience of committees' jurisdictions is indicated. While substantial variance exists within each of the categories, the broad differences between categories are easily deciphered from participants' comments.

Clearly, conflict in the public environment is positively related to salience; thus the parallel between House and Senate committees' salience is present for conflict as well. Major differences between House and Senate committees occur in the commerce and interior committees. The energy and health jurisdiction of House Energy and Commerce gives it sources of environmental conflict that are not present for Senate Commerce. Indeed, House Commerce's environment exhibits much more conflict than the Senate committee's. Democrat John Dingell of Michigan, chair of the House committee, quipped that "controversy follows the committee around like the Earth follows the Sun."[17] The

Table 3-3 Perceived Conflict and Salience of Committee Public Environments (Direction of Change in Conflict During Past 15 Years Indicated in Parentheses)*

Perceived Conflict	Salience		
	High	Moderate	Low
High	Budget (+) H. Commerce (+) Judiciary (+) Labor	S. Energy & NR S. Finance H. Ways & Means (+)	
Moderate	S. Commerce Foreign policy	Appropriations (+) Armed services Banking (−) Public works (−) H. Interior (−)	
Low			Agriculture Govt. Operations H. Science H. Mer. Marine (−) H. Post Office H. Dist. of Col. Veterans Small Business

* References are to both the House and Senate committees unless otherwise indicated. Excludes House Rules, House Administration, and Senate Rules and Administration, for which the public environment is not significant. The Appropriations and Budget committees have been classified on salience based on their role in spending and economic policy.

Source: Conflict: Authors' interviews with participants; Salience: Table 3-2.

Senate counterpart also has been a hotbed of political controversy, but, as consumer issues under its jurisdiction faded in significance during the 1970s, so did conflict in the committee's environment. The interior committees—House Interior and Insular Affairs and Senate Energy and Natural Resources—are more similar. Energy and Natural Resource's energy jurisdiction is substantially broader, though, bringing to it conflicts that take place before Commerce in the House. Other smaller differences exist between the chambers, but none that suggest that the committees should be placed in separate categories. For example, Senate

Environment and Public Works has experienced more intense conflict in air pollution and other environmental policy battles than has its House counterpart. The declining significance of environmental disputes has made these committees more similar in recent years.

Table 3-3 also indicates which committees have experienced substantial increases (+) or decreases (-) in their public environments' level of conflict since the late 1960s. Other sets of committees also deserve attention. The Judiciary committees' environments have been relatively high in conflict throughout this period, but the rise of abortion, school prayer, balanced budgets, and other issues involving proposed constitutional amendments has intensified conflict even more. An aide to Speaker Thomas P. "Tip" O'Neill declared that House Judiciary members now face "razor-sharp issues" because they confront diametrically opposed groups with intensely held beliefs. The conflict in the public environments of the Appropriations and especially the Budget committees increased as federal spending became a more salient issue in the late 1970s. The Appropriations committees' environmental conflict was exacerbated further by the increasing use of riders on appropriations bills. Riders, which are amendments designed to limit spending for some otherwise authorized purpose (for abortions, for example), have attracted the attention of many groups that previously had paid little attention to spending bills.

The Interbranch Environment

The character of interbranch environments also varies greatly. Four broad types of interbranch environments can be identified, as has been done in Tables A-4 and A-5 (Appendix) where types of witnesses appearing before each committee in the prereform 91st Congress and the postreform 96th Congress are provided. One group of committees interacts primarily with executive officials representing the viewpoints of the particular administration in power. A second set interacts with relatively large numbers of officials from many agencies, generally focusing on agency activities rather than activities directed by the White House. Committees in a third set normally deal only with officials from a narrow range of agencies. The second set of broad, agency-oriented committees has the most fragmented interbranch environments, while the other two groups' interbranch environments are more monolithic. The executive branch plays only a very small, explicit role in the environments of the Senate Rules and Administration, House Administration, and House Rules committees.

Top administration officials dominate the interbranch environments of the tax, budget, and foreign policy committees of both chambers.[18] The tax and budget committees' major legislation concerns fiscal policy on which the president is directly and regularly involved.[19] Presidential recommendations in these areas, of course, often are molded with public opinion in mind and, once proposed, they gain high public salience. Indeed, fiscal policy has formed the centerpiece of recent presidents' legislative agendas. Presidential proposals usually serve as the stimulus, and often the starting point, for major legislative action by the tax and budget committees. The committees' interbranch environment is thus highly focused on the president and his personal representatives. This is not to say that the administration is always of one mind; differences of opinion within the administration on fiscal policy are highly publicized events and the publicity indicates how focused the interbranch environments of the tax and budget committees normally are.

The foreign policy committees' interbranch environments are not so exclusively focused on the White House as are the tax and budget committees'. But the relatively centralized nature of foreign policy making in the executive branch still makes their interbranch environments more monolithic than most other committees'. Presidents have a special role in foreign affairs by virtue of their constitutional authority to make treaties and to appoint ambassadors and other foreign policy officials (with the consent of the Senate). The widely recognized need to have a single voice in world politics bolsters this authority. And foreign policy agencies, especially the State Department, operate more directly under the White House's supervision than do most domestic agencies whose mandates are more clearly specified in law. Even when the foreign policy committees are not dealing directly with the highest-level officials in the executive branch, their discussions usually concern administration policy with respect to some aspect of international affairs.

Despite the administration-orientation of both foreign policy committees, Senate Foreign Relations members traditionally have examined a wider range of foreign policy matters and interacted with a broader range of executive officials than have House Foreign Affairs members. In part, this was a product of the Senate committee's constitutional role in ratifying treaties and confirming presidential appointees.[20] But differences between the committees' interbranch environments have virtually disappeared. After a series of internal reforms in the early 1970s, the House committee's subcommittees became more active and began to explore a wide range of international issues comparable to those considered by Foreign Relations.[21] In fact, as the more recent witness tallies suggest, House Foreign Affairs has interviewed more executive witnesses in recent Congresses than has Foreign Relations. (See Tables A-4 and A-5, Appendix.)

Most committees with highly fragmented jurisdictions also have fragmented, agency-oriented interbranch environments, with a relatively large number of officials from many agencies appearing as witnesses. (These are the committees in the second groups of Tables A-4 and A-5, Appendix.) And yet, with two important exceptions, agency witnesses are not nearly so numerous as public witnesses. Except for House Appropriations members, these committee members generally view nongovernmental groups as the most important parts of their political environments. Nongovernmental groups' demands or needs are the focus of these committees' activities. For several committees, especially the energy, judiciary, and labor committees, the size or political significance of these outside groups frequently leads to the involvement of the president and his closest advisers.

The House and Senate Appropriations committees are the two committees in this group that hear more executive than public witnesses. For both committees, executive witnesses usually are officials who present justifications for their agencies' funding requests. The House Appropriations Committee, though, hears more than three times the number of executive (and other) witnesses than does its Senate counterpart, even though the proportion of executive witnesses is nearly identical. This is the product of several factors.[22] Senate Appropriations members have a somewhat narrower focus on constituency interests than do House committee members.[23] And, by custom, appropriations bills originate in the House. Consequently, senators' attention often is focused on appeals from officials and affected outsiders unhappy with House decisions.[24] Senate Appropriations members also have less time to devote to their committee's activities because they normally hold two or three other committee assignments—unlike House Appropriations members who usually are not permitted seats on other standing committees.[25] Agency officials, of course, are fully cognizant of the differences between the two committees and put more effort and manpower into their presentations before the House committee.

The House Appropriations Committee's environment has become less dominated by executive officials and more oriented toward nongovernmental groups (see Chapter 4). This is a direct result of House reforms that opened committee meetings and limited the Appropriations chair's involvement in subcommittee assignments. Members now are free to choose subcommittees related to the interests of constituency groups and are obliged to hear those groups' demands in open hearings. In fact, House Appropriations' public witnesses have increased from only 23 percent from 1969 to 1970 to about 40 percent from 1979 to 1980, rising to the Senate committee's figure for both periods. In short, House Appropriations' political environment has become more similar to that of Senate Appropriations. (See Tables A-4 and A-5, Appendix.)

The interbranch environments of the third set of committees differ little from the environments of other agency-oriented committees, except for their relevance to a small number of agencies. The Armed Services committees deserve to be noted, though, for executive officials' dominance of their environments. In both chambers, civilian and uniformed defense officials consume most of the Armed Services committees' time. And the president dominates their time when the issues involve major new weapons programs, the use of troops abroad, or are related to defense-oriented foreign policy issues. As a result, the armed services committees' environments closely resemble the foreign policy committees' when such issues arise. But most committee-department interaction concerns matters to which the president and his closest advisers pay little attention. Procurement practices, benefits for military personnel, activities at various military installations, and many other matters seldom attract the White House's attention. Thus the armed services committees, like the other committees in this · category, have interbranch environments that are somewhat more fragmented than those of the tax, budget, and foreign policy committees.

Finally, it should be noted that while the fragmentation and scope of interbranch environments vary considerably, conflict within the interbranch environments varies little over the long-run. This is not surprising because most potential conflicts among executive agencies and officials are resolved prior to presentation of executive recommendations to Congress or simply are suppressed by the administration. In any case, conflict within the executive branch does not appear to be distributed in any systematic, uneven way among congressional committees.

The Congressional Environment

Congressional colleagues are the final major ingredient in committee environments. Noncommittee colleagues may shape a committee's actions as claimants on committee decisions and as judges of decisions once they reach the floor. An average member's interest in a committee is likely to stem from the relevance of the committee's decisions to the member's own political circumstances.[26]

Two situations should be distinguished:

First, many House and Senate committees regularly receive demands from noncommittee members who are seeking benefits for their constituents. The agriculture, appropriations, armed services, commerce, interior, post office, public works, tax, and veterans' affairs committees of both chambers are in this group. Rank-and-file colleagues are not the dominant forces in these committees' environments, but they do play an important role in supporting outside clientele groups and, often on an individual basis, in committee members' efforts to build support for legislation that includes benefits for their own constituencies.

Second, highly salient, national issues affect members collectively by shaping public attitudes about the party to which they belong. Individual members believe that their own policy positions affect their reelection chances, but their party's performance on those issues is an additional concern. Not surprisingly, then, party leaders are a central component of the environments of those committees with jurisdiction over salient issues dividing the Democratic and Republican parties. In response to rank-and-file expectations, which often come in the form of explicit demands, party leaders assert themselves in policy areas likely to affect their party's electoral fortunes.[27] These areas typically are ones in which the administration also is involved, except for many foreign policy issues that are handled on a nonpartisan basis.

Issues handled by the tax and budget committees are highly salient, as previously noted, and long have divided the parties.[28] Thus these committees are under party leaders' constant surveillance. Party leaders take special care in making appointments to these committees, and they expect greater support for party positions from their appointees on these committees than from members of most others.[29] The commerce, energy, judiciary, and labor committees also regularly deal with salient issues dividing the parties, but not quite so exclusively as do the tax and budget committees. Overall, committees attracting party leaders' attention have the most complex, fragmented environments because they typically include the administration, affected clientele groups, and the general public.

Nearly all committee environments have been complicated by the congressional budget process, especially since 1980 when the reconciliation procedure began to be employed after the first budget resolution. By this procedure, Congress orders committees to devise legislation that will yield reductions in spending below otherwise projected levels. The Budget committees police this process, placing themselves squarely in

75

the environments of most other committees. As will be seen in Chapter 4, the roles of the budget process and budget committees have become particularly important for the appropriations committees, whose spending discretion has been constrained by the new process. Nearly three-quarters of standing committees were affected by orders to produce "legislative savings" in programs under their jurisdictions in the 97th Congress.

Three committees have environments almost entirely dominated by chamber colleagues. In the House Administration and Senate Rules and Administration committees, colleague interest is stimulated by their jurisdiction over chamber "housekeeping" matters and campaign laws. But, even here, the interest usually is not very consistent. The House Rules Committee, in contrast, is highly salient to House members because of its role in writing special orders for consideration of legislation on the floor. Approximately 80 percent of Rules hearings are devoted to members' requests for special orders, and most of the remainder concern the procedures, organization, and authority of the House.[30] On special orders for major legislation, party leaders are significant factors in Rules' decisions, especially since the 1974 reform giving the Speaker authority to nominate Democratic members of the Rules Committee.[31] Nonetheless, the environments of these committees tend to be fragmented among the individuals, factions, and committees that compose their chambers.

A crude indicator of a committee's jurisdictional salience among chamber colleagues is the number of pieces of legislation referred to it, as reported in Table 3-4. Clearly, a strong and positive, though far from perfect, correlation exists between the public salience of committee jurisdictions and the volume of legislation committees attract. The tax, judiciary, and commerce committees receive the most referrals. In the tax and commerce committees, the legislation includes both benefits for narrow constituencies (favorable tax status for local industry or broadcast licenses, for example) and items of broad public appeal (such as Social Security benefit increases and health research). The appropriations and budget committees' chamber salience is understated by Table 3-4 because nearly all of the legislation they consider is a self-initiated part of the budget cycle.

The armed services and foreign policy committees are obvious exceptions to the relationship between public salience and referred legislation. Chamber colleagues generally play a small part in the environments of these executive-focused committees, despite the consistently high salience of subjects under their jurisdictions. One senator, a member of Foreign Relations and Agriculture, reports that he has never

Table 3-4 Number of Public Measures Referred to House and Senate
Committees in the 94th-96th Congresses (1975-1980)

House		*Senate*	
Ways & Means	10,043	Commerce	3,487
Judiciary	7,928	Judiciary	3,120
Commerce	6,087	Finance	2,177
Post Office	3,689	Energy & Natural Resources	1,514
Education & Labor	2,718	Governmental Affairs	1,106
Interior	2,552	Labor	959
Rules	2,395	Environment & Public Works	798
Foreign Affairs	2,308	Rules & Administration	712
Public Works	2,191	Banking	706
Banking	2,054	Foreign Relations	704
Agriculture	1,950	Agriculture	676
Veterans' Affairs	1,767	Armed Services	421
Armed Services	1,490	Budget	364
Government Operations	1,366	Veterans' Affairs	307
House Administration	1,267	Appropriations	228
Merchant Marine	1,213	Small Business	80
Science & Technology	672		
Appropriations	410		
Small Business	318		
District of Columbia	221		
Budget	50		

Source: Congressional Research Service, calculated from the SCORPIO bill status system.
House Standards of Official Conduct is excluded.

received a request from a colleague for special consideration on a matter before Foreign Relations. "In contrast," he said, "it's a part of the routine on Ag[riculture]." In the case of Armed Services committees, chamber colleagues frequently take an interest in committee actions on military bases and personnel, but they seldom submit legislation detailing defense policy or weapons programs, areas in which noncommittee members and staff have little competence. The special role of the executive in defense and foreign policy making also means that congressional action is less frequently an appropriate response to a world event or executive action than it is in most facets of domestic policy.

The large number of bills referred to House Post Office and Civil Service, relative to its low public salience, may come as a surprise. Its high ranking results from the large number of measures it considers to create national holidays and other days of commemoration. These measures recently have numbered more than 600 per Congress. Few are given serious consideration, but members continue to find at least symbolic value in their introduction.[32] A handful are reported by the committee each year; in the 95th Congress, for example, legislation was reported that called for a National Grandparents Day, a National Joggers Day, and a National Good Neighbor Day.

The conflict in congressional environments is a product of the conflict in committees' public environments. In our interviews, we detected no significant differences in members' perceptions of conflict in their congressional and public environments. Indeed, noncommittee colleagues' demands on a committee were nearly always reported to be closely associated with the outside group or constituency interest they were representing. As noted earlier, however, three committees have congressional environments of much greater importance than their public environments. In the House Administration and Senate Rules and Administration committees, conflict among chamber colleagues is sporadic and usually only moderately intense. House Rules, on the other hand, regularly faces a conflictive environment as colleagues compete for special orders that give them procedural advantages on the floor or respect their jurisdictional claims. A senior adviser to former Rules Chairman Richard Bolling argued that the intensity of these disputes often exceeded the policy fights themselves because they frequently involved longstanding personality and status conflicts among members.

Despite the similarity of congressional environments in corresponding House and Senate committees, a marked difference continues to exist between chambers in the relative significance of the rank-and-file members and the party leadership. Chamber colleagues tend to be more important in the Senate than in the House. One thoughtful senator, a former House member, explains:

> When I wanted to influence a committee's decision in the House, all I could do is testify, talk to a few friends on the committee, and then, if I didn't like their bill, cast a lonely vote on the floor against it. But as soon as I walked into the Senate it became clear to me . . . that my options are better here. Even after just four years, I tend to know more of the fellows on the committee better than I often did in the House, and everyone seems to respect the fact that you can go to the floor if you're not happy about what went on in committee.

This senator describes what Richard Fenno has termed the "permeability" of Senate committees.[33] He also indicates two underlying causes of differences between the two chambers in this respect: the stronger personal relationships among senators and the greater importance of floor deliberations in Senate decision making. Fenno points out that the

Senate's smaller size and greater overlap in committee memberships, the product of a larger number of assignments per member, permit strong relationships to develop among a higher proportion of senators.[34] As a result, noncommittee members in the Senate generally have greater access to committee members and thus have more opportunities to influence committee decisions. The House has opened some additional access to its committees as a result of the 1970s reforms, but the underlying causes for the differences remain.[35]

In contrast, House party leaders play a more significant role in committee environments than do Senate party leaders. House leaders have firmer control of resources important to committee members. As will be seen in Chapter 8, House leaders more firmly control committee assignments. In the larger House, the party whip systems, which can be used to gather information about support and opposition to committee bills, are often an important tool for committee members; they operate under party leaders' supervision. And House majority party leaders face fewer effective challengers to their control of floor scheduling than do Senate leaders, who must worry about filibusters destroying their plans. As a result, House committee members concerned about the fate of a controversial bill on the floor are more likely to seek out party leaders for assistance. In part, the role of House leaders reflects the Democratic reforms of the 1970s, but, as we saw in Chapter 1, it also represents long-term differences between the chambers.

Conclusion

Committees vary widely in the character of their jurisdictions and environments. They also differ greatly in the degree to which issues under their jurisdiction attract attention and engender conflict among interested outsiders. Some committees, such as the budget, commerce, judiciary, labor, and tax committees, regularly consider highly salient and controversial issues. Others, such as agriculture, veterans' affairs, and small business committees, have legislative jurisdictions that attract little attention and conflict. Jurisdictional reform and evolving national issues also affect committees' agendas and the character of their environments. Thus, in addition to opportunities and constraints associated with change in formal structures and procedures, shifting agendas and environments alter opportunities and constraints perceived by members. How these two sets of factors mold members' attitudes about their committees is the subject of the next chapter.

NOTES

1. The claim that agendas and interested outsiders differ in important ways among committees would not be disputed by any observer of Congress, and yet identifying a useful set of properties to characterize committees' agendas and environments is a difficult task. One possible approach is to focus on the the subject matter or policy decision per se, that is, to identify properties inherent to the policy issue itself. Properties such as the pattern of costs and benefits, complexity, divisibility, volume, and newness have been noted. See, for example, John Ferejohn, *Pork Barrel Politics* (Stanford, Calif.: Stanford University Press, 1974), 5; James Q. Wilson, *Political Organizations* (New York: Basic Books, 1973), 330; Theodore J. Lowi, "American Business, Public Policy, Case Studies and Political Theory," *World Politics* 16 (July 1964): 677-715; John F. Manley, *The Politics of Finance* (Boston: Little, Brown & Co., 1970), 92-95. Committees' agendas may differ on each of these properties and may become more or less alike over time.

   Policy properties, unfortunately, have proven difficult to use for empirical research. Consequently, most scholars attempt to establish the empirical import of their concepts only by example or shift away from direct measures and rely instead on decision makers' perceptions of issues they face. The latter approach usually is justified further on the grounds that it is the participants' perceptions that are significant anyway, although it is often implied that perceptions are closely related to the objective characteristics of issues. Unfortunately, when dealing with the multifaceted jurisdictions of congressional committees, even perceptual measures are difficult to employ rigorously.

   Policy properties, in turn, usually are assumed to have a strong causal connection to the nature of committees' political environments. James Q. Wilson, for example, argues that a policy with very concentrated benefits for a small segment of society, but with widely dispersed costs, will engender less interest and opposition than a policy with concentrated benefits and costs. See Wilson, *Political Organizations*, 327-337. From committee members' point of view, it is often the political alignments stimulated by an issue, rather than the characteristics of the issue itself, that are significant.

2. David E. Price, *Policymaking in Congressional Committees* (Tucson: The University of Arizona Press, 1979), 45-50; also see David E. Price, "Policy Making in Congressional Committees: The Impact of 'Environmental' Factors," *American Political Science Review* 72 (June 1978): 549, 569-571.

3. Price, *Policymaking*, 564; E. E. Schattschneider, *The Semisovereign People* (Hinsdale, Ill.: The Dryden Press, 1975), Chap. 2.

4. Barbara Hinckley, "Policy Content, Committee Membership, and Behavior," *American Journal of Political Science* 19 (August 1975): 543-557.

5. Hinckley, "Policy Content"; Lowi, "American Business"; and Price, *Policymaking*.

6. For discussions of the problems of jurisdictional alignments, see U.S., Congress, Senate, Temporary Select Committee to Study the Senate Committee System, *The Senate Committee System*, 94th Cong., 2d sess., 151-187; Allen Schick, "Complex Policymaking in the United States Senate"; U.S., Congress, Senate, The Commission on the Operation of the Senate, *Policy Analysis on Major Issues*, 94th Cong., 2d sess., 4-24; U.S., Congress, House,

Select Committee on Committees, *Monographs on the Committees of the House of Representatives,* 93d Congress, 2d sess.

7. The Budget committees have not been included in the ranking because, strictly speaking, they do not have direct jurisdiction over specific agencies or programs, except for the area of budget policy.

8. Manley, *Politics of Finance,* Chap. 6; Richard F. Fenno, *Congressmen in Committees* (Boston: Little, Brown & Co., 1973), 152-154.

9. The 1982 tax bill was a unique exception to this pattern.

10. Catherine E. Rudder, "Committee Reform and the Revenue Process," in *Congress Reconsidered,* 1st ed., ed. Lawrence C. Dodd and Bruce I. Oppenheimer (New York: Praeger Publishers, 1977), 124-126.

11. *Congressional Quarterly Weekly Report,* October 28, 1983, 2067.

12. Ibid.

13. For present purposes, it does not matter whether television news stories represent editorial judgment about what the public already is concerned about or whether the stories actually stimulate public interest in a subject.

14. These data were collected from Vanderbilt Television News Archive, *Televisions News Index and Abstracts* (Nashville, Tenn.: Joint Universities Libraries, 1969-1980). This source provides a synopsis of each story and a running time count of each broadcast. Every other weekday news broadcast was used. Stories involving events that fell under no committee's jurisdiction, such as those on presidential election campaigns or World Series results, were excluded, as were features such as the daily stock market report. CBS stories were used because CBS consistently had more viewers than ABC's or NBC's evening news programs during the period examined.

    Three sets of news stories present special coding difficulties because they fall within the legislative jurisdictions of two or more committees. These sets are listed at the bottom of Table 3-2. The tallies for the affected committees do not include the time allocated to these stories and thus understate the media's attention to matters falling under their jurisdictions. In the case of the war in Indochina, the foreign policy and armed services committees shared common interests. No standing committee has explicit jurisdiction over the state of the economy, although committees with jurisdiction over fiscal and monetary policy, especially the appropriations, tax, and banking committees, have directly related jurisdictions. Finally, as noted in Chapter 2, several committees with jurisdiction over energy, especially the House Commerce Committee, have higher relative standing than their ranking indicates. Beginning in 1977, energy stories were placed under the Energy and Natural Resources Committee, reflecting the Senate's jurisdictional reforms.

15. This approach has two limitations. First, it provides a measure of national salience only. We have no comparable measure for salience within particular constituencies. Second, restricting the study to each committee's legislative jurisdiction means that topics a committee explores as a part of its wider oversight jurisdiction are neglected. This restriction, which is necessary for reducing coding ambiguities, should not affect the relative standing of committees, with the exception of House Government Operations and Senate Governmental Affairs committees.

16. Price, *Policymaking,* 46.

17. Andy Plattner, "Scrappy House Energy Panel Provides High Pressure Arena for Wrangling over Regulation," *Congressional Quarterly Weekly Report*, March 12, 1983, 502.
18. See Manley, *The Politics of Finance*, Chap. 7; Fenno, *Congressmen in Committees*, Chaps. 2 and 5; David E. Price, *Who Makes the Laws?* (Cambridge, Mass.: Schenkman Publishing Co., 1972), Chaps. 4 and 5.
19. These committees also have jurisdiction over Social Security and certain welfare and health areas that regularly involve the administration.
20. Fenno, *Congressmen*, 155.
21. See Fred Kaiser, "Oversight of Foreign Policy: The U.S. House Committee on International Relations," *Legislative Studies Quarterly* 2 (August 1977): 255-279.
22. Fenno, *Congressmen*, 154-155.
23. See Chapter 4.
24. This "appeals court" role was not so important in the early 1980s as Senate Appropriations began to mark up bills before the House passed appropriations bills. See Diane Granat, "Senate Appropriations: A Court of Appeals," *Congressional Quarterly Weekly Report*, June 14, 1983, 1214. Nevertheless, our interviews indicate that the role continues to be an important one for the Senate committee on most appropriations bills.
25. There has been an occasional exception to this rule. It also should be noted that five House Appropriations members now sit on the Budget Committee.
26. See Chapter 4 for a discussion of members' reelection goals.
27. Fenno, *Congressmen*, 24.
28. Fenno, *Congressmen*, 24, 152-153; Lance T. LeLoup, *The Fiscal Congress* (Westport, Conn.: Greenwood Press, 1980), 70-71. 29. See Chapter 8.
30. See the U.S. Congress, House and Senate, Rules Committees "Survey of Activities" for recent Congresses.
31. See Chapter 4 for a description of how this reform changed Rules Democrats' motivations.
32. The House Post Office and Civil Service Committee adopted a rule during the 95th Congress to restrict consideration of measures providing for celebrations or holidays to those that have the written endorsement of a majority of the House.
33. Fenno, *Congressmen*, 148.
34. Ibid., 145-148.
35. For a somewhat different view, see Norman J. Ornstein, "The House and the Senate in a New Congress," in *The New Congress*, ed. Thomas E. Mann and Norman J. Ornstein (Washington, D.C.: American Enterprise Institute for Public Policy Research, 1981), 367-369.

Member Goals | 4

Member goals provide a key to understanding how structural-procedural innovations and agenda-environmental changes alter committee decision-making processes. Reforms, if they are effective, restructure committee members' opportunities to pursue their objectives. Besides redefining issues that committees debate, agenda changes reshape the mix of personal goals that committee members can pursue. Generalizations about the effect of reform and agenda change on member goals are susceptible to great error, however, because members' goals vary from committee to committee. In this chapter, committee-specific effects on member goals are explored.

Types of Member Goals

The significance of personal political goals for understanding committee differences was established by Richard Fenno in *Congressmen in Committees*.[1] Through interviews with members of 12 congressional committees during the late 1950s and 1960s, Fenno identified three goals that motivate members' committee activity: reelection, good public policy, and influence within the chamber. He argued that

> all congressmen probably hold all three goals. But each congressman has his own mix of priorities and intensities—a mix which may, of course, change over time. . . . The opportunity to achieve the three goals varies widely among committees. House members, therefore, match their individual patterns of aspiration to the diverse patterns of opportunity presented by House committees. The matching process usually takes place as a congressman seeks an original assignment or a transfer to a committee he believes well suited to his goals. But it may occur when a congressman adjusts his personal aspirations, temporarily or permanently, to fit the opportunities offered by the committee where he happens to be.[2]

Fenno found that committees did indeed attract members differentially according to their personal goals, a finding that later was corroborated by Charles Bullock's interviews with House freshmen of the 92d Congress (1971-1973).[3]

Since Fenno's seminal work, scholars have disagreed about which of the three goals motivates most members most of the time, but the finding that some mix of the three goals motivates most committee activity remains valid in the 1980s. Table 4-1 gives the number of House and Senate members motivated by each goal in a recent Congress and in Congresses of more than a decade ago. The House figures and the 97th Congress's Senate figures were calculated from junior members' or their knowledgeable staff's responses to the questions: "What committees did you want to serve on (after you were first elected to your chamber)? Why?"[4] The responses include committees that members may not have requested formally, but that were viewed as attractive nevertheless. Unfortunately, no similar data are available for the Senate in an earlier Congress. The 1948-1971 Senate figures were collected by Bullock from the archived papers of two former members of the Senate Democratic Committee on Committees.[5] This written record is not quite so useful because it often represents a senator's attempt to sell himself to party leaders as a candidate for a particular committee assignment, instead of reflecting his or her genuine personal motivation for interest in a committee. The correspondence also excludes committee preferences expressed orally to party leaders and preferences that actually did not lead to a formal request for assignment.

Table 4-1 Motivations for Committee Preferences *(by percent)*

	House		*Senate*	
	1972	1982	Pre-1972	1982
Constituency	69	87	(49)	100
Policy	83	80	(49)	89
Power/Prestige	25	34	(3)	15

Source: See discussion and citations in text. The pre-1972 Senate figure in the constituency category combines Bullock's reelection, regional balance, and prescriptive right categories; the policy category combines Bullock's policy, political experience, and occupational categories.

The "constituency" label has replaced the "reelection" label in Table 4-1 because many members mention a richer set of constituency-oriented motivations than the reelection label suggests. Even so, the vast majority of constituency-oriented motivations are defined in terms of electoral needs.[6] Overall, such motivations are the most frequently mentioned reasons for preferring particular committees. Policy interests are a close second and influence or prestige a distant third, especially in the Senate. As Fenno noted, the great importance of floor deliberations in Senate decision making prevents a senator from substantially increasing his or her relative power by taking any particular committee seat. And because nearly all senators can gain a seat on one of the four "major" Senate committees (see Chapter 1), no special prestige within the chamber is associated with membership on those committees.[7] Nevertheless, mixed motives are the norm for members of both chambers (Table 4-2). Multiple motives, however, are infrequently expressed for the same committee. Usually only one goal is emphasized for each committee of interest, and several committees are mentioned for different reasons. Of the separate committee mentions in the 97th Congress interviews, 77.4 percent were associated with only one goal in the House and 73.4 percent were associated with only one goal in the Senate. These findings corroborate Fenno's assumptions about members' calculations when considering their options for committee assignments.

Table 4-2 Committee Preference Motivation Combinations, 1982 *(frequencies)*

	House	Seats
Constituency only	9	1
Policy only	5	0
Power/Prestige only	2	0
Constituency and Policy	27	20
Constituency and Power/Prestige	1	2
Policy and Power/Prestige	1	0
Constituency, Policy, and Power/Prestige	17	2
	62	25

Source: Authors' interviews (see text).

Goals, Agendas, and Reform _____

Whether a member seeks a committee berth for purposes of serving constituency interests, good public policy, or chamber influence, his or her interest is grounded in the committee's substantive jurisdiction. The relevance of a committee's activities to any member's personal goals therefore may increase or decrease as a function of formal jurisdictional changes. And the perceived opportunity to pursue certain goals can change as political events outside members' control affect a committee's informal agenda. As a result, the relationship between member goals and agenda/jurisdiction preferences requires examination.

First, consider a member motivated solely by constituency-oriented concerns. Such a member will, of course, seek a committee with jurisdiction salient to his or her constituents. But, as Morris Fiorina has indicated, the single-minded pursuit of reelection also leads to an avoidance of issues that alienate elements of one's constituency and to an emphasis on activities that alienate no one. Acquiring federal dollars for local projects and servicing constituents who have problems with the federal government would be two examples of this.[8] Avoiding controversial issues often means avoiding salient national issues and the committees that consider them. Successful efforts to bring federal dollars to a state or district often require avoiding national and broad congressional attention to the purposes for which the dollars are to be spent.[9] A committee with jurisdiction over programs that have concentrated benefits (for one's constituents) but widely dispersed costs (taxes, consumer prices) is well suited to these needs. House Judiciary Chairman Peter W. Rodino, Jr., a Democrat from New Jersey, makes this point in complaining about the lack of interest in his committee:

> ... we have no money to spread around. No grants. No loans. No loan guarantees. No subsidies. A spot on [a committee with such jurisdiction] permits a member to be hardly visible in controversy—while conspicuously dealing out federal dollars to grateful constituencies. It is a comfortable condition.[10]

Such a committee is typically one with a narrow jurisdiction over programs of interest to a limited number of members and constituencies. Thus a committee with low national salience, high local salience, low conflict, and a narrow jurisdiction is especially attractive to the constituency-oriented member.

A member motivated by an interest in a particular policy area, or perhaps merely an interest in getting involved in important issues, sees things from a far different point of view than does his or her reelection-motivated colleague. First, salient national issues are attractive because the policy-oriented member seeks to contribute to the shape of important policies.[11] If they are conflict-ridden issues, so be it. Conflict, after all, probably reflects the importance and complexity of the issues. Thus policy decisions with concentrated perceived costs, but only diffuse benefits, do not keep the truly policy-oriented member away from a committee facing such decisions. And the broader the committee's jurisdiction, the better it is for a member attracted to challenging issues.

Finally, consider a member seeking a committee on which he or she can pursue the goal of chamber influence and prestige. For this member, an agenda exceptionally salient to chamber colleagues is required, rather than one that is locally or nationally salient. Chamber salience may originate in the local or national significance of a committee attractive to this type of member, but the key feature is that nearly all of one's colleagues care a great deal about what the committee does.[12] Policy conflict may come with the territory and, at least to a certain extent, conflict is desirable. Without some minimal level of conflict, few real choices are present and little influence can be exercised. A broad committee jurisdiction facilitates chamber-wide salience and ensures that opportunities exist to make decisions that colleagues perceive as important to them.

Few members of Congress fit these ideal-types perfectly. Yet such ideal-types suggest how changes in committee agendas affect committee preferences and motivations for those preferences. First, a decrease in the local salience of a committee's decisions or an increase in the level of constituent policy conflict may decrease a committee's value for the pursuit of reelection and may detract from the overall value of a committee that is useful for other reasons. Second, a decrease in the national salience of a committee's agenda or a significant loss of formal jurisdiction will decrease the committee's value to members with policy motivations. Third, a decrease in the chamber salience of a committee's decisions or a loss of jurisdiction will decrease the committee's appeal to the influence- or prestige-motivated members.

Unfortunately for students of politics, the relationship between agendas and goals is not quite so simple as the ideal-types suggest. First, many members acquire their committee seats long before agenda changes modify their committees' value for achieving their particular goals. Even if changing events reduce that value for some members, the value of accumulated seniority and experience often makes it difficult to justify the search for a new assignment. Instead, most senior members retain their assignments and make do with what they have. In some cases this may mean adjusting to changing opportunities by shifting the emphasis from one personal goal to another, as Fenno suggested. In other cases members may neglect or resist the change. For example, opportunities to pursue a nationally salient, controversial issue may be bypassed by members of a committee primarily concerned about reelection. And members may simply shift the focus of their attention to another committee on which they serve. The importance of this has increased in the House since the early 1970s when most members gained additional committee assignments (see Table 2-2, p. 51).

Second, because most committee members have multiple goals, in the form of a combination of reelection and policy interests, the actual agenda preferences are likely to be a hybrid of preferences associated with these two goals. Specifically, as David Price has argued, exciting, highly salient policy areas with relatively low political conflict are well suited to most members' interests. Price cites medical research as an example of such a "motherhood" issue for members of the House and Senate Commerce committees.[13] Few members of any committee could be expected to ignore opportunities to be associated with such issues. Unfortunately for members of Congress, many, if not the vast majority, of the issues they face are not of this type, and they generally are forced to pick among their various goals when choosing committees.

Third, the role of committee decision-making practices in limiting or magnifying the effect of agenda changes also must be taken into account. Fenno's study of congressional committees led him to conclude that goals shape decision-making processes (rather than vice-versa): the major changes in decision-making processes that he observed were in the direction of making the processes consistent with longstanding member goals.[14] Yet, from the point of view of a new member considering committee assignment options, a committee's decision-making processes may shape his or her opportunities to pursue goals as much as does the committee's agenda.[15] An autocratic chair, for example, may so limit opportunities for rank-and-file members to place new issues on the committee's agenda that little reason exists for policy-oriented members to seek assignment to that committee. Moreover, externally imposed reforms, such as those experienced by many House committees during the 1970s, often cannot be interpreted as members' efforts to reshape committee procedures to their needs. Because the reforms did not affect all committees in the same way, it is important to consider how those reforms increased or decreased rank-and-file members' opportunities to pursue certain goals.

Finally, a committee does not necessarily lose attractiveness when reform or agenda changes reduce its value for the pursuit of a particular goal. Reform and agenda change may provide new opportunities to pursue goals that previously could not be "serviced" by the committee, an effect that may be stronger than the damage done to the committee's ability to pursue the old goals. Because members of Congress commonly hold multiple goals, at least some members on most committees can be expected to take advantage of new opportunities. In the case of altered opportunities due to agenda additions and subtractions, however, the effect is not symmetric. While additions to a committee's agenda often can be accommodated by members with multiple goals, agenda losses often mean that the committee is less useful for any purpose. As a rule, committees acquiring new agenda items already are useful to their members; committees experiencing agenda losses may suffer serious blows to their ability to service constituents, control important policy decisions, or exercise influence within the chamber. For just this reason, jurisdictional reform generates intense opposition. In terms of their ability to meet member goals, committees slated to lose legislative jurisdiction generally have more at stake than committees targeted to gain that jurisdiction. Indeed, as political scientist Roger Davidson, a consultant to the Bolling reform committee, observed,

> those who expected to gain were more muted in the expressions than those who saw themselves as losing.... In reorganization politics, defensive forces tend to be more potent than the forces of change.[16]

The prospect of losing known opportunities to pursue goals stimulates action more than uncertain opportunities of new jurisdictions.

Member Goals in the House

The committee-specific motivations reported in Table 4-3 indicate that, in making the important decision about which committee assignments to pursue, House freshmen distinguish among committees based on personal aspirations and goals. Interestingly, the survey of committee preference motivations also indicates that only a handful of committees attract members who share nearly identical motivations.

Influence and Prestige Committees

The Appropriations, Rules, and Ways and Means committees remain distinctively prestigious in House members' eyes. When describing these committees, House members use terms such as "important," "powerful," "*the* committee," "where the action is," and "the mover-and-shaker committee"—descriptions similar to those Fenno heard for Appropriations and Ways and Means in the 1960s. As seen in Chapter 3, each of these committees is unusually salient to a large number of House

Table 4-3 House Committee Preference Motivation Frequencies, by Committee

	Constituency		Policy		Prestige	
Congress	92	97	92	97	92	97
Prestige Committees						
Appropriations	5	5	3	6	7	11
Budget	—	0	—	4	—	5
Rules	1	0	0	1	0	3
Ways and Means	1	0	0	6	5	7
Policy Committees						
Banking	1	14	9	17	1	1
Foreign Affairs	1	2	4	8	0	0
Commerce	3	9	16	13	1	0
Judiciary	0	0	7	3	0	0
(Education and Labor)	5	3	7	2	0	0
Government Operations	0	0	0	9	0	0
Constituency Committees						
Agriculture	10	15	3	7	0	0
Armed Services	5	11	3	7	1	0
(Education and Labor)	5	3	7	2	0	0
Interior	7	12	4	2	0	0
Merchant Marine	3	5	0	0	0	0
Public Works	7	4	1	2	0	0
Science & Technology	0	9	1	5	1	0
Small Business	—	13	—	4	—	0
Veterans' Affairs	5	2	0	1	0	0
Undesired Committees						
District of Columbia	0	1	0	1	0	1
House Administration	0	0	0	0	0	0
Post Office and Civil Service	1	1	0	0	0	0
Standards of Official Conduct	—	0	—	1	—	0

Source: See discussion and citations in text.

members. Their importance is reflected by their formal designation, since 1946, as the only "exclusive" committees of the House. In general, their members may not sit on other standing committees (with the exception of Budget, as explained below). Other motivations for seeking these committees are common, but what makes them unique is their attractiveness to House members beyond their value for servicing constituents or pursuing personal policy interests. The importance of these committees in House politics dictates that attention be given to each of them.

Rules. The prestige and influence of the House Committee on Rules reside in its power to propose special orders or "rules" for the consideration of legislation on the floor.[17] Unlike the smaller Senate, which tolerates flexible floor procedures, the House more carefully structures its floor activity. Without special orders, House floor debate would be sheer chaos. Because rules are required to bring nearly all important legislation to the floor, to limit debate, and often to limit amendments, Rules members are in a position to block or expedite legislation important to individual members of the House. The committee's reach, then, is as broad as that of any committee in Congress, despite its limited jurisdiction. And its decisions are salient and often controversial within the chamber. Thus the Rules Committee is ideally suited to the member seeking influence and prestige within the House. With its small size (only 13 members in the 98th Congress), Rules is truly elite.[18]

As noted in Chapter 1, a conservative coalition of southern Democrats and Republicans controlled Rules after the mid-1930s and, often contrary to the wishes of most majority party Democrats, blocked floor consideration of many liberal bills. In the 1960s the committee's expansion, the addition of moderate and liberal Democrats, and the electoral defeat of conservative Chairman Howard "Judge" Smith changed the committee's political balance to one more supportive of the Democratic leadership's policy positions. And yet, some key Democratic legislation continued to face effective conservative obstructionism on Rules.

Most liberals hoped that a new era had arrived in 1973 when a fellow liberal, Democrat Ray J. Madden of Indiana, became chair and three new Democrats, each a leadership supporter, were appointed to the committee. Instead, Rules members, accustomed to independence, endured an uncomfortable transition period. At first, the committee frequently reported rules permitting floor consideration of liberal legislation opposed by the vast majority of the House, resulting in an embarrassing string of House votes rejecting the committee's proposed rules. Rules members, ever conscious of their status and prestige, were the subject of only partly friendly jokes about their floor defeats. One committee Democrat even complained that Rules members "were harassed by members for some of those rules we reported out."[19] Committee Democrats scrutinized legislation and potential floor opposition more carefully in 1974, rejecting two rules the Democratic leadership recommended. To support the leadership was important to Rules Democrats, but not at the expense of committee defeat on the floor. One Rules member, who understandably wished to remain anonymous, said that he hoped that the Speaker had "learned his lesson." [20] These are the words of a member concerned about his personal status in the House as much as his own policy preferences or party allegiances.

Two final changes made the Rules Committee a genuine arm of the Speaker. First, as was mentioned in Chapter 2, the reformist Democratic Caucus of the 94th Congress gave the Speaker the authority to name all Democratic Rules members, subject to caucus approval. Political independence was not to be a criterion applied in choosing Democratic Rules members. In fact, Democrats appointed to Rules in recent Congresses have been recruited by party leaders or the committee chair. Second, Richard Bolling of Missouri became chair of Rules in 1979. It was Bolling who made the motion to give the Speaker the power to nominate Democratic Rules members before the start of the 94th Congress. Bolling strongly believed that his committee should regain some of its historical status as the "Speaker's committee," helping to schedule and structure floor consideration of legislation as the majority party leadership desired.

Despite some temporary concern that Rules' importance and prestige would decline with the loss of independence from party leaders, the committee remains attractive to House members seeking chamber influence and prestige. Proponents and opponents of legislation still come to Rules to plead their case for a favorable rule, and, on legislation not vital to party leaders, Rules members have great discretion. Previously unnoticed or unpublicized problems with legislation occasionally are noticed and publicized by Rules members, and they often delay or structure floor consideration to permit the weaknesses they see in legislation to be corrected.[21] Committee and subcommittee chairs' reputations can be bolstered or damaged by these encounters with the Rules Committee.[22] In a large and highly decentralized chamber, the Rules Committee is one of the few remaining decision-making forums that regularly draw the attention of nearly all House members.

Nevertheless, the self-defined source of Rules' influence and prestige has changed in an important way. Bruce Oppenheimer has noted that many Rules members began to view themselves as "field commanders" for party leaders in the mid-1970s, a role perception that has been strengthened since that time.[23] In this role, Rules members serve as additional sets of eyes and ears for their party leadership. Rules members often spot legislation with political problems for the party and draw the attention of elected party leaders to it. Majority party leaders consult with Rules Democrats on nearly all major pieces of legislation—not only to inform Rules members of leadership preferences for a rule, but also to seek information and advice about legislative strategy. Indeed, Bolling was considered a part of the party leadership from the 95th to 97th Congresses and attended "leadership meetings" on a regular basis. As a result, Rules members' influence and prestige are closely tied to that of the party leadership, especially for majority party Democrats.

Appropriations. "It has everything," exclaimed a freshman Republican who sought a seat on Appropriations at the beginning of the 97th Congress. The committee's jurisdiction over spending bills makes it attractive to members seeking dollars for district programs and projects and to members interested in federal fiscal policy. But more importantly, the committee's significance in national fiscal policy making and importance to noncommittee members seeking district funding also make membership valuable to those seeking influence and prestige within the chamber.[24] As Democratic Appropriations member Norman Dicks of Washington asserted, "It's where the money is. And money is where the clout is."[25]

Reforms and agenda changes since the mid-1970s have affected the relative significance of the three goals for Appropriations members. First, the Democrats took away full committee chairs' power to appoint subcommittees at the beginning of the 94th Congress, including the power to appoint subcommittee chairs. Democrats now take turns, in order of seniority, choosing subcommittee assignments. As a result, an Appropriations chair no longer can appoint subcommittees in such a way as to minimize constituency pressure and maximize willingness to reduce spending requests, as had been the practice in the 1960s.[26] Appropriations Democrats now openly choose subcommittee assignments they believe are valuable to them at home. Senior Appropriations members complain that this change has meant that during hearings and markups members more frequently are advocates for, rather than critical overseers of, programs than they were in the late 1960s. Democrat David R. Obey of Wisconsin explained that "now the pro-defense people go to [the] Defense [subcommittee], public works people go to Energy and Water, pro-health and education people go to Labor-HHS."[27]

Appropriations subcommittee chairs now must be elected by the Democratic Caucus. In practice, they continue to be selected according to subcommittee seniority, as they were in the 1960s, but the subcommittee chairs are well aware that they are accountable to the caucus. Consequently, many participants note, subcommittee chairs are more responsive to the demands of noncommittee members than they were in the 1960s.

Members also point out that Appropriations' hearings and meetings were closed to uninvited outsiders until the 1970s. Opening hearings and meetings to the public made members less willing to set aside the demands of colleagues, constituents, and important clientele groups. In short, opportunities to pursue district-oriented interests have improved, and pressures to do so have increased for Appropriations' members.

Second, the erosion of Appropriations' control over expenditures, which was well under way in the late 1960s, was exacerbated in the 1970s, undermining the committee's source of influence and prestige in the House. The primary culprit has been "backdoor spending" that does not require the Appropriations committees' approval or that is mandated by law. For example, Social Security, which, since the early 1960s, has been one of the most rapidly expanding federal programs, does not require periodic appropriations from Congress. Other entitlement programs (entitlements are provisions that guarantee individuals or localities certain federal support if they meet specified criteria) give Appropriations no effective choice but to approve funds based on estimated demand. Because such permanent appropriations, entitlements, and similar outlays fall under the jurisdictions of the other committees, backdoor spending is uncontrollable from Appropriations' point of view.

Even more importantly, the loss of spending control was a partial cause of, and was compounded by, the creation of the budget process and Budget committees. Since the late 1970s, budget resolutions have placed constraints on Appropriations' decisions. In 1981 the Republican-backed first budget resolution went so far as to require that appropriations bills that were inconsistent with the budget resolution not be sent to the president until all appropriations bills were passed and found to meet the budget resolution's aggregate spending targets. An aide to Speaker Thomas P. O'Neill explained one effect of the change: "It's amazing, really, we seldom consult Appropriations members like we used to on spending politics; the ball game is now played in the Budget Committee." Appropriations members recognize the difference, as one member of both Appropriations and Budget commented:

> Appropriations is still a strong committee, but it's nothing like it used to be. Everybody in the Congress is becoming an expert on spending, and they are less likely to defer to us . . . Appropriations isn't top dog anymore.[28]

The ranking Appropriations Republican, Silvio Conte from Massachusetts, adds: "We're not eunuchs yet, but we've lost a lot."[29] Appropriations still attracts members because of its influence and prestige, but, in absolute terms, these qualities have declined in importance as its monopoly over spending decisions has eroded.

Finally, despite the budget process's encroachment into the committee's traditional role, an upsurge of policy-related interest in Appropriations occurred as federal spending became a more salient national issue in the late 1970s. This is especially true for conservative Republicans who, even in the 1960s, occasionally sought Appropriations for policy reasons.[30] All six freshmen of the 97th Congress who mentioned a policy-oriented motivation for interest in Appropriations consistently supported President Reagan's budget and tax proposals throughout the 97th Congress.

On balance, then, House Appropriations has become somewhat less attractive for reasons of prestige and influence (although these still dominate), decidedly more attractive to constituency-oriented members, and at least temporarily of more interest to conservative, policy-oriented members.

Ways and Means. The House Ways and Means Committee long has been considered one of, if not the most, powerful and prestigious committees of Congress.[31] Throughout the 1960s and early 1970s, Ways and Means' small size (25 members), its nationally salient jurisdiction (taxation, trade, Social Security, health insurance, public assistance, and unemployment compensation), and, for Democrats, its function as the Committee on Committees combined to make it especially attractive to the influence- and prestige-oriented member. Much of the committee's legislation, and nearly all of its tax legislation, was considered on the House floor under closed rules on the theory that tax bills were too complex and important for uninformed outsiders to tamper with. The Ways and Means chair for two decades, Wilbur D. Mills of Arkansas, was described as the most powerful member of Congress. Mills, a renowned expert on tax policy, operated the committee with a strong hand, closed markups, appointed no subcommittees, and was committed to the apprenticeship-seniority norm.[32]

Not surprisingly, Ways and Means became a chief target for reform in the 93d and 94th Congresses. Along with other House committees, Ways and Means was forced to open its hearings and meetings to the public; the Democratic Caucus established a procedure to make it easier to get an amendment to a Ways and Means bill considered on the floor; and the caucus forced the committee to create five subcommittees, its first since Mills' second term as chair; Ways and Means Democrats were stripped of their committee assignment authority; and the committee was expanded to 37 members. (Ways and Means escaped major changes in its jurisdiction, despite repeated attempts by House reformers.) These reforms have reshaped the opportunities of Ways and Means members and potential members to pursue their personal goals.

First, the committee was among those most strongly affected by the reforms because of the saliency of tax and social welfare issues and its previous practice of closing markups to outsiders. The percentage of closed Ways and Means meetings dropped from 63 percent in 1972 to just 5 percent in 1974.[33] As a result, one Democratic party leader observed, "Those fellows find it tougher to move on some things than they used to—every tax attorney in the city is sitting there noting their every word and reporting it to somebody back home when there's a surprise." Ways and Means members never have been insulated from special interests, of course, but political pressures now are felt more keenly by members, and when junior members were admitted to the committee after its enlargement in 1975, this sensitivity was heightened. Even so, Ways and Means does not attract members for reelection reasons. As was the case in the 1960s, it is difficult to please all constituents all the time in tax policy, and the openness of the process has made tax decisions even more difficult for many members.[34] For them, Ways and Means membership is often a political liability. As we saw in the previous chapter, Ways and Means sought to minimize this liability in 1983 by again closing some markup sessions to the public.

Reforms imposed on Ways and Means also have made it more valuable to members with strong policy motivations, although policy goals long have been important to at least a few Ways and Means members.[35] The creation of subcommittees and the availability of subcommittee staff to more members gave them the tools to pursue their own policy interests. Of the six freshmen in the 97th Congress who were attracted to Ways and Means for policy reasons, four mentioned the opportunity to pursue their own ideas for tax reform. Previously, under the watchful eye of Mills and the influence of an exceptionally strong committee norm of apprenticeship, similar hopes would have been "wild-eyed idealism," as one long-term Ways and Means aide commented. In the case of Ways and Means, reforms clearly succeeded in creating new opportunities for participation, especially for newcomers to the House.

Finally, Ways and Means members have lost some of their unique influence and prestige. In part, this has been due to the damage done to the committee's reputation of expertise and moderation in tax legislation, a reputation carefully cultivated by Mills and his select group of colleagues during the 1960s. Ways and Means members, particularly majority party Democrats, generally are less willing to suppress their personal policy preferences. In 1974 and 1975, for example, majority party Ways and Means members pursued their own amendments to committee bills on the floor with little regard for the committee's tradition of supporting its legislation on the floor. And in 1981 differences among Ways and Means Democrats on the nature of a Democratic tax cut alternative brought the issue to the Speaker; it was the Speaker who successfully demanded a particular approach, against the initial preferences of Chairman Dan Rostenkowski. These internal disputes, made more public by open meetings, have destroyed the mystique of writing tax legislation. When coupled with the reform of the closed rule, Ways and Means' longstanding reputation for expertise has been visibly tainted.

Ways and Means members' loss of chamber influence and prestige was compounded by the loss of the Committee on Committees function by the committee's Democrats. Catherine Rudder discovered in interviews with Ways and Means Democrats soon after the reforms that veteran members believed the loss of assignment responsibilities did not affect the committee's ability to get its bills passed on the floor.[36] In their view, the only loss was in the committee's prestige. Junior Democrats saw things differently: one junior Democrat told Rudder that the reform "constitutes a substantial diminution in power for the committee." A senior Republican concurred by noting that the assignment power had provided committee Democrats "an element of respect and gave House members second thoughts about crossing them on the floor." [37] Current members agree with these latter views. The committee retains substantial attractiveness for its influence and prestige, but its special influence now is more dependent on the committee's ability to satisfy noncommittee members' requests for special considerations when writing legislation. The committee's jurisdiction always has made opportunities to do so commonplace, but more policy concessions are required when few other sources of leverage are available. This further weakens the credibility of Ways and Means' claims that its legislation requires special treatment because of its complexity and makes it more difficult for the committee's leaders to build support on the floor.

Changes in the balance of goals were boosted by the exceptionally large turnover in Ways and Means' membership in the 1970s. Only two House committees exhibited less continuity in overall membership; only four Ways and Means members in 1971 served through the 97th Congress (1981-1983). The committee's expansion in 1975, along with normal retirements in the previous year, meant that 19 of the 37 committee members were new in that year alone. Many of the new

Democrats were strong liberals with well-defined policy goals. In sum, Ways and Means' previous attraction—primarily influence and prestige and secondarily policy—has changed to a more equal balance of influence and policy. But the committee remains one of the most attractive for House members seeking chamber influence and prestige. It continues to have little attractiveness for constituency-related reasons.

The common thread underlying changes in member goals in Rules, Appropriations, and Ways and Means is procedural reform. All three committees were directly affected by the democratizing reforms of the 1970s. Rules became more closely tied to an elected party leader, Appropriations' chairs lost their ability to dictate subcommittee memberships, Ways and Means' chairs lost their stranglehold over committee deliberations, and the entire committee lost vital sources of influence to the Democratic Caucus. Few jurisdictional changes directly affected these committees, and informal agenda changes were not major factors. In each case, the net effect was a recognition on the part of committee members that their influence within the House was reduced as their decision-making autonomy was weakened. Nevertheless, each continues to control enough decisions vital to many, if not all, House members to retain great attractiveness and to hold a special status in the eyes of the rest of the House.

Policy Committees

In contrast to the importance of reforms for influence-oriented committees, agenda change has driven most of the major shifts in members' attitudes about service on House committees viewed as policy-oriented. Two policy-oriented committees, Education and Labor and Judiciary, already had experienced internal democratizing reforms when the House and the Democratic Caucus imposed reforms on other committees during the 1970s. For most policy-oriented committees, however, the reforms allowed their members to pursue more vigorously policy interests already motivating their committee activity. This was the case for Banking, Commerce, Foreign Affairs, and Government Operations. Some members perceived externally imposed reforms as the only way to achieve their personal policy goals. Only in the Banking Committee did the reforms of the 1970s provide an opportunity for members to pursue a substantially different mix of goals in their committee activity. In each policy-oriented committee, though, the rise and fall of issues on the national agenda have affected the committee's attractiveness.

Except for the newly popular Government Operations Committee, the policy-oriented committees of the House are considered "semi-exclusive" or "major" by the majority party Democrats. Such a designation reflects the Democrats' view that these committees are important enough to require that no member of their party be allowed to sit on more than one of them, but not so important as to prevent major committee members from holding a seat on other committees designated as "nonmajor."[38] Consequently, except for members of the exclusive Appropriations, Rules, and Ways and Means committees, Democratic Caucus rules limit Democrats to two committee assignments on either (1) one major and one nonmajor committee or (2) two nonmajor committees. House Republicans do not distinguish formally between categories of committees for appointment purposes, although they informally recognize the three exclusive committees.

The House Commerce Committee long has been attractive to policy-oriented members. Within its huge jurisdiction are air pollution control, health, consumer protection, and energy issues, each widely recognized as nationally "important" and controversial policy areas. As Democratic Representative Ron Wyden of Oregon explained:

> The stakes are so high in Commerce.... It affects the regulatory relationship to every aspect of America, not only billions of dollars but the very nature of the relationship of citizens and government. There is no better issues committee.[39]

As a result, one senior Commerce aide pointed out, the committee draws members who are "independent, they have their own agendas, they are inclined to develop their own views, and they are not inclined to be led." This is an excellent definition of policy-oriented members.

In the late 1960s and early 1970s, consumer and environmental issues prominent on the public agenda were Commerce's special attractions.[40] These issues lost some of their national salience as the 1970s progressed, and they eventually were superseded by energy issues. This led to the committee's acquisition of new jurisdiction in 1974 and its renaming (as Energy and Commerce) during the 96th Congress. Commerce issues have been highly salient and controversial, as would be expected from the degree to which they involve costs that often are perceived to be highly concentrated on business, industry, and professional groups.

Commerce members always have perceived some policy areas in constituency-oriented terms, including transportation issues such as highways, mass transportation, and aviation. But these have not attracted many of its members; they finally were given to the Public Works Committee in the mid-1970s.[41] In contrast, the oil shortages of the

1970s stimulated midwestern and northeastern members to seek assignments to Commerce to protect their districts' interests, as did problems such as the storage of toxic wastes and financially troubled railroads. The comments of 97th Congress freshmen reflect this increase in district-oriented motivation (Table 4-3). Nevertheless, Commerce remains a very attractive committee to members with strong policy interests.[42]

The Banking, Finance, and Urban Affairs Committee is the only remaining equal of Commerce in popularity among policy-motivated members. Under strong chairs in the 1960s, Banking's policy focus was on financial and banking matters. With the reforms of the early 1970s diminishing the chair's ability to control the committee, the chair's ability to direct the committee's agenda toward financial matters was destroyed. Democratic liberals, who were responsible for the reforms and who had ousted Democrat Wright Patman of Texas from his chairmanship in 1975, were much more interested in the committee's housing and urban affairs jurisdiction. Interest in these issues is responsible for the Housing and Community Development Subcommittee's increased size: 33 members in the 97th Congress, up from 15 in the 93d Congress, making it the largest subcommittee in the House. In many cases, personal policy interests were wedded to district-oriented motivations to look out for the interests of urban constituents. This is reflected in the large number of constituency motivations mentioned by freshmen of the 97th Congress (Table 4-3). Some House members still are attracted by financial issues, but among the 97th Congress freshmen nearly all of those were Republicans with some background in banking or insurance.

Government Operations, which attracted very few members in the 1960s (none among the 92d Congress freshmen), is now a popular nonmajor assignment as a result of additions to its jurisdiction, agenda changes, and reform. For many years, Government Operations had broad oversight responsibilities over the administration of nearly all federal programs, but it had little legislative jurisdiction with which to attract members. During the 1970s, the committee was given legislative jurisdiction over revenue sharing, privacy, counter-cyclical aid, and other areas that appealed to many House members. Perhaps even more importantly, the greater salience of "waste and fraud" issues has made the committee's oversight responsibilities more enticing. And, once on the committee, Government Operations' members discover that broad oversight jurisdiction permits them to become involved in a much wider range of policy issues than would be possible elsewhere. One long-term member explained that "it's a very important committee; it has a wide jurisdiction and gives us a chance to look at everything." Finally, internal democratization in the early 1970s permitted policy-oriented members to pursue their interests more actively and attracted members to the committee who sought to take advantage of its opportunities.[43] The 1971 rule limiting members to a single subcommittee chair and the 1974 reforms, which were accompanied by a new Government Operations chair, gave subcommittees greater independence and resources. This appeared to unleash committee members who had strong interests in investigating agencies such as the Federal Bureau of Investigation, Central Intelligence Agency, Internal Revenue Service, and the Federal Reserve Board.

The Foreign Affairs Committee attracts House members almost exclusively for policy reasons, as it did in the 1960s.[44] Of the eight freshmen of the 97th Congress interested in Foreign Affairs, four mentioned their foreign travel as responsible for their interest in foreign policy. (One member remarked, "I bet I'm the only member of Congress who has been to the Falkland Islands.") Three members mentioned their academic training in the field, and two noted they had a personal interest in foreign affairs because they were foreign born. Most Foreign Affairs members see the committee's agenda as stimulating little interest in their home districts.[45] The only change in Foreign Affairs members' attitudes, and it is an important one, is that they are less deferential to foreign and defense policy officials in the executive branch than they were in the mid-1960s. The Vietnam War and other experiences during the 1960s and early 1970s have made committee members, especially liberals, more than mere spectators of the executive branch. In fact, in contrast to the 1960s, Foreign Affairs activists seek to develop a policy expertise to serve as a basis for their independent judgment.[46] If anything, committee members are more genuinely and completely policy-motivated in the 1980s than they were in the 1960s.

Foreign Affairs members' independent policy motivations, in part, were responsible for and reinforced by the committee's further decentralization in the early 1970s.[47] The committee's main activity in the 1960s—writing the foreign aid bill—took place at the full committee level where all members could contribute.[48] The committee had developed a large number of subcommittees during the 1960s that had been given substantial freedom to pursue their own interests by Chairman Thomas E. "Doc" Morgan, but many of the subcommittees remained dormant.[49] The subcommittees gained new vitality when four policy-oriented liberals assumed subcommittee chairs in 1971, three because of the limit on chairs.[50] Since then, members have experimented with the subcommittee structure in an attempt to create opportunities to pursue their own policy interests.

Two House committees that members motivated by personal policy interests once considered attractive have lost some of their appeal. The first, Education and Labor, was composed of prototypical, policy-oriented members during the 1960s when poverty, education, and labor issues were at the top of President Kennedy's and President Johnson's domestic agendas. Education and Labor members had exceptionally strong ideological goals, with only a few urban Democrats viewing their work as having electoral value in their urban districts.[51] Liberal Democrats dominated the committee; Republicans avoided it because they usually could do no more than offer symbolic opposition while risking the political consequences of opposing organized education and labor groups. Education and Labor members, especially the senior Democrats who have been on the committee since the 1960s, retain a strong motivation to support or oppose the federal role in these areas. Even in the 1960s, though, divisive labor issues had begun to fade as federal support for education, job training, and pensions became a more important part of the committee's agenda. Increasingly, protecting established programs, instead of creating new ones, became the committee's focus. As a result, Democrats lost much of their earlier enthusiasm for the committee. In the mid-1980s, education issues may be rekindling interest in Education and Labor. Republicans, especially, see education as an attractive issue. They frequently point out the political value of "going to bat for school loans for my middle-class constituents," as one of them put it.

The Judiciary Committee also has lost much of its appeal. Since the 93d Congress, very few House members have sought a Judiciary assignment.[52] In the 97th Congress, no Democrat requested Judiciary until the party caucus permitted Democrats to sit on the committee as an assignment beyond their normal two-committee limit. This change in interest is directly attributable to changes in the committee's agenda. Instead of facing the civil rights and liberties issues of the 1960s and early 1970s, Judiciary members now must manage issues such as abortion, school prayer, busing, and balanced budgets. The issues of the 1960s were very attractive to policy-oriented members, especially House liberals, but the new social issues force members to take positions on issues that most members would prefer to avoid. Chairman Peter Rodino explained the change this way:

> The truth be known, a Judiciary seat today is about as attractive to a member as the prospect of closing [Washington's] National Airport. . . . Through the 1950s and 1960s—and as recently as six years ago when the committee comprised 38 members—we had to turn away applicants. Judiciary was considered a choice and prestigious panel. Mem-

bers were eager to deal with the great and difficult issues of national moment. We were writing history and many wanted a hand in the writing.... The issues today are no less momentous ... but nowadays membership on the committee is considered by too many [as] too risky.[53]

Even among policy-oriented members, there is a limit to to the electoral risks they are willing to take to pursue personal policy preferences. Among freshmen of the 97th Congress, only two Republicans were attracted to Judiciary because of these issues. The other member with an interest in the committee wanted to utilize his legal expertise.[54]

The classification of these committees as policy-oriented and some of the changes just described are corroborated by House Democrats' patterns of committee assignment requests since the late 1950s (data provided in Table A-6, Appendix).[55] A strong tendency existed for members interested in one policy-oriented committee also to list other policy-oriented committees among their formal requests to party leaders. (Keep in mind that there were 20 effective choices during most of the period under study.) Three important differences between the 1960s and the 1970s and 1980s should be noted. First, Government Operations has been among the top choices of members requesting other policy committees only since the early 1970s. A great increase has occurred in the number of Democrats requesting Government Operations in the last decade, and that committee's requesters have sought other policy committees much more frequently. Second, Education and Labor requesters have been less likely to list other policy committees in recent years than in the 1960s, as have been the fewer members requesting Judiciary. And third, the Interior Committee has moved into or up the list of policy-oriented committees, which is a clue to the presence of more policy-oriented Interior members during the 1970s and 1980s.

The Budget Committee: A Hybrid

The House Budget Committee resembles Ways and Means in member motivation, as indicated in Table 4-3. Freshmen of the 97th Congress who were attracted to Budget mentioned their personal interest in budget policy and the committee's jurisdiction over increasingly important budget resolutions. Yet, unlike many members attracted to Ways and Means, those interested in Budget never mentioned Budget's reputation or status within the House. In fact, two freshmen, a Democrat and a Republican, indicated that they hoped their visibility and party service on the committee would lead to an appointment to Appropriations or Ways and Means. Budget is important and powerful, but not exceptionally prestigious.

A major contributing factor to Budget's odd combination of power and limited prestige is the restricted tenure of its members.[56] The Congressional Budget and Impoundment Control Act of 1974 provided that the committee be composed of five members from Appropriations, five from Ways and Means, and fifteen (later seventeen) members of other House committees. Each member's service was limited to four years out of any ten-year period, a limit that was extended to six years in 1979. Consequently, Budget members do not have the opportunity to develop long-term chamber influence by virtue of membership on the committee or the prestige that might come with that influence.

The Budget Committee also suffers from its nonexclusive jurisdiction.[57] The committee's main function, writing budget resolutions, entails making judgments about expenditures and revenues that fall under other House committees' jurisdictions. As a result, Budget exercises independent discretion only by directly challenging the decision-making autonomy of other House committees. Until 1981 the Budget Committee minimized direct conflict with other committees by setting spending targets at levels that permitted most of them to act freely, without violating the ceilings.[58] In 1981, faced with President Reagan's budget-cutting program, the committee produced resolutions forcing most House committees to find programmatic ways to sharply reduce projected spending, a move that stimulated efforts to revamp the budget process in the 98th Congress.[59] To the extent to which Budget is successful in influencing policy, it appears, it creates more enemies than admirers in the House.

These limitations led to a somewhat different definition of goals, at least for Budget's majority party Democrats. Lance LeLoup discovered in interviews with Budget members between 1975 and 1978 that Budget Democrats saw their major goal as ensuring that the new budget process worked.[60] While Budget Republicans were motivated strongly by their policy goal of reducing federal spending and deficits, Democratic members acted to establish a firm institutional footing for the new budget process and the new committee. Keeping the process alive meant avoiding direct conflicts with other powerful House committees whenever possible. LeLoup concluded that Budget Democrats in the mid-1970s should be classified as process-oriented rather than as policy- or influence-oriented. In fact, two or three Democrats had developed an excellent reputation for their expertise in understanding the details of budgeting and the budget process. He found, as we have, that members do not mention motivations related to reelection chances for their interest in Budget.[61]

Since the end of the 1970s the Budget Committee has become more attractive to Democrats for policy reasons. This change coincided with an increase in the salience of budgeting on the national agenda as President Carter, and then President Reagan, sought ways to reduce deficits.[62] None of the freshmen of the 97th Congress interested in Budget mentioned the personal goal of preserving or strengthening the budget process per se. Rather, their motivations were participating in the making of budget policy and belonging to an obviously "important" or "powerful" committee. Nevertheless, two Democratic members of Budget, appointed to the committee in the 95th and 96th Congresses, expressed continuing interest in preserving the budget process—one of them mentioning the importance of the process to Congress's institutional role in economic and budget policy making. In sum, Budget is a hybrid of influence and policy committees, with a continuing—but perhaps fading—element of process-motivated activity.

Constituency Committees

Eight House committees attract members primarily for constituency-oriented reasons. An additional committee, Post Office and Civil Service, also is district-oriented but is nevertheless desired by so few members that it is listed in the "undesired" category in Table 4-3. The most striking characteristic of member goals in the constituency committees is their stability. Only one of these committees, Science and Technology, has changed markedly in attractiveness during the past 15 years. The others have retained moderate attractiveness for the same balance of reasons observers noted 10 or 15 years ago.

The classic constituency committee is Agriculture. Its members distinguish themselves as "cotton men," "tobacco men," "wheat men," "cattle men," and "dairy men," mirroring the dominant agricultural products of their districts. With only one exception, the 97th Congress freshmen interested in the committee commented on the importance of agriculture to their constituents. Several members noted that they had made campaign promises to seek a seat on Agriculture. This pattern is true for most of the district-oriented committees. For Agriculture, this has resulted in a geographical bias in the committee's membership, as Table 4-4 demonstrates. Throughout the 1960s, the committee exhibited a substantial southern and slight midwestern bias in composition. Southern overrepresentation resulted in the dominance of cotton interests for several decades, with southerners chairing the committee for 34 years between 1931 and 1975. Turnover during the 1970s, however, brought more members to the committee from the Midwest and West

Table 4-4 Regional Representation on Selected House Committees, 89th to 90th and 96th to 97th Congresses *(percent from each region)*

Region	House Seats Per Region		Agriculture		Interior		Merchant Marine	
	89-90	96-97	89-90	96-97	89-90	96-97	89-90	96-97
East	25%	24%	11%	5%	24%	14%	33%	31%
South	24	25	36	27	12	12	21	23
Border	6	6	4	4	9	8	7	10
Midwest	29	30	34	39	24	18	19	13
West	16	15	15	25	32	48	19	23

Regions: East: Conn., Del., Maine, Mass., N.H., N.J., N.Y., Pa., R.I., Vt. South: Ala., Ark., Fla., Ga., La., Miss., N.C., S.C., Tenn., Tex., Va. Border: Ky., Md., Okla., W.Va. Midwest: Ill., Ind., Iowa, Kans., Mich., Minn., Mo., Nebr., N.Dak., Ohio, S.Dak., Wis., Iowa. West: Alaska, Ariz., Calif., Colo., Hawaii, Idaho, Mont., Nev., N.Mex., Oreg., Utah, Wash., Wyo.

and created a better balance among supporters of various agricultural commodities.

Agriculture also attracts members for policy reasons, as indicated in Table 4-3. For all 97th Congress freshmen mentioning Agriculture, the policy goals were expressed by members who were farmers, had some farming background, or had state legislative experience in agricultural policy. The policy interest always appeared to dictate behavior consistent with constituent interests. Throughout the period under study, there have been policy-oriented members on Agriculture. In the 1960s, one Agriculture staffer explained, the committee had two or three Republicans who often would oppose federal commodity programs on the grounds that the federal government should not upset market forces. And, in the early 1970s, the committee acquired a handful of members who represented nonrural districts.[63] While these nonrural members emphasized different issues, such as nutrition and consumerism, their interest in the committee's decisions on issues such as food stamps often were strongly related to reelection concerns. The committee remains nearly as constituency-oriented as it was 15 years ago.

Armed Services is very similar to Agriculture in its mix of motivations. Eight of the 97th Congress's freshmen said that their primary interest in Armed Services rested on the committee's jurisdiction over military installations in their districts. Three others mentioned the importance of defense contracts with industries in their districts. Many members of Armed Services also have strong, and generally conservative, views about national defense policy that are compatible with their support of district military installations. Former Armed Services Chairman L. Mendel Rivers expressed the committee's attitude when he welcomed a new Secretary of Defense in 1969:

> Now Mr. Secretary, we welcome you, and it is our fervent hope, and believe me this is the truth, that this is going to be the beginning of a long, happy, and cooperative effort between the two of us, your Department and ours, and I am sure you know, better than anybody, that this committee is the *only official spokesman for the DOD* on the floor.[64]

In the 1970s, the committee attracted four or five liberal, policy-oriented members who challenged the committee's promilitary bipartisan majority. One member observed, "The result of the Vietnam experience was to make the defense establishment the target of liberals, and they finally made their way to Armed Services." Nonetheless, the committee remained predominantly promilitary and constituency-oriented.

Fenno discovered that the House Interior Committee was primarily reelection-oriented, but that members added to it in the late 1960s and early 1970s were more policy-motivated and environmentalist in orientation than their predecessors.[65] The committee's jurisdiction over water development, public lands, and mining is its attraction to constitutency-oriented members. These concerns are especially important to western states, and the committee traditionally has attracted a disproportionate number of members from those areas (Table 4-4). Yet current Interior members concur with Fenno's observation that many members drawn to the committee around 1970 were motivated by newly salient environmental concerns. The influx of policy-oriented members was given a boost by the 1971 designation of Interior as a nonmajor committee and the simultaneous increase in the number of Democrats given two assignments, allowing members with only a secondary interest in Interior a chance to seek assignment to the committee. As a result, a handful of eastern members with strong preservationist views came to Interior in the late 1960s. And several Interior members in the late 1970s came with a strong interest in the newly acquired jurisdiction over nuclear power regulation. Despite these changes, western members made up an even larger portion of the committee in recent Congresses than in the mid-1960s. And, as Table 4-3 indicates, Interior still attracts members primarily for constituency-related reasons; only two members mentioned environmental concerns, and one of them was more concerned about a salient local pollution problem than with pursuing any personal policy interest.

Pegged a "pork-barrel" committee by its detractors, the House Committee on Public Works and Transportation has been known for its value to members seeking political credit for federally funded projects in areas such as rivers and harbors, public buildings, and, since the mid-1970s, highways and airports. James Murphy discovered in the 1960s that 25 of 34 Public Works members believed their membership was useful for meeting their districts' needs.[66] A similar pattern was found by Bullock for the freshmen of the 92d Congress and in our interviews with members and potential committee members in the 97th (Table 4-3). Even so, the "pork barrel" label and its disparaging connotations are resisted strongly by committee members and staff. They feel projects supported by the committee are "in the public interest of our districts," as one member explained. Despite the clear district orientation of Public Works, strong policy-oriented motivations are present among some of its members. The addition of aviation to the committee's jurisdiction has drawn the attention of at least three or four members whose personal enthusiasm for aviation motivates most of their activity; both of the freshmen of the 97th Congress who mentioned policy reasons for interest in Public Works noted its aviation jurisdiction. The committee's jurisdiction over water treatment plants and related construction was seized by several Public Works members who were interested in pollution control problems in the early 1970s. And at least one member, Democrat Robert Edgar of Pennsylvania, has gained some notoriety for challenging the pork-barrel character of his committee colleagues' decisions. A Methodist minister elected in the post-Watergate election of 1974, Edgar's policy orientation is evidenced by his claim that "a healthy sense of outrage is not bad for the policy process. . . . I'm not a good wheeler-dealer. I'm thought of as one person who rattles the chains of the system." [67] But even Edgar has not bypassed opportunities to seek funding for maintenance of mass transit systems, such as the one in his district. In any case, the fact that Edgar stands out among his committee colleagues indicates Public Works' continuing district orientation.

Merchant Marine and Fisheries, Post Office and Civil Service, Small Business, and Veterans' Affairs also attract members predominately for constituency-related reasons. In the case of Post Office and Civil Service, however, the creation of the Postal Service as an independent government corporation in 1970 took away the committee's jurisdiction over postal employees' salaries and postal rates. This reduced the committee's ability to provide direct benefits to affected clientele groups and diminished House members' interest in serving on the committee.[68] The constituency focus of Merchant Marine and Fisheries is reflected in the geographical bias in its membership (Table 4-4). While not directly inferrable from the table, Merchant Marine and Fisheries' membership is taken almost entirely from coastal districts and midwestern districts bordering the Great Lakes.

The Committee on Science and Technology is the only constituency-oriented committee to experience a substantial gain in attractiveness among new House members during the 1970s and early 1980s. Many more freshmen were interested in Science in the 97th Congress than in the 92d, as Table 4-3 indicates. The situation in the late 1960s and early 1970s was described by former representative Ken Hechler, author of the committee's authorized history:

> ...the House committee ... experienced some difficulty in attracting Members with interests outside of space and science. The turnover in committee membership became unusually large, as many Members sought to be on those committees which helped their own districts to a greater extent. This was especially true after the Moon landing in 1969, as it became apparent that the decline in the space program might mean a decline in the significance of the Science Committee.[69]

The committee fought for and received jurisdiction over more aspects of scientific research and gained special oversight authority over all nonmilitary research in 1974. In the minds of House members, one longtime aide explained, the committee's image changed from the "Space Committee" to the "Science Committee." These changes occurred just as high technology research and industry were becoming important to many areas of the country. Members and interested freshmen of the 97th Congress frequently mentioned district-oriented motivations: "My district is a junior Silicon Valley now," "the largest private research concern in the nation is in my area," "the aerospace business is the number one industry in my district," and "the regional center for nuclear power is within my district." The committee's constituency orientation also is reflected in the continuing significance of the geographical distribution of federal research support to its members.[70] But, like Agriculture and Armed Services, Science is attractive to members for policy reasons as well (Table 4-3). Many Science members express great personal interest in science and technology issues, believing that matters vital to the future of the nation are within the committee's jurisdiction. This is especially true of an increasing number of members with academic, engineering, or science backgrounds and occupations.

As was the case for the policy committees, the pattern of requests for members seeking each constituency committee reinforces our interpretations (see Table A-7, Appendix). While the tendency is not so strong as for policy committees, there is a tendency for requesters of a constituency committee to list other district-oriented committees as well. Several features of these request patterns deserve to be noted here. First, Commerce appears high on many of the lists, an indication of its general attractiveness to House members. Foreign Affairs and Education and Labor, on the other hand, appear infrequently. Second, Interior exhibited a great increase in requests in the 1970s. A breakdown of Interior requests by Congress would show that the bulk of requests occurred in the early 1970s, as the above discussion suggested. Third, Science showed a small drop in the 1970s; a tally of each Congress would show that the real drop occurred in the early 1970s and that since that time interest in the committee has risen. Finally, Post Office and Veterans' Affairs have been unattractive since the late 1950s, with Post Office's drawing power nearly disappearing in the 1970s.

Except for Science and Technology and Interior, neither agenda changes nor procedural reforms have had a major effect on the goal orientation of constituency committees. Most new issues retain a district orientation for members concerned about them. The constituency orientation is not surprising for committees with jurisdictions concerning clear benefits for limited constituencies. Of course, dramatic shifts in agendas are not likely to occur on constituency committees with very narrow jurisdictions and, when shifts do occur, they are likely to be short lived. Procedural reforms alone do not make these committees any more attractive to members without relevant constituency interests or to members seeking committees for policy or chamber influence reasons. In the absence of significant national issues, policy- and influence-oriented members will continue to see membership on other committees as more useful. Science and Technology, the only constituency committee that acquired substantial new formal jurisdiction, also increased in attractiveness to members for policy reasons.

Undesired Committees

In addition to Post Office and Civil Service, three House standing committees consistently attract few members. The first, Standards of Official Conduct, is a special case because of its unique jurisdiction over ethics violations by House members. As one party leader described it, "Anyone who wants a seat on Standards doesn't deserve a seat on Standards,"—reflecting the discomfort felt (or that ought to be felt) by members sitting as judges of colleagues' behavior. The second committee, District of Columbia, attracts members of three types, a committee member explained: (1) members from districts bordering the District who have constituency-related reasons for membership, (2) urban and black members who have a personal interest in District problems, and (3) members who serve as a favor to the chair, ranking minority member, or party leaders. The pool of potential interest is small and the actual interest is even smaller. The committee's previous attractiveness—its ability to influence personnel decisions, police activity, and other aspects of District of Columbia government (for personal benefit or the benefit of colleagues)—was eliminated after the Home Rule Charter was enacted in the early 1970s. The committee now is in the hands of a small number of members who look out for the District's interests on Capitol Hill. Finally, House Administration's previous control of office accounts and supplies, which gave it special chamber influence under the chairmanship of Wayne L. Hays, was substantially reduced after Hays resigned in the midst of the Elizabeth Ray sex scandal and the House reformed its accounting and personnel procedures in 1976.[71] The committee's jurisdiction over election laws and campaign finance regulation is its only substantial policy attraction, but that alone is not enough to attract members.

Member Goals in the Senate

Member goals are less easily characterized in the Senate than in the House. There are several reasons for this. First, as noted earlier in the chapter, mentions of chamber influence or prestige are less common in the Senate; for no Senate committee was this objective the most frequently mentioned motivation (Table 4-5). Second, reelection and other constituency-oriented motivations were mentioned by a higher proportion of Senate respondents than House respondents—despite the fact that senators are up for reelection only every six years. As a result, a number of Senate committees whose House counterparts are clearly policy-oriented are also constituency-oriented to a substantial extent. And the desire to be reelected appears to lead to a greater emphasis on publicity in the Senate than in the House, perhaps as a consequence of senators' larger and more diverse constituencies and their greater dependence on the electronic media for communicating with their constituents. For many senators, the publicity emphasis makes it more difficult to differentiate personal policy interest from reelection interest because both goals often entail attracting public attention to an issue.

Table 4-5 Senate Committee Preference Motivation Frequencies, by Committee

	Constituency		Policy		Prestige	
Congress	Pre-92	97	Pre-92	97	Pre-92	97
Policy Committees						
Budget	—	1	—	4	*	0
Foreign Relations	3	1	19	5	2	0
Governmental Affairs	*	1	*	3	*	0
Judiciary	*	2	9	7	*	0
Labor	2	3	4	4	*	0
Mixed Constituency/Policy Committees						
Armed Services	4	4	4	6	*	0
Banking	*	2	*	3	*	0
Finance	4	8	13	9	*	4
Small Business	—	4	—	4	*	0
Constituency Committees						
Agriculture	4	13	*	2	*	0
Appropriations	31	6	15	3	2	2
Commerce	13	5	5	2	*	0
Energy and Natural Resources (formerly Interior)	4	6	2	3	*	0
Environment & Public Works	5	5	4	1	*	0
Undesired Committees						
Rules & Administration	*	0	*	1	*	0
Veterans' Affairs	*	2	3	0	*	0

* Bullock does not report N's for cells with fewer than 2 cases.

Source: See discussion and citations in text.

Most importantly, distinguishing committee types in the Senate is difficult because senators simply have a lower level of certainty and intensity about committee preference motivations than do representatives.[72] The lack of intensity sensed among the 97th Congress Senate respondents also reflects the larger number of opportunities the Senate committee system offers its members to pursue their goals. First, as mentioned earlier, nearly all senators receive a seat on one of four top committees (Appropriations, Armed Services, Finance, and Foreign Relations). Senators of both parties are permitted only one assignment on these committees. Second, senators' larger number of committee assignments permits them to pursue more easily both state and personal policy goals. In the 97th Congress, for example, the average Republican senator had 2.9 standing committee assignments and the average Democratic senator had 2.7 assignments, in contrast to 1.6 and 1.8 for House Republicans and Democrats, respectively.[73] Third, several Senate committees have larger jurisdictions than their House cousins. This allows senators to pursue a wider range of personal political objectives on those committees. Finally, it is easier for Senate noncommittee members to influence a committee's decisions. This greater permeability is reinforced by the Senate's more open and flexible floor procedures, which make it easier for noncommittee members to amend bills after they are reported to the floor, to filibuster, or to place a "hold" on a bill. (In recent years, senators have been able to ask the majority leader to delay action on a bill and, as a matter of courtesy, the majority leader has felt bound by their requests.)[74] And senators, with memberships on more committees and subcommittees and the ability to filibuster on the floor, often are in a better bargaining position than House members.

Policy Committees

Five Senate committees contain a majority of members who are policy-oriented in their approach to committee activity. Of the five, Foreign Relations is the most exclusively policy-oriented. Members of Foreign Relations mention such things as "personal interest," "my previous job sent me to Central America often," "I wanted to broaden my experience," and "no real political reason" when commenting on why they sought the committee. Foreign Relations' members do not consider the committee especially powerful or prestigious within the Senate.[75] As one Foreign Relations member said,

> Well, you know, it is fun to hobnob with foreign leaders and discuss world affairs, but it doesn't get me any place with my Senate colleagues. . . . Foreign Relations doesn't have much legislative jurisdiction that's important to other senators—it's nothing like Finance or Appropriations.

Only one senator mentioned a state-related reason for seeking a seat on Foreign Relations. He explained that his predecessor was on the committee, and he believed a Foreign Relations seat would help him build the "statesman image" his predecessor had acquired back home. The strong policy-orientation of Foreign Relations' members parallels Fenno's findings for the 1960s.[76]

Senate Budget members also list policy goals for their committee activity. "Where the action is" was a phrase used by three junior committee members during the 97th Congress. Because Senate Budget members are not encumbered by the strict tenure or representational limits placed on their House counterparts, they are free to pursue policy interests over the long term. Nonetheless, interest in the committee, like the House Budget Committee, has varied with the salience of budget issues.[77] Generally, the committee has been of secondary importance to its members, except its ranking members. Most consider their seats on one of the four major Senate committees to be more important to them.[78] No member or prospective member mentioned special influence or status within the Senate as a product of Budget membership, although senators do believe that Budget membership allows them to protect some programs important to their states.[79] As with the House Budget Committee, Senate Budget's lack of direct substantive jurisdiction over programs and the congressional budget process's high level of aggregation do not permit its members to take much positive action on behalf of constituents or colleagues.

Senate Governmental Affairs is much like House Government Operations in its members' policy motivations. Although Governmental Affairs in 1977 gained jurisdiction over areas that have a constituency orientation in the House (civil service, postal service, District of Columbia), the committee's main attractions are its broad oversight authority and a few issues such as government regulation and intergovernmental relations. Committee leaders of both parties take pride in the committee's moderate political composition, though, and have sought to maintain it during recent Congresses. No chamber influence or prestige is gained by membership on Governmental Affairs, but some members perceive electoral value accruing to them from publicity they receive in oversight hearings. One senior committee aide explained that this is especially true of liberal Democrats who can establish their credentials as opponents of government waste and fraud by sponsoring legislation, hearings, and investigations through Governmental Affairs.

Senate Labor and Human Resources and Senate Judiciary also are similar to their House counterparts in their policy orientation. Both attract members of ideological extremes who push their personal policy views on divisive issues. Senate Labor differs from House Education and Labor in that it has additional jurisdiction over health issues, which senators see as a constituency-oriented, low-conflict policy area. Labor lost a strong constituency-oriented area, veterans' affairs, when the Veterans' Affairs Committee was created in the early 1970s. Senate Judiciary, like House Judiciary, is a difficult assignment for some members because of the salient social issues under its jurisdiction. At least four members attempted to leave Judiciary in the early 1980s for that reason. Not surprisingly, Senate party and committee leaders have had difficulty attracting members, especially of certain types, to these two committees over the last few years. In both cases, ideological factionalism within the parties has been a stumbling block to finding "acceptable" members and placing them on the committee involved.

Mixed Policy/Constituency Committees

Senators seeking assignment to the Finance, Armed Services, Banking and Urban Affairs, and Small Business committees express an even mix of policy- and constituency-related goals. In the case of Finance, no change has occurred in the blend of members' motivations since the 1960s when Fenno concluded that its members "emphasize about equally the pursuit of policy and reelection goals."[80] Senators find the committee's jurisdiction over tax, trade, and social security matters both personally interesting and electorally useful. In contrast to Fenno's findings, however, a few members of the 97th Congress, both within the committee and outside of it, viewed Finance as an influential and prestigious Senate committee. These senators clearly perceived Finance's tax jurisdiction as salient to the entire chamber, and several of them mentioned Finance members' ability to do favors for noncommittee members in writing tax legislation, applying terms such as "powerful," "influential," and "prestigious." Many senators identify Finance as the most powerful and prestigious Senate committee.

The difference between the 1960s and the 1980s was due in large part to the 16-year chairmanship of Democrat Russell Long of Louisiana. Long, as Fenno noted, bolstered the committee's staff and gradually developed a reputation for political savvy equal to Wilbur Mills' reputation for technical expertise in the House. An aide to one senior Finance member said, "It's simple—Finance is powerful because Long is powerful. . . . Long not only wants to hear what you want in that bill, he uses what you want to his advantage." Participants believe the committee's reputation survived its transition in 1981 to Republican control under Chairman Robert Dole of Kansas. Dole shepherded several major bills, including a politically divisive and electorally risky $95 billion tax bill, through the Senate in his first three years as chair.

Armed Services, Banking and Urban Affairs, and Small Business also are seen as useful for both policy and constituency reasons. The Senate Armed Services Committee is comparable to House Armed Services in that the significance to individual states of military installations, personnel, and defense contractors attracts many members. Similarly, on the policy side, a large number of Senate Armed Services members have strong and usually conservative policy views that coincide with their constituencies' interests. Nevertheless, the Senate committee attracts a larger contingent of members with insignificant state connections to the defense establishment who also have a personal policy interest in the committee's activities. Especially important in recent years has been the membership of Democratic liberals Gary Hart of Colorado and Edward M. Kennedy of Massachusetts.

Senate Banking, in contrast, is more constituency-oriented than its House counterpart. According to one Senate Banking member, the committee lost some of its appeal to liberal activists when issues such as urban decay and redevelopment slipped from the national agenda during the 1970s. Urban and housing issues still attract members for state-oriented reasons, but personal interest in these issues appears to have declined substantially. Small Business has had legislative jurisdiction only since 1977. While interest in Small Business is very low, it does attract members looking for another state-oriented committee and who have a small business background—members with a personal interest in the committee's jurisdiction.

Constituency Committees

Six Senate committees attract senators primarily for constituency-related reasons. So few senators desire Veterans' Affairs that it has been placed in the "undesired" category. All six have exhibited little change in member goals during the past 15 years.

Senate Agriculture is the chamber's most purely constituency-oriented committee. Like its House counterpart, Senate Agriculture's membership is disproportionately southern and midwestern, with the midwestern bias having grown during the 1970s (Table 4-6). This state orientation has been the same for years. Energy and Natural Resources (Interior before the 1977 reforms) has retained primarily state-related interest for senators and, like House Interior, has retained a distinct western bias in its composition. But world events and the regrouping of energy jurisdiction in 1977 have changed the geographic composition of Energy and Natural Resources. A handful of senators from energy-poor states have been attracted to Energy and Natural Resources to protect their states' interests in the face of energy shortages and rising energy prices. Also, the addition of domestic atomic energy production, coal, and other energy matters to the committee's jurisdiction has attracted senators seeking to serve state interests. Energy issues have enticed

Table 4-6 Regional Representation on Selected Senate Committees, 89th to 90th and 96th to 97th Congresses *(percent from each region)*

Region	Senate Seats Per Region	Agriculture		Energy & Natural Resources	
		89-90	96-97	89-90	96-97
East	20%	12%	5%	0%	27%
South	22	47	36	0	18
Border	8	6	9	0	9
Midwest	24	23	40	17	5
West	26	12	9	83	40

Regions: East: Conn., Del., Maine, Mass., N.H., N.J., N.Y., Pa., R.I., Vt. South: Ala., Ark., Fla., Ga., La., Miss., N.C., S.C., Tenn., Tex., Va. Border: Ky., Md., Okla., W.Va. Midwest: Ill., Ind., Iowa, Kans., Mich., Minn., Mo., Nebr., N.Dak., Ohio, S.Dak., Wisc. West: Alaska, Ariz., Calif., Colo., Hawaii, Idaho, Mont., Nev., N.Mex., Oreg., Utah, Wash., Wyo.

several senators with personal policy interests in energy to the committee, but, for the most part, jurisdictional changes have reinforced its constituency orientation.

Throughout the 1960s, senators' primary objective on Appropriations was to provide funding for programs in their states, with chamber influence and good public policy of secondary interest.[81] No evidence exists to indicate that this has changed in any important way. Appropriations still provides an opportunity for members seeking money for programs in their states to do favors for colleagues and thus provides some extra influence and prestige in the Senate. But when more than half of the states are represented on the committee, opportunities to serve noncommittee members are not nearly so numerous as they might be. If a change has occurred during the last decade or so, it has been toward a lighter emphasis on chamber influence or prestige. Personal policy goals seldom have been significant to most Appropriations' members, although Republicans appointed to the committee since the late 1970s express some personal concern about holding down federal spending. The strength of their state orientation is indicated by the fact that the same Republicans were unhappy about spending cuts imposed on them by the budget resolutions of the 97th and 98th Congresses. This change in the budgeting environment has shifted their role away from one of merely an appeals court for agencies and affected interests that suffered cuts in House action to one of more actively protecting established programs.

Senate Commerce's balance of goals is the opposite of the balance on House Energy and Commerce. While Senate Commerce has had a core of strongly policy-oriented members for many years, the majority of senators attracted to the committee have had state-related goals.[82] As they have for House Commerce, consumer protection, some environmental protection issues, and other areas have stimulated strong policy interest, as well as state-related interest, in Senate Commerce—but its broad jurisdiction over constituency-oriented areas such as the merchant marine, U.S. Coast Guard, space programs, transportation, and tourism attracts most members. Space programs were added to Commerce's jurisdiction when the Aeronautics and Space Sciences Committee was abolished in 1977. That jurisdiction remains under Science and Technology in the House. Senate Commerce also lacks most of the health and energy jurisdiction that attracts policy-oriented members to House Commerce, having lost some energy jurisdiction in the 1977 reforms. The Senate committee, in the view of two former aides, has become somewhat more constituency-oriented as a result of these agenda changes.

Finally, Senate Environment and Public Works has become even more constituency-oriented since the early 1970s. In the late 1960s and early 1970s, major air and water pollution control legislation was written in the committee, which, in turn, attracted senators with personal policy interests in the field. "Since then," one senior aide explained, "the committee has not been as much fun as it was. Those big issues are gone and we don't attract the same kind of member that we once did." In original proposals for jurisdictional reform, Public Works was slated to pick up additional jurisdiction over pesticides, ocean policy, coastal management, and other environmental areas that, eventually, were left under other committees' jurisdictions. Such a change may have boosted the interest of policy-oriented senators in the committee. Instead, the committee remains attractive to senators primarily for its jurisdiction over rivers and harbors, water projects, highways, and other constituency concerns.

Undesired Committees

Many members of both Rules and Administration and Veterans' Affairs indicate that they did not seek assignment to these committees. Rules and Administration primarily is concerned with Senate housekeeping matters, although it does have jurisdiction over election and campaign practices. But no special influence or reelection benefits are gained by membership on this committee. Veterans' Affairs members mention their association with veterans programs and veterans groups as electorally useful, but most members discount its value.

Conclusion: Member
Goals and the Committee Systems ⸻⸻⸻⸻⸻⸻⸻⸻

Even though students of Congress have disagreed about what motivates members to seek one assignment rather than another, most of them agree that the committee systems play a central role in member goal attainment. David Mayhew notes that "if a group of planners sat down and tried to design a pair of American national assemblies with the goal of serving members' electoral needs year in and year out, they would be hard pressed to improve on what exists." [83] In contrast, Rochelle Jones and Peter Woll claim that "understanding the drive for internal power and status explodes the misconception that the activities of Capitol Hill are geared to reelection." [84] They argue that the fragmented committee systems are designed to fill members' insatiable hunger for bases of personal power.[85] In fact, Congress's committee systems are remarkably well suited to these and other member goals. Jurisdictional fragmentation certainly helps. Members representing similar constituencies can join together to determine policy affecting those constituencies with minimal interference from disinterested members; influence-oriented members thrive on their committees' exclusive jurisdictions; and members with particular policy interests are given an opportunity to focus on and have a major influence over policy decisions in those areas. Just as importantly, legislative jurisdiction, in terms of its salience and conflict potential, is not evenly distributed among congressional committees. As a consequence, members with different goal emphases can seek out committees suited to their needs and separately pursue those goals enthusiastically in their committee activities. This is more true in the House than the Senate, where fewer committees with more evenly divided jurisdictions make committee distinctions more difficult for members. But in both chambers the uneven distribution of jurisdiction, agendas, and environments facilitates the achievement of members' multiple goals.

NOTES

1. Richard F. Fenno, *Congressmen in Committees* (Boston: Little, Brown & Co., 1973).
2. Fenno, *Congressmen*, 1-2.
3. Charles S. Bullock III, "Motivations for U.S. Congressional Committee Preferences: Freshmen of the 92d Congress," *Legislative Studies Quarterly* 1 (May 1976): 201-212.
4. Bullock used this question in his study of the 92d Congress House freshmen. We used the same question during interviews with freshmen of the 97th Congress. See Steven S. Smith and Christopher J. Deering, "Changing Motives for Committee Preferences of New Members of the U.S. House," *Legislative Studies Quarterly* 8 (May 1983): 271-281.
5. Charles S. Bullock III, "U.S. Senate Committee Preferences and Motivations," paper prepared for the 1982 meeting of the American Political Science Association, Denver, Colorado, September 2-5, 1982.
6. Two additional motivations, predecessor cues and a delegate-model philosophy, were mentioned by members. Nine House freshmen in the 97th Congress indicated that they listed a committee because their predecessor was on the committee. In some cases, the predecessor's cue was tied directly to the reelection goal because freshmen saw the predecessor's assignments as an indicator of which committees would be useful at home. In most instances, though, the predecessor's assignments served merely to direct a member to certain committees, or state delegation colleagues had explicit expectations that someone from that state or district should fill the vacancy. Delegate-philosophy motivations were expressed by many House and Senate members who believed that someone from their district or state ought to serve on a certain committee to properly represent its constituency. These members made no mention of reelection needs.

   These variations in constituency-oriented motivations may stem from this data's focus on preference motivations rather than on goals pursued after assignment. The predecessor version can lead merely to assignment to a certain committee (dictating no particular behavior once on the committee) and thus would be difficult to detect when focusing on participation in committee activities after appointment. The delegate motivation is more similar to the reelection motivation in that it usually requires further pursuit of district interests after appointment to the committee. Indeed, it is difficult to distinguish delegate-motivated from reelection-motivated behavior in committee activities, despite the fact that the two goals are clearly separable in members' responses about committee preferences. This interpretation is similar to Herbert Weisberg and his colleagues' discovery that Ohio State legislators often distinguish between service to their constituents and reelection as goals for their activity. See Herbert S. Weisberg, Thomas Boyd, Marshall Goodman, and Debra Gross, "Reelection and Constituency Service as State Legislator Goals: It's Just Part of the Job," paper prepared for the American Political Science Association's 1982 meeting, Denver, Colorado, September 2-5, 1982.
7. Fenno, *Congressmen*, 145-148.
8. Morris P. Fiorina, *Congress: Keystone of the Washington Establishment* (New Haven: Yale University Press, 1977), 41-46.

9. See Randall Ripley and Grace A. Franklin, *Congress, the Bureaucracy and Public Policy* (Homewood, Ill.: Dorsey Press, 1980), 92-110.
10. Peter W. Rodino, Jr., "That Old Judiciary Just Ain't What She Used To Be," *Washington Star*, March 19, 1981, A15.
11. Fenno, *Congressmen*, 9.
12. Ibid., 4.
13. David E. Price, "Congressional Committees in the Policy Process," in *Congress Reconsidered*, 2d ed., ed. Lawrence C. Dodd and Bruce I. Oppenheimer (Washington, D.C.: CQ Press, 1981), 181.
14. Fenno, *Congressmen*, 284-285, for example.
15. David E. Price, *Who Makes the Laws?* (Cambridge, Mass.: Schenkman Publishing Co., 1972), 93, 176-177, 275, 318.
16. Roger H. Davidson, "Breaking Up Those 'Cozy Triangles': An Impossible Dream?" in *Legislative Reform and Public Policy*, ed. Susan Welch and John G. Peters (New York: Praeger Publishers, 1977), 42-43.
17. Rules reported from the Rules Committee are in the form of simple resolutions that are passed by a majority vote on the House floor prior to a bill's consideration in the committee of the whole. The resolution stipulates in detail the conditions for debate on a piece of legislation.
18. Few Democrats actively consider Rules because the Speaker has virtual control over appointments; thus, few freshmen mention it as a committee preference.
19. Alan Ehrenhalt, "House Rules Committee Regains Image of Independence," *Congressional Quarterly Weekly Report*, March 30, 1974, 804.
20. Ibid., 810.
21. Bruce I. Oppenheimer, "The Rules Committee: New Arm of Leadership in a Decentralized House," in *Congress Reconsidered*, 1st ed., ed. Lawrence C. Dodd and Bruce I. Oppenheimer (New York: Praeger Publishers, 1977), 103.
22. Ibid., 105-112.
23. Ibid., 103-105.
24. See Fenno, *Congressmen*, 3-4.
25. Quoted in Diane Granat, "House Appropriations Panel Doles Out Cold Federal Cash, Chafes at Budget Procedures," *Congressional Quarterly Weekly Report*, June 18, 1983, 1209.
26. Fenno, *Congressmen*, 97; also see Richard F. Fenno, *The Power of the Purse* (Boston: Little, Brown & Co., 1966), 141.
27. Quoted in Granat, "House Appropriations," 1210.
28. Lance T. LeLoup, *The Fiscal Congress* (Westport, Conn.: Greenwood Press, 1980), 123.
29. Quoted in Granat, "House Appropriations," 1215.
30. Fenno, *Congressmen*, 4.
31. See Malcolm E. Jewell and Chu Chi-Hung, "Membership Movement and Committee Attractiveness in the U.S. House of Representatives, 1963-1971," *American Journal of Political Science* 18 (May 1974), 433-441.
32. See John F. Manley, *The Politics of Finance* (Boston: Little, Brown & Co., 1970), Chap. IV.
33. See "Committee Secrecy: House Opens Up Its Session in 1973," *Congressional Quarterly Weekly Report*, February 16, 1974, 377 and "Open Committee Trend in House and Senate," *Congressional Quarterly Weekly Report*, January 11, 1975, 83.

34. Catherine E. Rudder, "Committee Reform and the Revenue Process," in *Congress Reconsidered,* 1st ed., ed. Dodd and Oppenheimer, 124-126.
35. Fenno, *Congressmen,* 4-5.
36. Rudder, "Committee Reform," 128-130.
37. Ibid., 129.
38. Rules of the House Democrats in caucus distinguish committees as follows. Exclusive—Appropriations, Rules, Ways and Means. Major—Agriculture, Armed Services, Banking, Commerce, Education & Labor, Judiciary, Public Works. Nonmajor—Budget, District of Columbia, Government Operations, House Administration, Interior, Merchant Marine, Post Office, Science & Technology, Small Business, Standards of Official Conduct, Veterans' Affairs.
39. Andy Plattner, "Scrappy House Energy Panel Provides High Pressure Arena for Wrangling Over Regulation," *Congressional Quarterly Weekly Report,* March 12, 1983, 501.
40. See David E. Price, "Policy Making in Congressional Committees: The Impact of 'Environmental' Factors," *American Political Science Review* 72 (June 1978), 560-568.
41. Price, "Policy Making," 550-560.
42. It should be noted that members and other participants also see Energy and Commerce as an attractive committee because its members easily attract campaign contributions from private interests affected by its highly salient, broad jurisdiction. In fact, Energy and Commerce ranked fourth among House committees in mean contributions from political action committees in 1982. There is, however, no simple relationship between the salience or breadth of a committee's jurisdiction and political action committee contributions for all House committees.
43. Norman J. Ornstein and David W. Rohde, "Shifting Forces, Changing Rules, and Political Outcomes: The Impact of Congressional Change on Four House Committees," in *New Perspectives on the House of Representatives,* 3d ed., ed. Robert L. Peabody and Nelson W. Polsby (Chicago: Rand McNally & Co., 1977), 246-252.
44. Fenno, *Congressmen,* 9.
45. One example: a Foreign Affairs freshman, Tom Lantos of California, was criticized by his 1982 opponent for membership on a committee that did so little for the district.
46. Fenno, *Congressmen,* 28.
47. Ornstein and Rohde, "Shifting Forces," 252-261.
48. Fenno, *Congressmen,* 107.
49. Ibid., 108.
50. See Fred Kaiser, "Oversight of Foreign Policy: The U.S. House Committee on International Relations," *Legislative Studies Quarterly* 2 (August 1977): 255-279.
51. Fenno, *Congressmen,* 9-12.
52. See Lynette P. Perkins, "Influences of Members' Goals on their Committee Behavior: The U.S. House Judiciary Committee," *Legislative Studies Quarterly* 5 (August 1980), 391.
53. Rodino, "That Old Judiciary," A15.
54. Perkins, "Influences," found many House Judiciary members of the 93d Congress to be motivated by reelection (p. 376). This is contrary to Bullock's findings for 92d Congress freshmen. The difference probably is due to

Perkins' using a direct question about each of the goals to members already sitting on Judiciary as opposed to Bullock's use of an open-ended question about preference motivations to potential members. Perkins' approach probably stimulates positive responses and thus tends to yield a multiple goal characterization even when one or more goals are of relatively little significance. In addition, Perkins' discussion suggests that the reelection-oriented members were not so much driven by reelection desires in their Judiciary activity as they were in avoiding Judiciary involvement because the committee did not serve the reelection goal well. The active participants were policy-oriented.

55. We are grateful to Professor Kenneth Shepsle of Washington University for use of his data on Democratic committee requests for the 86th to 93d Congresses. Request data are unavailable for the 91st Congress. The authors collected the 94th to 97th Congress request data and thank several participants in the Democratic committee assignment process for their generosity. For background, see Kenneth A. Shepsle, *The Giant Jigsaw Puzzle* (Chicago: University of Chicago Press, 1973).
56. Allen Schick, *Congress and Money: Budgeting, Spending and Taxing* (Washington, D.C.: The Urban Institute Press, 1980), 100.
57. Ibid., 110.
58. Ibid., Chap. 8.
59. The House Budget Committee rejected strong reconciliation orders to other House committees in 1980, in contrast to its Senate counterpart.
60. LeLoup, *Fiscal Congress*, 53.
61. Also see John W. Ellwood and James A. Thurber, "The Politics of the Congressional Budget Process Re-examined," in *Congress Reconsidered*, 2d ed., ed. Dodd and Oppenheimer, 254.
62. Schick, *Congress and Money*, 118, 129.
63. Ornstein and Rohde, "Shifting Forces," 196-197.
64. U.S., Congress, House, Armed Services Committee, No. 91-14, March 27, 1969, 170-172. Emphasis added.
65. Fenno, *Congressmen*, 59, 285-287.
66. James T. Murphy, "Partisanship and the House Public Works Committee," paper presented at the American Political Science Association's 1968 meeting, September, 1968. Washington, D.C.
67. Margot Hornblower, "An Angry Man's Education on Getting Along Without Going Along," *Washington Post*, July 6, 1982, A2.
68. Fenno, *Congressmen*, 281.
69. U.S., Congress, House, *Toward the Endless Frontier: History of the Committee on Science and Technology, 1959-1979* (Washington, D.C.: Government Printing Office, 1980), 695.
70. Ibid., 536-540.
71. Bruce F. Freed, "House Elects Thompson to Replace Hays; Controls on Perquisites Tightened," *Congressional Quarterly Weekly Report*, June 26, 1976, 1631-1633.
72. This observation is consistent with Fenno's findings, of course. See Fenno, *Congressmen*, 148.
73. Note that majority party members do better. See Bruce A. Ray and Steven S. Smith, "Leverage, Reward, Accommodation, and Administration: Four Theories on the Growth of Congressional Committee Seats," paper prepared for

Committees in Congress

the Southern Political Science Association's 1982 meeting, October 28-30, 1982, Atlanta, Georgia.

74. In mid-1983, Republican Senate Majority Leader Howard Baker of Tennessee announced that he would no longer feel compelled to honor "holds" on legislation. Holds had become so commonplace that Baker found it very difficult to set the schedule for the floor.

75. Fenno, *Congressmen*, 161-162.

76. Ibid., 141-142.

77. Schick, *Congress and Money*, 95, 99.

78. But Senate Republicans also included the Budget Committee as an exclusive committee until 1980.

79. Schick, *Congress and Money*, 124.

80. Fenno, *Congressmen*, 144; Price, *Who Makes the Laws?* 167-176.

81. Fenno, *Congressmen*, 142-143; Stephen Horn, *Unused Power* (Washington, D.C.: The Brookings Institution, 1970), 10-11.

82. Price, *Who Makes the Laws?*, 79.

83. David Mayhew, *Congress: The Electoral Connection* (New Haven: Yale University Press, 1974), 81-82.

84. Rochelle Jones and Peter Woll, *The Private World of Congress* (New York: The Free Press, 1979), 235.

85. Ibid., Chaps. 3 and 6; also see Lawrence C. Dodd, "Congress and the Quest for Power," in *Congress Reconsidered*, 1st ed., ed. Dodd and Oppenheimer, 270-272.

Subcommittees and Committee Decision Making | 5

Despite the variety of decision-making patterns in congressional committees, "subcommittee government" has replaced "committee government" as the term most frequently used to characterize the nature of congressional decision making.[1] Subcommittee government is said to exist, according to one definition,

> when the basic responsibility for the bulk of legislative activity (hearings, debates, legislative markups, that is, the basic writing of a bill) occurs, not at a meeting of an entire standing committee, but at a meeting of a smaller subcommittee of the standing committee. The decisions of the subcommittee are then viewed as the authoritative decisions—decisions that are altered by the standing committee only when the subcommittee is seriously divided or when it is viewed as highly unrepresentative of the full committee.[2]

The term subcommittee government has been applied broadly—to both chambers and to most committees.[3] In this and the following two chapters, committee structure, activities, leadership, and staff are examined to determine the degree to which committee decision-making processes approximate subcommittee government. The argument is that, while generalizations about subcommittee government capture the direction of change in congressional decision making, they tend to oversimplify patterns of committee behavior and to overstate the degree to which many committees have changed during the past 15 years. Even House committees, which experienced externally imposed procedural reforms, reacted in a number of ways, and Senate committees retained the great variety that was present in the late 1960s.

Modal decision-making patterns of the House and the Senate were reflected in the manner in which the House Energy and Commerce Committee and the Senate Energy and Natural Resources Committee handled legislation in 1983 to decontrol natural gas prices. In the House, Energy and Commerce's Subcommittee on Fossil and Synthetic Fuels held a lengthy series of hearings and markup sessions before sending the legislation to the full committee. Thus two battlefields existed for this highly divisive legislation because losers in the subcommittee would wage another battle at the full committee level. The split-level nature of participants' strategies in the House was reflected in an exchange between two staff assistants about a proposal offered by the subcommittee chairman, Democrat Philip R. Sharp of Indiana.

> As Nancy Williams of Sharp's staff began explaining the proposal section by section, she was questioned by Roy Willis, legislative assistant to Democrat W.J. "Billy" Tauzin of Louisiana, the No. 1 gas-producing state in the country.
>
> "You call this a compromise?" asked Willis, whose boss had co-sponsored the Reagan administration's bill to decontrol all natural gas prices by 1986, a concept that was not part of Sharp's committee draft. "There is nothing in it for us at all. But that's all right; we'll deal with *you* in the subcommittee."
>
> "Well, Roy," responded Williams, according to the recollections of others in the room that day, "we'll handle *you* in the full committee." [4]

In contrast, the Senate committee held all of its hearings and markups in full committee, a practice far different from what was typical in the same committee in the late 1960s.

The Structure of Congressional Committees

Both the nature of committee structure and the location of effective member participation in decision making are essential ingredients of subcommittee government. In this case, structure refers to the number and composition of subcommittees, and the location of effective participation concerns full committee versus subcommittee activity. As Chapter 2 outlined, House reforms directly affected both structure and participation by forcing the creation of at least four subcommittees on most committees and giving those subcommittees the authority and resources to conduct investigations and to write legislation. Senate reforms did neither directly. Indeed, by limiting subcommittee memberships the 1977 reforms indirectly reduced the number of Senate subcommittees. [5]

Subcommittee Growth

As noted in Chapters 1 and 2, the number of subcommittees in both chambers increased dramatically during the 1950s and 1960s. Subcommittees were almost as difficult to eliminate as committees had been in the nineteenth century. When subcommittees were challenged—a rare occurrence—their defenders often devised ingenious responses to protect positions they found to be valuable. One such instance stands out. In 1967 Republican Sen. Everett M. Dirksen of Illinois, one of the few minority party members permitted to chair a subcommittee after the 1946 reorganization, sought a $7,500 authorization from the Senate for his subcommittee's only employee. He was challenged by conservative Democrat Allen J. Ellender of Louisiana, who took the opportunity to question the need for the subcommittee itself:

> As I recall, that committee has 16 subcommittees, almost one for each member of the committee. I cannot for the life of me understand why legislation pertaining to Federal charters, holidays and celebrations could not be handled by the full Committee on the Judiciary.[6]

Senator Dirksen, who was known for his sharp wit and his deliberate, mellifluous speech, defended his subcommittee and its activities:

> Mr. President, in the first place, I am against disposing of this subcommittee, and the most important reason that I can assign is that I am the chairman. I want no legislative throatcutting here.... I have been the chairman or a member of this subcommittee for so long that the memory of man runneth not to the contrary. You are not going to do this to me, are you, and destroy my one and only chairmanship? Why, that is discrimination....
>
> The second reason, Mr. President, is that I am a stickler for tradition.... I have to let the Senate in on a little secret. Once upon a time there was a distinguished member of this body by the name of William Langer, from North Dakota, and at the time he was ranking Republican member on the Committee on the Judiciary. The distinguished chairman was the Honorable Pat McCarran of Nevada. I recall the day when Senator Langer went to Senator McCarran and said: "There is no justice. There ought to be at least one Republican chairman of one subcommittee on Judiciary." And Senator McCarran, with all the grace and all the generosity in his soul, said: "You are on and you are it. You name the subcommittee that you want." And Senator Langer said: "I'll take Charters, Holidays, and Celebrations."
>
> That is how that subcommittee came into being. It was an absolute, unadulterated, unmitigated, unrefined, unconfined deal. But I did not make the deal. I am only the inheritor of the deal. And I do not want my inheritance destroyed since I came by it very honestly. So you see, this is in the great tradition.
>
> The third reason I assign is that I think this is probably the most important subcommittee in the Senate of the United States. Just think of the question of charters that we have to pass on ... in due course there may be organizations like the Sons of Rest or the Association of Indigent Senators, or what have you, and maybe they want a Federal charter, and if they do, they march up to my subcommittee door and

they get good attention. So, you see, this is an important subcommittee, because it involves a lot of people. . . .

So, do not destroy this little subcommittee of two men and do not destroy this responsibility of the chairman of this little subcommittee. . . . I stand here today to protect this little subcommittee, and lay no profane hand on it because it will be a charge on your conscience.[7]

Dirksen's position was supported by a voice vote.

The House nevertheless has managed to halt the proliferation of subcommittees in recent Congresses and, in the case of three committees, to trim the number of subcommittees. Once we exclude Ways and Means' subcommittees, which were not created until after the 1974 reforms, and the two new standing committees, the number of standing subcommittees in the House actually fell from 120 to 118 between 1973 and 1983. This is partly the result of the cap on subcommittees adopted by House Democrats in 1981. The caucus rule provides that, except for Appropriations, standing committees are limited to eight subcommittees; committees with more than 35 members and fewer than six subcommittees may increase the number to six or, with Steering and Policy Committee approval, may have seven subcommittees. Agriculture and Banking reduced the number of their subcommittees in order to meet the eight-subcommittee limit. Education and Labor was forced to disband its Task Force on Welfare and Pension Plans to comply with the limit because the rule explicitly counted task forces and other special subunits as subcommittees. No incumbent subcommittee chair was forced to give up a chair, although three members in line for a chair could not assume one. The effect of the cap was that no House committee increased its number of subcommittees at the start of the 97th or 98th Congresses, the first Congresses in which that had happened since 1947. And the average number of subcommittee assignments per member dropped back to about 3.5 after exceeding 4 subcommittees per member in 1975-1976. The House, then, has an effective floor under the number of subcommittees set by chamber rules and a ceiling on the number of subcommittees set by majority party caucus rules. This has homogenized House committee structure: nearly 70 percent of standing committees had between six and eight subcommittees in 1983.

Despite its 1977 attempt at control, the Senate may be repeating its pattern of incrementally adding subcommittees. The number of Senate subcommittees on standing committees fell from 127 to 90 between 1973 and 1979, a result of the 1977 limits on the number of subcommittee assignments and chairs senators could hold. The mean number of subcommittee assignments per senator also dropped from nearly 10 to just under 7. But when the Republicans gained control of the Senate in 1981, they increased the number of subcommittees by two on Judiciary and by one on Commerce. Commerce and Small Business each added a subcommittee two years later when Banking also added two subcommittees—giving Banking more subcommittees than it has had at any time since 1949. The average number of subcommittees per member also began to creep back up, increasing by nearly half-a-seat per member between 1977 and 1983. The change is seen in Figure 5-1. In 1977 nearly 80 percent of senators had between six and eight subcommittee assignments on standing committees. The distribution reflects that year's

Figure 5-1   Distribution of Subcommittee Assignments on Standing Committees among Senators, 1977 and 1983

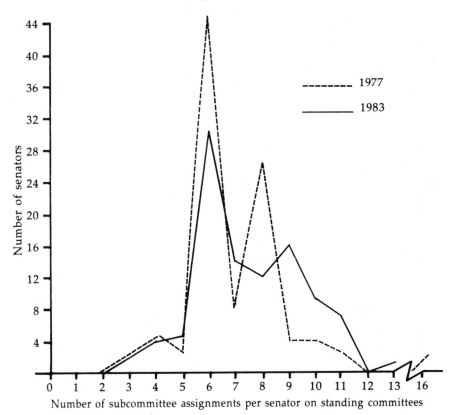

Source: *Congressional Staff Directory* (Mount Vernon, Va.: Congressional Staff Directory, Ltd., 1977, 1983).

reforms, which limited most senators to three subcommittees on each of two major committees and to two subcommittees on the minor committee on which they served. By 1983 senators regularly were ignoring the 1977 limits; in fact, the number of senators serving on more than eight subcommittees nearly tripled to 32 by 1983.

The Senate retains far greater variation in committee structure than does the House because of the absence of an explicit floor or ceiling for the number of Senate subcommittees. The Senate has had more committees with a large number of subcommittees and more committees with few subcommittees than has the House. In the 98th Congress, for example, the average number of subcommittees per committee was nearly identical for the two chambers, but the Senate had five committees with nine or more subcommittees and three with no subcommittees. The House had only one committee with more than nine subcommittees and one with no subcommittees, despite having more committees than the Senate.

Stimulants of Subcommittee Growth

Committees of all types, large and small, policy- and constituency-oriented, and active and less active, have faced internal or external circumstances that prompted them to create more subcommittees. In fact, 65 percent of current standing committees that have existed for more than a decade experienced net increases in the number of subcommittees during the past 30 years. This may indicate that there is an underlying motivation, common to members of nearly all committees, that stimulates subcommittee proliferation. Lawrence Dodd, for example, has argued that

> each member wants to exercise power—to make the key policy decisions. This motive places every member in a personal conflict with every other member: to the extent that one member realizes her or his goal personally to control all key decisions, all others must lose. Given this widespread power motive, an obvious way to resolve the conflict is to disperse power—or at least power positions—as widely as possible.[8]

In Dodd's view, subcommittee chairs have been the primary goal of members seeking more positions of power since the 1946 consolidation of standing committees. Unfortunately, no definitive evidence on members' ultimate objectives exists to test Dodd's thesis, but there is little doubt that subcommittee growth represents an effort by members to control those factors that affect their ability to achieve their personal goals, whatever they may be. Nonetheless, our discussions with committee members and staff strongly suggest that there are multiple motivations and circumstances that produce subcommittee growth. Subcommittees, like committees themselves, serve a variety of purposes for members and, as will be seen later in this chapter, the role of subcommittees varies widely among committees. Power is no more an end in itself than is reelection for members. Creating new, well-staffed subcommittees gives their chairs more independence and thus adds to their influence over policy decisions. But it also provides new opportunities to pursue policy interests and to gain publicity vital to reelection. Indeed, any quick review of congressional observers' explanations for the number of subcommittees will demonstrate that there are many sufficient causes for subcommittee growth, but few necessary ones.[9]

Nevertheless, committees with large jurisdictions have had the most opportunities and experienced the greatest pressure to create new subcommittees. There is a distinct tendency for committees of high jurisdictional fragmentation to have more subcommittees than other committees. This is most obvious at the extremes. The Appropriations committees have the most fragmented jurisdictions and the most subcommittees, while the rules, administration, and veterans committees are low in both jurisdictional fragmentation and subcommittees. Overall, the correlation between jurisdictional fragmentation and subcommittees has been positive and moderately strong in recent Congresses (the cross-sectional rank-order correlation has been more than .60 for the House and more than .36 in the Senate in each of the last six Congresses—93d to 98th).[10]

Other factors, such as member goals and workload, probably reinforce the effects of jurisdictional fragmentation, but do not have a measurable effect on the number of subcommittees independent of jurisdictional fragmentation. In 1969 House policy and constituency committees averaged 6.2 and 6.0 subcommittees, respectively, but their averages increased to 7.8 and 6.7 by 1977. Personal policy interests clearly were important in the subcommittee expansions in Banking, Commerce, Education and Labor, and Judiciary. These committees' large, multifaceted jurisdictions, of course, provided ready-made foundations upon which new subcommittees could be created. In the 98th Congress, policy committees averaged more than one subcommittee more than constituency committees in both the House and Senate.[11]

Aggregate Patterns of Activity

The presence of numerous subcommittees, even when bolstered by rules that grant subcommittees some independence from parent committees, does not guarantee a decision-making pattern properly labelled subcommittee government. Independent activity does not necessarily entail autonomy in decision making, although independence is probably a precondition for autonomy. The simple fact is that subcommittees remain creatures of parent committees that may ignore or emasculate subcommittee recommendations. The question is how much legislation is written in subcommittee and how much of it survives the parliamentary hurdle presented by the full committee.[12]

The percentage of legislation referred to House subcommittees more than doubled between the 91st Congress (before the reforms) and the 96th Congress at the end of the 1970s (Table 5-1). Until the 1970s, many full committee chairs did not bother to refer to a subcommittee legislation that was not likely to be taken up by the full committee. This meant, of course, that full committee chairs could retain control of legislation they did not support. But since 1975, when the 1973 Subcommittee Bill of Rights was implemented in most House committees, subcommittees have become the dungeons of Congress in which most legislation dies.[13] Much less change occurred in the path of legislation eventually reported to the House floor. Even in the late 1960s, most legislation brought to the floor had been referred to a subcommittee at some point in committee deliberations. But since the reforms, several House committees have adopted rules to keep certain types of legislation at the full committee level. And several hold Senate bills at the full committee, especially late in a congressional session when there is no chance of further action or when similar legislation

Table 5-1 Percentage of Legislation Referred to and Reported from Standing Committees that was Referred to Subcommittee or was the Subject of a Subcommittee Hearing

		91st Congress	96th Congress
House:	Referred	35.7	79.8
	Reported	75.4	80.0
Senate:	Referred	41.5	41.1
	Reported	40.0	44.8

Note: Excludes House and Senate Appropriations and House Rules committees because they do not produce comparable committee calendars. Excludes matters related to nominations.

Source: Committee Calendars

already has been reported to the floor. Thus not all referred or reported legislation is sent to subcommittee.

In contrast, the aggregate Senate pattern has remained unchanged. Most referred and reported legislation is not sent to subcommittee. The Senate is far more full committee-oriented, and senators can participate more fully in shaping major legislation there than in the House.

The pattern of committee and subcommittee meetings and hearings confirms these chamber differences. The percentage of House meetings and hearings held by subcommittees increased greatly during the 1970s, as Table 5-2 indicates. Nearly all House hearings now are held by subcommittees. Subcommittee chairs control the timing and content of their hearings and full committee chairs usually pursue their own interests through subcommittees they chair rather than through the full committee. But the key change in the House is that a majority of the meetings at which substantive policy decisions are made also now are held in subcommittee. The reforms had a clear effect, as is suggested by the presence of greater change in the number of subcommittee meetings in the 1970s than in the 1960s. Subcommittees gained the authority and resources with which to make substantive policy decisions. And yet the figures also demonstrate that full committee meetings still are not greatly outnumbered by subcommittee meetings, even though sub-committees outnumber House full committees by more than six to one. The pattern of meetings indicates, therefore, that while the House clearly has moved toward subcommittee government, existing commit-tee activities represent a mixed pattern of subcommittee and full committee involvement.

Table 5-2 Percentage of All Standing Committee Meetings and Hear-ings Held by Subcommittees

		86th Congress	91st Congress	96th Congress
House:	Meetings	45.6	47.9	56.1
	Hearings	72.3	77.0	90.7
Senate:	Meetings	27.1	30.6	19.1
	Hearings	77.7	79.6	65.2

Note: House Appropriations excluded because it does not report its meetings in the Daily Digest. Excludes meetings and hearings on nominations.

Source: Daily Digest of the *Congressional Record*

The continuing significance of full committee activity in House members' daily routines after the reforms was demonstrated in a 1977 study of their allocation of time. Based on daily logs of members' activities, the study showed that about 53 percent of time spent on committee activities by House Democrats was spent in full committee. While only 37 percent of the time spent in hearings was in full committee hearings, 64 percent was spent by Democrats in markups at the full committee level. Similar allocations of representatives' time were found for Republicans.[14] A survey conducted a year earlier disclosed that 82 percent of responding House members rated their work "in subcommittees to develop legislation" as "very important," while 71 percent considered their full committee work in developing legislation very important.[15] Again, the appropriate interpretation is that the most frequent House decision-making pattern is one of mixed full committee and subcommittee participation.

The Senate retains its longstanding modal pattern of subcommittee hearings and full committee markup (Table 5-2). Most Senate committees operate on the assumption that subcommittee markups are an inefficient use of senators' limited time and that their efforts often will be repeated at the full committee level. As one Senate committee staff director explained:

> We tried a subcommittee markup a couple of years ago, but we could only get two senators to show. They just decided to get together over lunch and make some recommendations to the committee without taking formal action. We haven't tried it since.

Despite the Senate's propensity to create new subcommittees regularly, subcommittee government is not widely institutionalized in that chamber, and there has not been any general movement toward it, at least as is discernible in the pattern of meetings and hearings. Indeed, the percentage of Senate meetings held in subcommittee in recent Congresses is lower than the House percentage of more than 20 years ago.

House Committee Decision Making Patterns

With three notable exceptions, House committees now routinely refer nearly all legislation to subcommittees, where most hearings are held. On several committees, this represents a sharp break with the past. Armed Services, for example, referred only 12 percent of its legislation to subcommittee during the 91st Congress (1969-1971). Conservative Democratic Chairman L. Mendel Rivers of South Carolina and his equally pro-Pentagon successor, Democrat F. Edward Hebert of Louisiana, retained careful control over legislation, selectively referring it to subcommittees as their political preferences dictated. Subcommittees were not given fixed, written jurisdictions; they merely were numbered. This permitted Rivers and Hebert to assign legislation to subcommittees that they had stacked with members favorable to their own views. In contrast, nearly all of Armed Services' legislation was referred to subcommittee in recent Congresses (99 percent in the 96th Congress), a direct result of the 1970s' reforms. In the 98th Congress, this meant that two new subcommittee chairs, who have been among the Pentagon's sharpest critics in Congress (Democrats Ronald V. Dellums of California and Les Aspin of Wisconsin), became overseers of legislation traditionally of great interest to the constituency-oriented Armed Services members—military installations and personnel benefits. Similar but less politically dramatic changes in the treatment of legislation occurred on Banking, Merchant Marine and Fisheries, Public Works, and Science and Technology.

The three important exceptions have been Foreign Affairs, Ways and Means, and House Administration. Foreign Affairs increased the percentage of bills referred to subcommittee from 17 to 76 percent between the 91st and 96th Congresses, but still holds some important legislation for the full committee. In 1979, for example, the full committee retained control over legislation implementing the Panama Canal treaties, the Taiwan Relations Act of 1979, and several foreign assistance bills. These are among the core issues of interest to policy-oriented Foreign Affairs members, and they make up a large part of the legislation the committee reports to the floor (Table 5-3). Nevertheless, Foreign Affairs' subcommittees have been nearly as active in holding hearings as those of most other policy committees since the early 1970s.[16]

Ways and Means, as noted above, holds income tax legislation for the full committee, but refers most other legislation to subcommittee. This represents a major change from the Wilbur Mills era when there were no subcommittees. Health, social security, trade, and welfare measures have been routinely referred to subcommittee since 1975. House Administration treats campaign election law, its only major policy jurisdiction, at the full committee level. As a result of these practices, approximately one-fourth of Ways and Means and House Administration hearings are still held by the full committee, a fraction two or three times as large as for other House committees.

Treatment of legislation eventually reported to the floor is of even greater importance than simple referral. Most House subcommittees were active in committee decision making as the 1970s began (Table 5-3). At least two-thirds of reported legislation was considered by subcommittees in 13 committees (and for Appropriations, which does not publish a committee calendar). Significant exceptions in the 91st Congress were Banking, Public Works, and Ways and Means. By the 96th Congress, only Small Business, which gained standing committee status in 1977, handled a large proportion of legislation strictly at the full committee level. The figure in Table 5-3 for Foreign Affairs in the 96th Congress is misleading because it includes many resolutions of no statutory significance that merely express the opinion of the House or Congress on some issue. Once these resolutions are excluded, nearly 70

Table 5-3 The Role of House Subcommittees: Percent of Reported Legislation with Subcommittee Action and Percent of Committee Meetings Held by Subcommittees*

Congress	Reported Legislation with Subcommittee Action		Meetings Held by Subcommittees	
	91st	96th	91st	96th
Constituency Committees:				
Agriculture	78	83	53	79
Armed Services	81	94	61	62
Interior	97	72	49	50
Merchant Marine	92	99	63	57
Post Office & Civil Service	82	87	34	48
Public Works	18	99	50	68
Science and Technology	83	91	48	63
Veterans' Affairs	66	91	59	47
Small Business	—	58	—	44
Policy Committees:				
Banking	10	85	37	63
Commerce	67	92	58	60
Education and Labor	69	81	61	47
Foreign Affairs	67	57	18	43
Government Operations	100	100	63	70
Judiciary	94	88	76	76
Prestige Committees:				
Ways and Means	0	77	0	46
Others:				
District of Columbia	86	92	58	55
House Administration	100	89	79	71

* See notes to Table 5-1 and 5-2.

percent of Foreign Affairs legislation is considered by subcommittees, a percentage still lower than nearly all other committees.

House committees display greater variety in the proportion of meetings held at the subcommittee level. Even in the 96th Congress, a majority of meetings (which are almost entirely markup sessions) were held at the full committee level on 11 of the 18 committees for which comparable data is available, which represents no net change since the 91st Congress. These include both constituency and policy committees. In three cases, Agriculture, Veterans' Affairs, and Education and Labor, a significant drop occurred in the percentage of meetings held by subcommittees. In all three cases, however, the absolute number of meetings also dropped, reflecting a decline in the size of these committees' legislative agendas during the 1970s. Only District of Columbia and Post Office exhibited similar declines in activity. The number of hearings held by the subcommittees of the three committees remained constant or increased.

Policy Committees

The role of subcommittees expanded most on Banking, Commerce, Foreign Affairs, and, obviously, Ways and Means. In each case, personal policy motivations play a great role in members' activities and, in each case, those motivations have played an important part in changing the role of subcommittees.

Banking's subcommittees had been constrained in the late 1960s and early 1970s by Wright Patman, a strong, activist chair who controlled the composition of subcommittees and the flow of legislation to them.[17] Only the housing subcommittee retained some freedom from Patman because of all other senior committee members' presence on it. The other subcommittees, all dealing with some aspect of banking and finance, Patman's specialty, were permitted to hold dozens of hearings, often with Patman present, but held few meetings. In the 91st Congress, for example, there were fewer than 10 meetings. Patman's strategy was to withhold clear jurisdiction from subcommittees. This allowed him to refer nearly any legislation he desired to his own subcommittee, although he often preferred not to refer legislation to subcommittee at all. The full committee, with Patman carefully controlling its agenda and proceedings, held 35 meetings to mark up legislation during the 91st Congress. Patman simply used the tools at his disposal to further his own deeply held policy beliefs. Committee Democrats were frustrated by Patman's control, but not because they differed strongly with him on policy matters; in fact, Patman's populist attitudes on

137

banking matters found substantial support among committee liberals. The problem was that the liberals could not pursue their own interests effectively. With Patman's ouster and the implementation of the Subcommittee Bill of Rights in 1975, all of Banking's subcommittees became much more active and began to mark up legislation before sending it back to the full committee.

The role of subcommittees on the Commerce Committee also was transformed during the 1970s.[18] After Democrat Harley O. Staggers of West Virginia became full committee chair in 1966, he gradually enhanced the role of subcommittees and eventually gave them the duty of holding hearings on most legislation. Thus the percentage of reported legislation treated by subcommittees was not particularly low in the late 1960s, as Table 5-3 indicates. Staggers, nonetheless, limited subcommittee chairs' access to staff, appointed subcommittees so as to maintain control over their activities and decisions, and even set agendas for subcommittee hearings, occasionally refusing subcommittee chairs' requests for hearings on their own legislation. As a result, several issue-oriented liberals, such as Democrats John E. Moss of California, John D. Dingell of Michigan, and Paul G. Rogers of Florida, repeatedly found obstacles placed in their path by Staggers and his full committee staff. An effort was made to implement the Subcommittee Bill of Rights in the committee soon after the Democratic Caucus adopted the policy in January 1973, but Staggers and a conservative majority on the committee were able to block the insurgents. Two years later, with the help of 12 new Democrats, Dingell, Moss, Rogers, and other subcommittee chairs forced a revision of the committee's rules and stripped Staggers of his subcommittee chair. Since that time, Commerce subcommittees have been well staffed and, as a group, have been the most active subcommittees in Congress.[19]

As a part of their revolt, the Commerce rebels expanded the number of subcommittee assignments members were permitted. Staggers had limited members to one subcommittee assignment, a practice unique to Commerce and Armed Services as the 1970s began. Many Democrats are now able to obtain three subcommittee assignments; others who want two assignments can receive them. Even Commerce Republicans, whose seats are limited by the majority party Democrats' generosity, were able to give all but the ranking subcommittee members and some freshmen two subcommittee seats in recent Congresses. As a result, 17 of the 27 Democrats (but only 6 of 15 Republicans) sat on the two energy subcommittees during the 98th Congress; 5 other Democrats were members of the oversight subcommittee, which could investigate energy matters as well. These changes greatly expanded Commerce Democrats' opportunities to pursue their policy interests and to participate in exciting policy debates.

The enhanced role of Foreign Affairs' subcommittees is the product of both the 1971 reform limiting members to a single subcommittee chair and the 1973 Subcommittee Bill of Rights. As noted in the previous chapter, the reforms were accommodated by Democratic Chairman Thomas E. "Doc" Morgan of Pennsylvania and resulted in immediate increases in subcommittee activity. At first, the vitalized subcommittees continued the 1960s practice of limiting themselves to hearings, as Fenno described:

> The crucial fact about these subcommittees is simply that very little happens there. With the exception of the subcommittee handling State Department regulations, the[y] report out almost no legislation. Their function is one of information gathering, to which end they hold hearings and consume information.[20]

Since the mid-1970s, however, even the annual foreign aid bill has been segmented for markup by the subcommittees and then packaged by the full committee. The increase in the percentage of Foreign Affairs' meetings held by subcommittees reported in Table 5-3 reflects the more active role of subcommittees in drafting legislation of all kinds.

Changes in Banking, Commerce, and Foreign Affairs completed the development of independent and active subcommittees on all six policy committees. And yet, with the sole exception of Government Operations, the subcommittees of these committees are not autonomous decision-making units. In fact, the same policy motivations that lead to membership on these committees and produce active subcommittees also lead to frequent battles over subcommittee recommendations at the full committee level.[21] Instead of establishing a decentralized decision-making process in which numerous groups of subcommittee members make decisions for the committee, the reforms on Banking, Commerce, and Foreign Affairs created more opportunities for members to influence policy decisions at both full committee and subcommittee levels. Subcommittee recommendations frequently are challenged at the full committee level, with losers at the subcommittee level appealing to the full committee. Minority party members often find that their chances of blocking certain provisions in proposed legislation are better at full committee than in subcommittees dominated by strong majority party advocates of a particular point of view. When the full committees ratify subcommittee recommendations, it is a product of policy agreement rather than a norm of deference. Any reciprocity that develops between subcommittees is a matter of temporary political convenience. Thus, for the affected policy committees, at least, the reforms of the 1970s have not decentralized decision making as much as they have broadened participation within committees.

For example, in April 1981, the Foreign Affairs' Subcommittee on International Security and Scientific Affairs, which was chaired by full committee Chairman Clement J. Zablocki of Wisconsin, rejected the Reagan administration's request for authorization to offer loans at low interest rates to other governments seeking to purchase American arms. The administration's "direct credit" plan would have cost the federal government nearly a billion dollars, the difference in cost between market interest rates and the rates offered other governments. Zablocki's subcommittee insisted that these credits were unreasonable at a time when the administration was demanding that Congress reduce domestic spending by billions of dollars. But the subcommittee's cuts ran counter to the preferences of other committee members who wanted a more generous foreign aid package. Zablocki was forced to compromise when the full committee took up the bill, although the administration succeeded in getting only about one-quarter of the funds requested.

Government Operations stands as a slight exception to the pattern for policy committees because of its focus on oversight. The primary products of subcommittee activity on Government Operations are formal reports on the results of investigations. The reports are sent to the full committee before they are published, but "seldom is the expertise of the investigating subcommittee challenged," as a senior Republican member explained. A committee aide added that a subcommittee's findings "are never questioned by anyone at the full committee," although modifications in subcommittee recommendations for legislative action included in the reports are made occasionally. Most of Government Operations' legislative jurisdiction is assigned to the Subcommittee on Legislation and National Security, chaired since 1975 by full committee Democratic Chairman Jack Brooks of Texas, whose legislative recommendations are scrutinized and frequently amended by the full committee.

Constituency Committees

Although the policy committees already had established independent subcommittees or were being transformed rapidly by committee insurgents, some constituency committees were much slower to change the role of their subcommittees. Two reasons underlie this difference. First, several constituency committees exhibit a greater consensus about legislative goals than do policy committees, a consensus that already had shaped committee operations at the time of the reforms. Consequently, the internal frustrations that had accumulated in some policy committees were less intense in district-oriented committees. Second, the sheer level of interest in constituency committee activities is often so low that members tolerate assertive chairs more than their policy committee counterparts do. Nevertheless, even constituency committee members were not single-minded seekers of benefits for their constituents. They also had their own policy and influence goals that eventually led to an evolution of committee decision-making patterns.

For example, between 1967 and 1975 House Agriculture Chairman W.R. "Bob" Poage of Texas retained centralized control of subcommittee appointments, jurisdiction, and bill referral, like most other committee chairs of his time.[22] In using these prerogatives, Poage accommodated most committee members' demands. He granted subcommittees recognized, if not written, jurisdictions that he usually respected in assigning legislation to subcommittee, appointed members to subcommittees related to their constituencies' interests, and gave subcommittees substantial discretion to hold hearings and write legislation on matters uniquely important to them. Even so, subcommittees were not given separate staff, and most hearings and markups on important legislation—for example, the omnibus farm bill that comes up every four years—were held at full committee. This was not a major problem for committee members, even for the few liberals on the committee, because they recognized the importance of developing a balanced package of subsidies for producers in their various constituencies. Without such a package, most subsidies for producers of individual commodities would not gain majority support in the House. A strong chair responsible for creating a package with majority support was viewed by members as an expedient means to servicing constituency interests and their own political goals.

Understandably, few Agriculture members had much interest in undermining Poage by fully exploiting the Democratic Caucus reforms. Although the committee adopted a rule providing for automatic referral of legislation to subcommittee in 1973, it was not until Democrat Thomas S. Foley of Washington became chair in 1975, after the Democratic Caucus deposed Poage, that the committee reformed its rules to implement the Subcommittee Bill of Rights. Poage's ouster, it should be noted, was not caused by an uprising among Agriculture members; in fact, the committee's three notable liberals openly supported Poage as a chair who met the needs of his committee. After the rules change, the commodity subcommittee chairs were not significantly more active because they had few personal policy interests that had been suppressed by Poage.[23] In 1977, when Foley had his first opportunity to usher through a general farm bill, the full committee held all hearings. Foley's goal, one committee aide explained, continued to be to make the subsidy programs as large as the administration and the House would permit, an aspiration appreciated by most of his committee colleagues. And yet Foley, himself a reformer when he chaired the Democratic Study Group, readily tolerated independent subcommittees on most matters, although he successfully resisted the creation of large subcommittee staffs (see Chapter 7).

Even the farm bill has been handled with more subcommittee participation in recent years. When the subsidy programs came up for reauthorization in 1981, more than 70 percent of the hearings were held in subcommittee. Agriculture's new chair that year, Democrat E. "Kika" de la Garza of Texas, did not attempt to restrain commodity subcommittee chairs who were anxious to garner support for programs that were under attack from the Reagan administration. At first, the full committee proceeded merely to package the recommendations of supporters of the various commodity programs—in the committee's traditional fashion of accommodating the various demands. But it later was forced to consider changes to bring down costs, pitting the producer groups and their representatives on the committee against each other. The task was particularly distasteful to a committee that prides itself on meeting members' demands.

Science and Technology also evolved slowly and less completely to a system of independent subcommittees. Even in the 97th Congress, subcommittees sent "their plans for hearings to the full committee for approval and recommendations," as a top committee aide explained. A member indicated that one purpose of the procedure was to ensure that subcommittees were not pursuing "irresponsible investigations of our pet agencies." The staffer suggested that it was only to double check the "efficacy of using the committee's time and resources in a certain way." But a more convincing rationale for this system of "checks and balances," as one participant called it, involves the belief that the committee's jurisdiction over highly technical subjects and scientific programs requires careful attention to the "professional quality" of its investigations and decisions. Subcommittee chairs, who would prefer not to embarrass themselves in front of experts and knowledgeable constituencies, tolerate the system because they have found that "it works for them," a full committee aide asserted.

Science and Technology subcommittees mark up most legislation before it is sent back to the full committee, as they did before the reforms (Table 5-3). But the subcommittee markups are closely observed by full committee staff who occasionally guide subcommittee members in a direction consistent with the views of the full committee chair. One aide went so far as to claim:

> There are no autonomous subcommittees. . . . The reforms didn't call for fiefdoms to be created in subcommittees and the chairman and full committee staff are on the look out for it. The chairman is aware of these tendencies and works to avoid them. . . . [If a subcommittee] tries to sneak something through, we'll clobber them with it.

The result is that subcommittees generally take into account other committee members' views when writing legislation, and their products usually are respected by the full committee. Similar patterns of observation and accommodation are mentioned prominently by members and staff of Armed Services, Merchant Marine and Fisheries, and Public Works.

Despite these examples of constituency committee adaptation to the reforms, more constituency committees come closer to meeting the definition of subcommittee government than do policy committees. As a group, the percentage of markup sessions held by their subcommittees is not significantly different from the percentage for policy subcommittees, as before the reform period. But interviewees on all constituency committees noted a full committee presumption in favor of subcommittee recommendations, even though amendments are common on several of them. No such presumption was mentioned by anyone associated with policy committees except for Government Operations, a finding similar to Fenno's for the 1960s.[24] Participants on Interior, Merchant Marine, Public Works, and Veterans' Affairs go a step further when they report that subcommittees face few serious challenges to their recommendations at the full committee level. Consider these comments:

> Interior: "The Committee is a rubberstamp of subcommittee decisions. . . . We often do not even have a quorum in the full committee when we pass on subcommittee bills."
> Merchant Marine: "With the exception of environmental issues—which have a strong ideological flavor—nearly everybody's taken care of by the subcommittee so often there's not much to do when it's sent up to us."
> Public Works: "Subcommittees are seldom challenged because everyone's requests are usually incorporated by the subcommittee. Problems are taken care of well in advance if we can."
> Veterans' Affairs: "The subcommittees are almost always unanimous and . . . the full committee rarely attempts to rehash what they have done."

In each of the four cases, subcommittee success at the full committee level is a pattern that committee observers believed was affected very little by changes in membership and procedure that occurred in the 1970s.

While autonomy is a word occasionally mentioned to describe the role of subcommittees on constituency committees, it certainly is not true that these subcommittees are insulated from nonsubcommittee members. This is illustrated by the Agriculture and Science and Technology examples. As two of the individuals quoted above suggest, participants often cite the openness of subcommittee members to suggestions from nonsubcommittee members as the major reason for subcommittee success. The close observation of subcommittee activity by full committee staff is in large part an effort to ensure that subcommittees are made aware of nonsubcommittee members' views and to signal outsiders about matters affecting their interests. Without exception, constituency committees' subcommittees appear to be consciously willing to listen to and take into account the other members' demands.

The permeability of constituency committee subcommittees seems to be a product of several factors. First, the nature of issues faced by many constituency committees permits them to accommodate outsiders' demands more easily than is possible on most policy committees. In many cases, the issues are not perceived in zero-sum terms; that is, the accommodation of outsiders' demands does not require that a subcommittee member or faction give up something in return. Because there is no direct conflict, it is relatively easy to add funding, projects, or subsidies for nonsubcommittee members. According to committee members and staff, this is often the case on three Armed Services subcommittees, three or four Interior subcommittees, most Post Office and Civil Service subcommittees, and at least two major subcommittees of both Public Works and Science and Technology. In contrast, subcommittee members of policy committees are more likely to be forced to compromise their own policy preferences to accommodate outsiders' demands.

The composition of the subcommittees of constitutency committees also contributes to their success. Constituency committee members are far more likely than policy committee members to acquire a seat on each of the subcommittees whose jurisdiction is of interest to them. In part, the difference reflects the specificity of constituency-oriented interests and the great breadth of many policy committee members' interests. While an Agriculture Committee member from Wisconsin has little interest in the cotton or tobacco subcommittees, few members of Commerce lack an interest in the energy, consumer protection, environmental, or commerce subcommittees they must choose among. As a result, members of district-oriented committees are somewhat more likely to be members of subcommittees in which they have an interest and less likely to challenge other subcommittees' recommendations. This is clearly the case on Agriculture, Interior, Merchant Marine, and Public Works.

Closely related to the match of interest and subcommittee assignment on constituency committees is the size of their subcommittees. At the beginning of the 1970s, the subcommittees of constituency committees averaged nearly 40 percent of the size of the full committee (Table A-7, Appendix). In four cases, Interior, Merchant Marine, Public Works, and Veterans' Affairs, major subcommittees were nearly 60 percent of the full committee's size. In each case, subcommittee jurisdictions were arranged in such a way that there was a large proportion of committee members who had direct constituency interests related to two or three subcommittees. No policy committee's average subcommittee size was as large as it was for these constitutency-oriented committees. Constituency committees' subcommittees were more likely to be representative of the full committee, and the full committee was more likely to be satisfied with subcommittee recommendations.[25] It also meant that nonsubcommittee members were more likely to have close friends who would look out for their interests on most subcommittees.

Those constituency committees with relatively small subcommittees either have fragmented constituency interests into numerous subcommittees (Agriculture and Armed Services) or are of low interest to their members (Post Office and Civil Service, Science and Technology, and Small Business). Because House Democratic Caucus rules limit Democrats to five subcommittee assignments, committees whose members have little interest in their activities simply are unable to have large subcommittees. Constituency committees with no participation problems also have been affected by the subcommittee assignment limit, as the drop in the size of Interior and Public Works subcommittees reflects (see Table A-7, Appendix). But Merchant Marine, Public Works, and Veterans' Affairs subcommittees still remain larger than most policy committee subcommittees relative to full committee size.

Prestige Committees

All three prestige committees have experienced change in the function of subcommittees in committee decision making. The changes are least obvious on Appropriations, whose 13 subcommittees continue to do nearly all of its work. The extremely large workload and size of Appropriations requires a division of labor and a heavy dependence by the full committee on subcommittee recommendations.[26] A senior Appropriations aide explained: "The full committee tends to rubberstamp the work of the subcommittees. Not too much has changed here." If anything, another staffer added, the workload has increased, making it even less feasible for nonsubcommittee members to check the work of a subcommittee. Appropriations' subcommittees continue to be the most autonomous in the House, and the members restrict their attention to their own subcommittees.

In the mid-1960s, Appropriations members specialized in the work of two subcommittees—to which they had been assigned by the full committee chair—and served an apprenticeship period before taking an active part in subcommittee hearings and deliberations.[27] Subcommittees were relatively small, specialized, decision-making instruments. Fenno noted, for example, that Appropriations subcommittees averaged only seven members in 1964. All meetings were closed until the 1970s, a practice that members believed protected them from pressure by special interests.[28]

The specialization and apprenticeship norms, which served to strengthen the role of subcommittees, have been undercut by subcommittee self-selection, open meetings, and growth. As noted in Chapter 4, the reform of subcommittee assignment procedures has allowed (some participants say "forced") Appropriations members to choose subcommittees closely related to their districts' interests. Along with the Appropriations Committee's role as a claimant in the budget process, subcommittee self-selection encourages more members to assume the role of advocate for a program serving constituent needs rather than as expert critics of agency spending practices. Open hearings and markup sessions have further exacerbated district pressures by making members' behavior more visible to representatives of key constituency groups. A subcommittee clerk complained that

> the members seem to be playing to the audience. They are not prone in an open markup or conference to say what they want to say. This year we had five or six members who showed up at our conference and some of the projects they wanted were dogs. But our members are not likely to criticize another member's feelings, so you don't have the kind of exchange we used to have when markups and conferences were closed.[29]

A by-product of these changes has been the apprenticeship norm's demise; all members feel compelled to participate right from the beginning because of the presence of important constituency groups in the audience.[30]

The number of Appropriations members with three subcommittee assignments has greatly increased since the mid-1960s, compounding the effects of subcommittee self-selection and open meetings. In the

1960s members normally held only two subcommittee assignments. There were always several members who held three, but these were primarily the most senior members. In contrast, in the 98th Congress nearly half of the majority party Democrats held three subcommittee assignments—as did six Republicans—and subcommittees averaged 10.4 members. An aide with the committee since the 1960s believes that many members now are overburdened and do not have the time to concentrate and specialize in a subcommittee's subject matter the way they had previously. They come to hearings and markups less prepared and consequently are less able to effectively challenge budgets proposed by administration officials. A junior member of the committee added that with large subcommittees (two with 13 members, three with 12 members) the typical member generally has less time to question witnesses than he or she did in the past, reducing the incentive to come well-prepared. There is no evidence that the decline in specialization has undermined subcommittees at the full committee level—after all, nonsubcommittee members are also overburdened—but Appropriations may be moving in that direction.

The role of Ways and Means' six subcommittees fits the mold of policy committees, as we would expect from its members strong policy orientation. The Ways and Means subcommittees are smaller than most constituency committee subcommittees, the full committee does not hesitate to amend subcommittee bills, and there is little genuine deference to subcommittees by nonsubcommittee members. The creation of subcommittees in 1975 permitted the policy-oriented liberals, who came to Ways and Means when it was expanded that year, to pursue their own policy interests in areas other than tax legislation. Members are able to become involved in more than one subject at a time, as had been impossible before the reform. All hearings and the first markup on legislation other than tax bills are held in subcommittee. But the burden of tax matters on members' time leaves less time for subcommittee activities than is the case on most policy committees. And there is a greater dependence on full committee staff and a more clearly defined interest in expert staff support by subcommittees than on most policy committees. In major part, this appears to be a legacy of the pre-1975 days when there were no subcommittees or subcommittee staff. It also represents the continuing interest of Ways and Means members in "not giving any subcommittee too long a leash," as an aide to Chairman Dan Rostenkowski explained.

When Richard Bolling, the foremost reformer of the House, became chair in 1979, the Rules Committee created two standing subcommittees for the first time. Bolling also created a task force on the budget process in the 97th Congress, which was reconstituted at the start of the 98th, that held hearings on a wide variety of proposals to modify the congressional budget process. But the vast majority of Rules' activity still concerns special orders that continue to be handled solely by the full committee. And the subcommittees are not autonomous. Both subcommittees had six members in the 98th Congress, nearly half of the 13-member full committee. The subcommittees are fairly independent of the full committee chair in scheduling hearings, but, like the full committee, they are carefully watched and strongly influenced by the majority party leadership. In fact, the Subcommittee on Legislative Process has been chaired since its creation by Democrat Gillis W. Long of Louisiana, who chaired the Democratic Caucus during the 97th and 98th Congresses. The Subcommittee on Rules of the House was chaired in the 97th and 98th Congresses by Democrat Joe Moakley of Massachusetts, a close political lieutenant of Speaker Tip O'Neill. Thus, while Rules members now have more opportunities to explore matters of House procedure and structure, their options for legislative solutions are circumscribed by the same factors that now constrain the full committee.

Consequences of Independent Subcommittees

While subcommittee independence has not led to subcommittee autonomy in the tradition of House Appropriations, several important negative consequences of greater subcommittee independence in the House exist. At a minimum, House members have become more like senators in the number of meetings and hearings they must attend, although House members do not yet match senators in this regard. As a result, they are now less able to concentrate on just a handful of topics at a time or, in the long run, to specialize as they have in the past, although they remain far more specialized as a group than do senators. Even so, it should not be assumed that nearly all members believe that their circumstances are less desirable today than they were in the 1960s. But there is a widespread feeling among House members that they lack control over their own legislative schedules.[31]

More significantly, the structure of the policy process in the House has been altered in many policy areas as a result of having smaller work groups—the subcommittees—assigned initial responsibility for more narrowly defined policy areas and related programs.[32] First, less continuity exists in subcommittee membership than in full committee membership. This is a product of more frequent transfers by members between subcommittees than between full committees and the frequent shifting of subcommittee jurisdictions within many committees. The "institutional memory" of the unit with immediate responsibility for writing the first draft of legislation, building coalitions, and conducting oversight of established programs is therefore less complete than it was before the 1970s. Thus, while subcommittees have more resources at their disposal, subcommittee members are not able to take full advantage of them.

Most subcommittees' small size also has narrowed the political interests represented on units with initial policy and oversight responsibility. In part, this is simply a matter of having greater sampling error as the "sample" of members decreases in size. But with subcommittee self-selection it is not a matter of chance. Those with special interest in a policy area usually can find their way onto a related subcommittee. House reformers of the 1970s noted that a problem of full committee structure was that they were stacked with members representing a narrow segment of the political spectrum: subcommittee independence gives members even more opportunities to develop strong political ties to special interests and agency officials in an environment where more neutral or critical members and outside interests are absent.

The spawning of independent subcommittees also adds obstacles to the legislative process. Even if full committees frequently change subcommittee recommendations, subcommittee involvement in drafting legislation adds at least one more stage to the law-making process. All committees may discharge a bill from a subcommittee at any time, and some House committees still permit the full committee chair to do so, but the anger engendered usually makes it difficult to do so without substantial cost. Jurisdictional fights between the more active subcommittees further complicate and often delay committee deliberations. Intercommittee disputes over jurisdiction also are more common as members pursue their personal interests through independent subcommittees. And, if nothing else, independent subcommittee chairs have increased dramatically the number of members who insist they be consulted by party and committee leaders on policy and party matters, adding to the time and effort it takes to make decisions and to move legislation through the bill process.

Senate Committee
Decision-making Patterns

The distinctiveness of decision-making patterns in Senate committees was seen in the aggregate patterns earlier in this chapter, but the committee-specific patterns reflected in Table 5-4 indicate even more

Table 5-4 The Role of Senate Subcommittees: Percent of Reported Legislation with Subcommittee Action and Percent of Committee Hearings and Meetings Held by Subcommittees*

Congress	Reported Legislation with Subcommittee Action		Meetings Held by Subcommittees		Hearings Held by Subcommittees	
	91st	96th	91st	96th	91st	96th
Constituency Committees:						
Agriculture	78	68	11	16	59	79
Appropriations	*	*	42	46	100	99
Commerce	44	81	78	0	81	56
Interior	94	92	45	0	86	69
Public Works	0	14	51	60	97	74
Veterans' Affairs	—	0	—	0	—	0
Mixed Constituency/Policy Committees:						
Armed Services	30	51	23	37	50	53
Banking	25	14	29	0	76	46
Finance	13	24	0	0	13	81
Policy Committees:						
Budget	—	0	—	0	—	17
Foreign Relations	0	0	7	3	42	20
Governmental Affairs	22	62	60	22	98	67
Judiciary	47	25	35	25	96	60
Labor	72	72	54	38	96	74
Other:						
Rules & Admin.	3	0	15	0	14	0

* See notes of Table 5-1 and 5-2.

important differences. First, Senate decision-making patterns in the 96th Congress show much greater variety than do House patterns. Second, the significance of subcommittees in decision making declined in at least as many Senate committees as it had increased during the 1970s. In at least four Senate committees, subcommittees have played a much smaller role in writing legislation in recent Congresses than they did at the beginning of the 1970s. The subcommittees of six Senate committees in the 96th Congress held fewer hearings, both in absolute numbers and relative to the number at full committee, than they did in the 91st Congress. Third, the vast majority of Senate committees show only little or no change in the significance of subcommittees in their decision-making processes. And finally, Senate subcommittees generally are much less significant than House subcommittees in committee decision making. Senate subcommittees are very active in holding hearings, but on most committees they play virtually no formal role in writing legislation. Even on Judiciary and Labor, committees often cited as among the Senate's most "decentralized," a clear majority of meetings in which legislation is written are held by the full committee.

The most immediate reason for the chamber differences is the absence in the Senate of chamber and party rules dictating committee procedure in any great detail. As was seen in Chapter 2, the Senate did not adopt any significant reforms affecting committee procedure when it readjusted its committee jurisdictions and set new limits on committee and subcommittee memberships. There was some interest in procedural reform, such as guaranteeing fixed subcommittee jurisdictions and bill referrals, but intense dissatisfaction about opportunities to participate was limited to a handful of members and only a couple of committees.

In the previous chapter senators were described as less dependent upon their committee memberships as their avenue of participation than are members of the House. Senators' ability to propose amendments or to filibuster on the floor, the absence of protective rules for floor consideration, and the Senate's practice of allowing individual senators to put a "hold" on legislation all give members of that chamber many strategic options outside of their committees that are not available to most House members. Senators are even less dependent on subcommittees. With nearly twice as many subcommittee assignments, senators rely less on any one or two subcommittees as a means for pursuing their personal political goals. Senate committees also are smaller, giving members more opportunities to contribute at the full committee level. Senators' larger personal staffs also permit them to investigate, develop, and publicize issues without committee or subcommittee staff support (see Chapter 7). Stated negatively, senators' parliamentary and personal resources make the Senate fully capable of slow, fragmented decision making without powerful subcommittees.

Certain practical considerations also affect the use of subcommittees by Senate committees.[33] First, senators are burdened by more committee and subcommittee assignments and other responsibilities than are most House members. On only one Senate committee, Finance, did members and staff fail to report to us that member attendance occasionally was a problem. As a result, committees often do not hold subcommittee markups simply because members do not have time to attend them at both the subcommittee and full committee levels. Two committee staff directors admitted that this sometimes is a convenient excuse for the full committee chair and staff to keep a bill under their control. The excuse usually works, despite its transparency. Not surprisingly, gaining the necessary quorum to take formal actions is also more of a problem for Senate subcommittees, a problem exacerbated by the subcommittees' small size. While Senate subcommittees are composed of a larger proportion of their full committees than House subcommittees, their absolute size is generally quite small. In the 98th Congress, Senate subcommittees averaged 7.2 members in contrast to 11.4 in the House. Subcommittee size became a more difficult problem in the Senate after the 1977 reform limiting senators' subcommittee assignments. The new rule forced senators to give up assignments, shrinking the average size of subcommittees on all Senate committees.

The requirement that committee meetings be open to the public also has discouraged subcommittee markups. In comparison with the House, where we heard complaints about open sessions only from Appropriations and Ways and Means members and staff, dissatisfaction with open markups in the Senate is widespread. The breadth and intensity of Senate dissatisfaction appears to stem from several related factors that make open sessions cumbersome and encourage the use of one-step full committee markups. To begin with, Senate committee meetings generally attract more attention than do House committee meetings. Television cameras are more likely to be present, making it more likely that a senator's committee actions will be visible to constituents and that senators will alter their behavior accordingly. Open meetings have led nearly all Senate committees to move their markup sessions to large hearing rooms, as have most of the larger House committees. Such an open environment is not conducive to give-and-take between members, discourages junior members from admitting ignorance by asking questions of knowledgeable colleagues, and puts a premium on grandstanding in front of the audience. These problems are especially acute in the Senate because senators are less specialized than House members and therefore are generally less well-qualified to participate effectively without obtrusive staff assistance. One staff director indicated that members of his committee even have developed hand signals so that they can communicate from their seats around the wide, horseshoe-shaped platforms used at most committee hearings. Finally, the political dangers associated with making decisions in public view are greater for senators because they have larger, more heterogeneous constituencies that are more likely to be composed of conflicting political interests.

As Table 5-4 indicates, committees in each of the three groups arranged by member goals display no distinctive patterns of hearings, markups, or the treatment of reported legislation. There are differences within each group, however, that reflect the committees' particular policy jurisdictions and political environments. On a handful of committees, significant changes also have occurred in the balance between full committee and subcommittee legislative activities that demonstrate that agenda change and full committee chairs' political objectives continue to play a major part in shaping the role of Senate subcommittees.

Constituency Committees

Among the constituency committees, Agriculture, Appropriations, and Environment and Public Works have changed little in the use of their subcommittees in committee decision making. At one extreme, Agriculture subcommittees are free to hold hearings on most matters of interest to them, but both hearings and markups on important legislation, such as the omnibus farm bill, are held for the full committee by the full committee chair. Subcommittees can and do mark up less significant legislation, though, and members and staff have "a strong tendency" to defer to subcommittee members on those bills. Like their House counterparts, Senate Agriculture members express a uniform desire to suppress partisanship and to develop a consensus before acting whenever possible, a desire consistent with their interest in assisting as many members as possible to meet constituency demands. In the case of subsidy programs, Senate strategists agree completely with House strategists that an omnibus bill is the best way "to keep us all together in committee and on the floor." Member goals have not changed on this committee, nor have the essential ingredients of its political environment. Therefore, Agriculture has retained a mode of organization and operation that has worked in the past.

In contrast, Senate Appropriations' subcommittees seem to play much the same role as they did when Fenno studied the committee in the early 1960s: the committee, because of its pressing workload, depends heavily upon its subcommittees to write legislation.[34] Senate Appropriations members did not specialize in the work of just a couple of subcommittees in the 1960s, and they do not now. An interest in maximizing opportunities to influence spending decisions affecting their states continues to dictate members' desire to belong to many subcommittees, to keep subcommittees open to nonsubcommittee members' demands, and to allow members to amend subcommittee recommendations at the full committee level.

And yet, even on Appropriations where decision-making practices fit members' goals well, the role of subcommittees is not set in concrete.

Fenno reported that under Chairman Carl Hayden, Appropriations subcommittees averaged 14 members and each member averaged seven subcommittee assignments. Hayden frequently adjusted subcommittee sizes to accommodate members' preferences.[35] In contrast, after Democrat John L. McClellan of Arkansas replaced Hayden in 1966, the average subcommittee size was reduced by more than three members, the number of subcommittee assignments per member was cut to just more than five, and staff assigned subcommittee duties were placed under closer supervision by the full committee staff. Long-term and former Appropriations aides indicate that the result was somewhat greater member participation on their remaining subcommittees and a better "staffed" product that was less frequently amended by the full committee. Subcommittee assignments fell again to under five per member, and the average subcommittee size dropped to just under 10 members in 1977, even though Appropriations was exempted from the subcommittee assignment limitation adopted that year. Senate Appropriations members remain less specialized than their House counterparts.

Environment and Public Works long has had more independent subcommittees than Agriculture but has depended more on full committee meetings to write legislation than has Appropriations. In the late 1960s and early 1970s, subcommittee investigations and hearings stimulated legislative action on major environmental legislation as Democrat Edmund S. Muskie of Maine and other subcommittee chairs were given great freedom by the full committee chair, Democrat Jennings Randolph of West Virginia. And yet, then, as in the early 1980s, deference to subcommittees depended entirely on member interest. An aide who has been with the committee since the 1960s explained that "subcommittees are often almost controlling, but when other members have any interest there's nothing stopping them from digging into the bill at full committee." Deference is greater on the public works side of the committee's jurisdiction, where narrower state interests that bring most members to the committee dominate. In this respect, Environment and Public Works is much like its House cousin. But even this committee has held many important bills at the full committee level for hearings and markup, in large part because the full committee chair occasionally has desired a strong hand in setting the agenda for hearings and ushering the bill through committee. This occurs almost exclusively on the environmental side of the committee's jurisdiction, as in the case of the Clean Air Act legislation of the 97th and 98th Congresses where chairs have had a strong personal policy interest in the legislation.

Greater changes have occurred on Commerce and Energy and Natural Resources. The personality of the Commerce Committee during the 1960s and most of the 1970s was shaped by Democrat Warren G. Magnuson of Washington, who chaired the committee between 1957 and 1978. By the early 1970s, Magnuson was permitting Commerce subcommittees to take an active role in holding hearings and writing legislation.[36] While Magnuson and his activist staff kept much consumer and other legislation at the full committee, subcommittee chairs were allowed to propose legislation in many areas of the committee's large jurisdiction (Table 5-4).

Magnuson relinquished his Commerce leadership position in 1978 to become chair of Appropriations, however, and was replaced by Democrat Howard W. Cannon of Nevada. Cannon, who was considerably more conservative than Magnuson and less willing to tolerate subcommittees devising new legislation on their own, immediately sought to exercise more centralized control. He described his outlook soon after taking over:

> I want the subcommittee chairmen to take a firm and an aggressive role, but I want that to be taken in conjunction with the chairman and the full committee. I look to them as being technicians who can do a lot of basic groundwork for us and then come back to us with some recommended solutions. We may or may not adopt their solutions. I don't say that we look completely to the subcommittees. I think they have a very, very important role to carry out in the full committee, but I think the full committee has the ultimate decision to make and I want to have a good hand in making that decision.[37]

A former Cannon aide to whom Cannon's comments were read pointed out that Cannon's qualifications on the role of subcommittees are what clearly distinguished him from his predecessor. In fact, as is corroborated by Table 5-4, Cannon "reserved for himself and the full committee all markups, as I recall," the aide noted. The same pattern has been continued by Cannon's Republican successor, Bob Packwood of Oregon. Subcommittees occasionally pass along informal recommendations to the full committee, but votes are not taken in subcommittee and markups are reserved for the full committee. As under Magnuson and Cannon, Packwood holds some legislation of personal or broad interest at the full committee level, even for hearings.

In large part, then, the change in Commerce's decision-making patterns is attributable to the assertiveness of the two most recent full committee chairs. Senate and Commerce Committee rules do not force the chair to refer legislation to subcommittee, and they often do not do so. In fact, Commerce participants refer to the procedure as "assigning" legislation to subcommittee as opposed to "referring" legislation to

subcommittee, thereby denoting the deliberate character of the procedure in the committee. The equally assertive House Energy and Commerce Committee chair, Democrat John Dingell of Michigan, cannot
mold committee decision-making processes similarly because of caucus
and committee rules limiting his discretion (see Chapter 6).

The changing character of the committee's agenda and membership
also appear to have contributed to the committee's tolerance of Cannon's
moves to limit subcommittee activity. Even before Magnuson switched
committee chairs, consumer protection issues lost much of their national
salience, and several policy-oriented liberals were replaced by members
without large policy agendas. A Magnuson staffer, who left in the mid-
1970s because "the wind was no longer in our sails," said that the "old
members were tired and the new ones were not taking over." Thus
many of the new members seemed to agree with Cannon's view that the
committee should "pause here and look at where we've been and where
we're going and not rush in with a lot of new legislative proposals."[38]

Like Commerce, Energy and Natural Resources (formerly Interior
and Insular Affairs) has discontinued subcommittee markups, although
the new pattern evolved more slowly than it did on Commerce. Fenno
explained that in the 1960s the committee organized "itself internally to
implement the same basic constituency-reelection goals as does House
Interior. And this accounts for the considerable similarity in their
internal structure."[39] He described how its members specialized in their
constituency interests through their participation in subcommittees
where the "bulk of the work . . . is done." [40] The committee's chair from
1963 to 1983, Democrat Henry M. Jackson of Washington, was "a
prototypically parttime Senate Committee chairman" who gave his
subcommittees the freedom to pursue issues and to produce legislation.
These committee practices are reflected in Table 5-4, which indicates
that in the 91st Congress nearly half of the markups were held in
subcommittee and that nearly all reported legislation was referred to
subcommittee or at least was the subject of a subcommittee hearing.

While Energy subcommittees continued to be active at the hearing
stage, even on matters that eventually were the subjects of reported
legislation, markups no longer were held in subcommittees by the end
of the 1970s. Two mutually reinforcing factors contributed to the
gradual disuse of subcommittees. First, the emergence of energy issues
in 1972 and 1973 greatly expanded the size of the committee's potential
agenda and shifted attention away from legislation of only local interest
(such as water projects) to issues of interest to a large number of
subcommittee members. Because "no significant leverage could be
gained by having a subcommittee markup," one of Jackson's staff

directors explained, "there wasn't much point to doing those things in subcommittee first." Second, the staff found it increasingly difficult to get members to attend subcommittee meetings. To reduce senators' burdens, the staff sought to keep the duplication of effort at the full and subcommittee levels to a minimum and, although there was no explicit plan to do so, subcommittee markups were phased out in the mid- and late 1970s. Jackson did impose a rule that matters related to more than one subcommittee or "are of exceptional national significance in which all Members wish to participate fully" be held at full committee, but genuine member interest in energy and the practical problems of attendance in subcommittees appear to have been the decisive factors. Unlike Commerce, the chair made no deliberate effort to reassert control over committee decision making. Instead, Energy exhibited a typical Senate committee response to issues of broad interest to members with little time: keep the activity at the full committee. Generally, that option is not available to full committee chairs in the House.

Policy Committees

Other than Appropriations, the Senate committees that continue to have the most independent subcommittees are those whose members use the committees to pursue personal policy interests: Governmental Affairs, Judiciary, and Labor and Human Resources. Judiciary and Labor have had numerous subcommittees during most of the post-World War II period, and Governmental Affairs increased its number of subcommittees when its jurisdiction was expanded in 1977. In all three cases, members use subcommittees to investigate areas of personal interest and to write legislation.[41]

As is the case for other Senate committees, activist chairs occasionally keep legislation at the full committee. For example, Democrat Harrison A. Williams, Jr., of New Jersey reserved many labor bills for the full Labor Committee during the 96th Congress, just as Republican Orrin G. Hatch of Utah kept much health legislation for the full committee during the 97th. Similarly, on Judiciary, Democrat Edward M. Kennedy of Massachusetts held criminal code revision and Law Enforcement Assistance Administration legislation for the full committee during the 96th Congress, and his successor, Republican Strom Thurmond of South Carolina, held antitrust legislation for full committee consideration. And Governmental Affairs Republican Chairman William V. Roth Jr. of Delaware reserved Department of Energy reorganization for the full committee during the 97th Congress. In some cases, chairs deliberately sought to keep legislation out of the hands of subcommittee chairs

157

with whom they had policy differences. In other cases, the full committee chair simply wanted to be in charge of managing legislation of great personal interest. Because their House counterparts have no such option, the Table 5-4 indicators of the role of subcommittees show lower values than do the parallel House subcommittees in Table 5-3.

What distinguishes these policy committees from the constituency-oriented committees is that the members of policy committees never would permit their full committee chairs to usurp completely their independence in drafting legislation. In all three cases, recent full committee chairs have attempted to reassert some central control over subcommittees, but have had only minimal success in doing so. When Kennedy became chair of Judiciary in 1979, he floated a reorganization plan that would have reduced the number of subcommittees from 10 to 4.[42] He also quickly expanded the size of the full committee staff, raising fears that he intended to handle many significant issues himself at the full committee level. In the end, Kennedy was forced to agree to keep seven restructured subcommittees in operation, and most legislation continued to flow to the subcommittees. Democratic Sen. Max Baucus of Montana, one of the subcommittee chairs, observed that Kennedy "knows to be successful there has to be give and take, even though earlier in the year his staff tried to grab a large number of the marbles here. They learned it wasn't working."[43] Similar skirmishes have occurred on Governmental Affairs and Labor. The full committee chairs have been partially successful, though, as dips in the percentage of meetings held in subcommittees indicate (Table 5-4).

Like the subcommittees of House policy committees, the subcommittees of Judiciary and Labor may be independent, but they are not autonomous. Participants report that no deference to subcommittees occurs except on insignificant legislation. Governmental Affairs is different from the other two in this regard because a large proportion of its legislation is insignificant from members' points of view. In fact, since the Republicans took over the committee in the 97th Congress, the full committee often does not even meet formally to report subcommittee legislation to the floor, as Senate rules require. Instead, the staff polls the members and, if there is no vociferous opposition, sends the bill to the floor as if the committee had met. When asked about complaints regarding this process, a committee aide responded, "Why should anyone complain? We're saving them from having to come to meetings to cast unanimous votes."

Neither Senate Budget nor Foreign Relations has subcommittees with legislative jurisdiction. Although the scope of their formal jurisdictions is broad, and thus of interest to policy-oriented members, the potential for producing legislation is limited on both committees and does not require using subcommittees to process legislation efficiently. Moreover, the legislation they consider is associated with monolithic, administration-focused political environments. On only a handful of occasions since the 1960s, such as in handling foreign assistance matters in 1975 and 1976, has Foreign Relations used subcommittees for legislative purposes. There have been occasional expressions of interest in creating more independent subcommittees on both committees, but the full committee chairs easily resisted the temptation to succumb to these demands.[44]

Why has Foreign Relations not followed House Foreign Affairs in developing more independent subcommittees? No member or staffer seems to have a good reason, although two general Senate characteristics also apply to Foreign Relations. First, Foreign Relations members have many other burdens and, while foreign policy issues are of personal interest to these senators, they usually are not vital to members' political interests. As long as their subcommittees are free to hold hearings, as they were under Democratic Chairman Frank Church of Idaho and have been under his successor, Republican Charles H. Percy of Illinois, there is no real need for subcommittees to write legislation. In contrast, House Foreign Affairs subcommittee chairs' careers are linked closely to their subcommittee positions. Second, Foreign Relations' chairs retain greater discretion in handling legislation and other committee business than the House chair does. Without serious challenges, Foreign Relations' chairs have been decisive.

Mixed Constituency/Policy Committees

As noted in Chapter 4, Finance members remain about equally motivated by state interests and personal policy interests, although at least a few members perceive some special prestige accruing from their membership. Fenno noted that the constituency and policy motivations yield an individualism common to many Senate committees that in turn produces "a decision-making process comprising high participation with low specialization."[45] In the 1960s, this translated into no subcommittees and free-for-all full committee meetings. This changed little, Fenno explained, after Russell Long became chair in 1966:

> Russell Long's accession to the chairmanship did not change the individualistic pattern of decision making. Indeed, Long was described by his colleagues as one of the most "unpredictable," "erratic," and "flighty" members of the group. "You never know where he's going to be, with you or against you. He's always off on some damn idea of his own."[46]

159

Over the years, however, Long settled down considerably, gained leverage over some members with the accumulation of favors done, and developed close personal relationships with most Finance members. By 1977, one Finance member, Democrat Spark M. Matsunaga of Hawaii, could claim about Long, "there's no doubt he runs the committee. Not even Wilbur Mills was like this."[47] Long clearly had developed a reputation for power in the Senate, and Finance members believed they benefited from it.[48]

A by-product of Long's control was dissatisfaction among some members about the centralized operation of the committee. Long temporarily mollified those members by creating subcommittees in 1973. The subcommittees were given substantial freedom to hold hearings, but they were not given any legislative responsibility. Four years later, when the Senate was pushing ahead with its committee reforms, two Finance liberals, Democrats Floyd K. Haskell of Colorado and William D. Hathaway of Maine, tried to force Long to grant subcommittees greater independence. While Long promised to increase the role of subcommittees, the insurgents failed to gain support from other committee Democrats, including Democratic liberals Abraham A. Ribicoff of Connecticut and Walter F. Mondale of Minnesota, and so failed to get the committee to formally change its rules or the distribution of staff support.[49] In fact, Finance retains a rule that "all legislation shall be kept on the full committee calendar unless a majority of the members present and voting agree to refer specific legislation to an appropriate subcommittee." Even with the switch to Republican Chairman Robert Dole of Kansas, Finance subcommittees play no formal function in writing legislation, although they are active in holding hearings (Table 5-4).

The Senate Banking Committee has had active subcommittees since John Sparkman became chair in 1967. Legislation never has been formally referred to subcommittee, although subcommittee chairs have been free to conduct investigations and to hold hearings as they see fit. Except for the housing subcommittee, however, on which nearly all Banking members sit, legislative drafting typically has been reserved for the full committee.[50] In part, this reflects occasional efforts by Sparkman and his successors, Democrat William Proxmire of Wisconsin and Republican Jake Garn of Utah, to control legislation personally. But the major motivation appears to have been to save time. A senior aide to Proxmire explained: "Banking has long been a second-tier committee of low interest to most of the senators. Subcommittee sessions would not have been attended by most of them." Under Proxmire, an activist in banking policy, using subcommittees to write legislation was almost completely discontinued (Table 5-4). Proxmire kept nearly all important legislation at the full committee level for both hearings and markup—to the consternation of two or three subcommittee chairs—leaving little legislation of interest for the subcommittees. Garn has taken a similar tack.

In contrast, Senate Armed Services subcommittees have become somewhat more active in writing legislation since the 1960s (Table 5-4). In fact, they have become more "institutionalized," a senior committee staffer noted, because the committee stopped using ad hoc subcommittees following the 1977 reform limiting subcommittee assignments. Most subcommittee efforts go into producing various parts of the annual military authorization bill, and they are "rarely overturned." As reasons for subcommittee autonomy, participants explain that nearly all members are in basic agreement about defense policy and that the subcommittees are so large that "its like having meetings of the full committee." In the 98th Congress, for example, four of the six subcommittees were composed of half of the committee's members and one had 11 of the 18 members on it. Even so, the subcommittees have been under close observation by recent full committee chairs and their centralized staffs. Hearings and meetings are scheduled only with the approval of the full committee chair. So, while more independent and autonomous than the subcommittees of most other Senate committees, Senate Armed Services subcommittees do not have the independence and autonomy of their House counterparts.[51]

Conclusion: The Extent of Subcommittee Government

Subcommittee government has not been fully institutionalized in either chamber, although House committees have moved farther in that direction since the early 1970s. Senate committees, if anything, on balance have moved away from forming independent subcommittees. Senate committees remain permeable to noncommittee members and challengeable on the Senate floor; Senate subcommittees generally remain highly permeable to outsiders. Their permeability, in turn, reduces senators' incentives to demand greater independence for subcommittees. Subcommittee independence, after all, is not of much use when full committees are not autonomous in the Senate. And subcommittee autonomy, which by definition means restricted participation, is simply not consistent with the participatory individualism of the Senate.

The distinction between subcommittee independence and autonomy is important, yet it often is obscured in discussions of changing congressional politics. In the House, subcommittees with the greatest independence and activity are least autonomous. The activism that demands subcommittee independence produces little deference to the work of others. In the Senate, this relationship can be seen in the differences between Governmental Affairs and Labor. With no constraining chamber or party rules, however, Senate chairs are able, and seem likely, to retain jurisdiction for the full committee when interest in subcommittee activity declines. That is, unlike House committees where low interest and participation sometimes have led to greater subcommittee autonomy, low interest and participation in Senate committees have led to a decline in subcommittee independence and autonomy as full committee chairs recentralized committee activity. With large personal staffs, multiple committee and subcommittee assignments, and many burdens on their time, senators have fewer incentives to strongly defend inactive subcommittees than do members of the House.

In addition to the important effects of reform, member goals and committee agendas and environments continue to play an important role in shaping committee decision-making patterns. The relationship is complex, and it is even more complex when viewed across time. Minor changes in the balance of goals held by rank-and-file members generally have little effect, but, at least in the Senate where few constraints have been imposed, a change in the committee chair's goals can alter the legislative functions performed by full and subcommittees rather quickly. Also, the effects of House reforms also were clearly influenced by the degree to which they reinforced member goals on committees and the degree to which decision-making patterns already had conformed to those goals. And finally, the changing salience of issues to members and interested outsiders clearly affects decision-making patterns and helps to determine subcommittee resistance to strong full committee chairs.

NOTES

1. Roger H. Davidson, "Subcommittee Government: New Channels for Policy Making," in *The New Congress*, ed. Thomas E. Mann and Norman J. Ornstein (Washington, D.C.: American Enterprise Institute for Public Policy Research, 1981), 99-133; Lawrence C. Dodd and Bruce I. Oppenheimer, "The House in Transition: Change and Consolidation," in *Congress Reconsidered*, 2d ed., ed. Lawrence C. Dodd and Bruce I. Oppenheimer (Washington, D.C.: CQ Press, 1981), 31-61.

2. Dodd and Oppenheimer, "The House in Transition," 41.

3. See Lawrence C. Dodd and Richard L. Schott, *Congress and the Administrative State* (New York: John Wiley & Sons, 1979), 124. For example, Dodd and Schott argue that "by the mid-1970s, Congress had institutionalized subcommittee government."

4. David Maraniss, "Competing Interests Snarl Gas Debate," *Washington Post*, June 26, 1983, A1.

5. The term "institutionalization" has been applied to some of the processes of change we discuss in this and the next two chapters. We choose not to package the changes in structure and process we discuss under such an umbrella concept. One reason is that the decade and a half examined here is an insufficient baseline for saying much about long-term processes like institutionalization. Second, there is a tendency to pile up indicators of such broad-based concepts without examining the relationship between the various features of committee operations. At this stage it is preferable not to obscure the separate features by putting a broad label on them. A third reason is that institutionalization is often associated with viability, a topic beyond the scope of this and the next two chapters. As the choice of concepts for the model suggests, we also do not believe it is particularly useful or necessary to adopt alternative packages of concepts, such as those that might be suggested by organization theorists or systems modellers. See Nelson W. Polsby, "Institutionalization in the U.S. House of Representatives," *American Political Science Review* 62 (1968): 144-168; Steven Haeberle, "The Institutionalization of the Subcommittees in the U.S. House of Representatives," *Journal of Politics* 40 (1978): 1054-1065; Joseph Cooper and David W. Brady, "Toward a Diachronic Analysis of Congress," *American Political Science Review* 75 (1981): 988-1006.

6. *Congressional Record* (bound), February 17, 1967, 3784. We thank Roger Davidson for bringing this story to our attention.

7. Ibid., 3784-3785.

8. Lawrence C. Dodd, "Congress and the Quest for Power," in *Congress Reconsidered*, 1st ed., ed. Lawrence C. Dodd and Bruce I. Oppenheimer (New York: Praeger Publishers, 1977), 272.

9. For example, see Richard F. Fenno, *Congressmen in Committees* (Boston: Little, Brown & Co., 1973), 94, 97-98, 105, 107, 110, 172, 175-177, 189; George Goodwin, Jr., *The Little Legislatures* (Amherst: University of Massachusetts Press, 1970), 48-52; John F. Manley, *The Politics of Finance* (Boston: Little, Brown & Co., 1970), 73-74; Donald R. Matthews, *U.S. Senators and Their World* (New York: Vintage Books, 1960), 161-163; Polsby, "Institutionalization," 167-168; and Randall B. Ripley, *Power in the Senate* (New York: St. Martin's Press, 1969), 142-143.

10. The reported correlation coefficient is Spearman's r.

11. Excludes Senate Budget, which was created in 1974.

12. Ideally, we could trace subcommittee recommendations to the full committee and to the floor to examine the role of subcommittees. Unfortunately, House and Senate policies for archiving committee records make this very difficult or impossible. The House and Senate now require committees to send their noncurrent records to the National Archives. House records are unavailable to the public for 50 years; Senate records are unavailable for

20 years, unless specific approval to see particular documents is gained from each committee chair.

13. Woodrow Wilson, *Congressional Government: A Study in American Politics* (1885; reprint, Baltimore: The Johns Hopkins University Press, 1981), 63. Wilson asserted that when a bill is referred to committee "it crosses a parliamentary bridge of sighs to dim dungeons of silence [whence] it will never return. The means and time of its death are unknown, but its friends never see it again."

14. Calculated from Thomas J. O'Donnell, "Controlling Legislative Time," in *The House at Work*, ed. Joseph Cooper and G. Calvin Mackenzie (Austin: University of Texas Press, 1981), Table 5.2, 131.

15. Cited in U.S., Congress, House, Select Committee on Committees, *Final Report*, H. Rept. No. 96-866, 96th Congress, 2d sess., 198.

16. See Fenno, *Congressmen*, 108.

17. See Ralph Nader Congress Project, *The Money Committees* (New York: Grossman Publishing, 1975), 40-46.

18. See Norman J. Ornstein and David W. Rohde, "Shifting Forces, Changing Rules and Political Outcomes: The Impact of Congressional Change on Four House Committees," in *New Perspectives on the House of Representatives*, 3d ed., ed. Robert L. Peabody and Nelson W. Polsby (Chicago: Rand McNally & Co., 1977), 186-269; Ralph Nader Congress Project, *The Commerce Committees* (New York: Grossman Publishing, 1975).

19. Reported in U.S., Congress, House, *Final Report*, 197-198.

20. Fenno, *Congressmen*, 108.

21. Ibid., 101-102.

22. Ralph Nader Congress Project, *The Agriculture Committees* (New York: Grossman Publishing, 1975), 157-159.

23. Ornstein and Rohde, "Shifting Forces," 230-231.

24. Fenno, *Congressmen*, 101-103.

25. Ibid., 98-100.

26. Ibid., 94.

27. Ibid., 94-97.

28. Richard F. Fenno, *The Power of the Purse* (Boston: Little, Brown & Co., 1966), 113.

29. Allen Schick, *Congress and Money* (Washington, D.C.: The Urban Institute Press, 1980), 429.

30. In the 96th and 97th Congresses, however, Appropriations subcommittees began to close or fail to give advance notice of some of their meetings. Staff justify this by saying they have sought to reduce the number of outsiders attending meetings. As one staffer said, members do not like "the hordes of lobbyists standing over their shoulders."

31. Norman J. Ornstein, "The House and the Senate in a New Congress," *The New Congress*, 367-369.

32. On these topics, see Davidson, "Subcommittee Government," 108-114; Dodd and Oppenheimer, "The House in Transition," 47-48; Ornstein, "The House and Senate," 367-369.

33. See Fenno, *Congressmen*, 148, for similar comments.

34. Ibid., 184-187.

35. Ibid., 185.

36. Ralph Nader Congress Project, *The Commerce Committees* (New York: Grossman Publishing, 1975), 43-46.

37. Linda E. Demkovich, "The Cautious Approach of Cannon's Commerce Committee," *National Journal*, May 27, 1978, 848.
38. Ibid.
39. Fenno, *Congressmen*, 177.
40. Ibid., 178.
41. On Labor, see Fenno, *Congressmen*, 174-177; David E. Price, *Who Makes the Laws?* (Cambridge, Mass.: Schenkman Publishing Co., 1972), 268.
42. Nadine Cohodas, "Kennedy and Rodino: How Two Very Different Chairmen Run Their Panels," *Congressional Quarterly Weekly Report*, February 2, 1980, 269.
43. Ibid.
44. See Schick, *Congress and Money*, 119-121, on Budget; Fenno, *Congressmen*, 188-189, on Foreign Relations.
45. Fenno, *Congressmen*, 182.
46. Ibid., 183-184.
47. Alan Ehrenhalt, "Senate Finance: The Fiefdom of Russell Long," *Congressional Quarterly Weekly Report*, September 10, 1977, 1909.
48. Ibid., 1905-1907.
49. Ibid., 1910.
50. Ralph Nader Congress Project, *The Money Committees* (New York: Grossman Publishing, 1975), 69.
51. Rules and Administration no longer has subcommittees. Small Business, which gained legislative jurisdiction in 1977, has active subcommittees but holds markups at the full committee level.

Leadership in Committees 6

"I love to think of those Southerners going in for a piece of pork and having to talk to Ron Dellums," observed Democrat Patricia Schroeder of Colorado in 1983. She had been asked to comment about Democrat Ronald Dellums of California, one of two new liberal subcommittee chairs on the House Armed Services Committee. "I don't think anyone has ever said no to those good ole boys before," she added.[1] Only a couple of years earlier, the incoming Republican chair of the Senate Banking and Housing Committee, Jake Garn of Utah, suggested that similarly dramatic consequences would follow the wholesale replacement of Senate Democratic committee chairs by the new majority party: ". . . organized labor is going to scream to high heaven, but I think we may have the votes now," Garn said.[2]

Times had changed on Congress's committees. New, more active leaders had taken the place of conservative, senior chairs of House committees and subcommittees, giving them positions from which to question existing policy more effectively. New procedures opened up their committees and ensured the independence of subcommittee chairs. And House changes in committee funding and staff allowance practices distributed resources more equally among members. Meanwhile, the Senate changed partisan hands for the first time in 25 years. Younger, more conservative opponents of big government, federal spending, and deficits were installed as new committee chairs. They, too, inherited a chamber structurally and procedurally distinct from that of their predecessors. Committee jurisdictions had been overhauled, staff assistance had increased, and new procedures had opened up committee operations. With resources more evenly distributed and members of Congress freer to pursue their personal goals, leadership had changed as well. For committee chairs, the art of leadership became less dependent on the use of formal procedures and special privileges to command compliance. More frequently it was dependent on the ability to persuade and—almost always—on the ability to bargain.

The Problem of Leadership

Leadership, Charles Jones notes, typically is approached from two different perspectives.[3] The first, a *personalistic* approach, emphasizes the traits, styles, or characteristics of individuals as they perform their leadership tasks. From this perspective, individuals might well control the formal power and authority of leadership positions and yet fail to perform adequately for some personal or idiosyncratic reason. The second, *contextual*, approach to leadership emphasizes the political or social circumstances within which people serve as leaders. From this perspective, individuals might well bring some personal talents to a position of authority, but the institutional context within which they serve will be the primary determinant of their styles and their success or failure.[4]

While both sets of factors are important to an understanding of leadership, most previous studies of congressional leadership, especially of committee leadership, have emphasized personalistic factors. Wilbur Mills' intelligence and memory, Adam Clayton Powell's eccentricities, J. William Fulbright's scholarship, Wayne Aspinall's fairness, or Russell Long's shrewdness appropriately have been used to explain their leadership. Yet, as case studies have begun to accumulate and observers have been able to compare a number of leaders, increasing emphasis has been placed on the political contexts in which leaders operate.

The ability of personalisitic and contextual factors to explain aspects of leadership varies from one situation to another.[5] For example, where committee structures and procedures are only vaguely defined, personalistic factors are more likely to be the primary determinants of leadership strategy and success. In contrast, where committee structures and procedures are specified clearly, leadership options are more limited and personal qualities are less likely to distinguish various committees.

In the House, where greater formalization of internal committee structure and procedure occurred in the 1970s, contextual factors have become more useful in explaining differences among committee chairs' approaches to committee politics. This is not to say that personal factors no longer help to distinguish among House committee chairs. With their formal powers curtailed, House chairs became even more dependent on personal skills, expertise, and shrewdness to get things done. These factors still help to separate successful leaders from unsuccessful leaders. But remember that contextual factors severely constrain even the most talented House committee leaders. In this regard, House full committee chairs have become more like Senate full committee chairs, who long have operated in an environment characterized by a relatively equal distribution of resources among participants. Nonetheless, Senate full committee chairs continue to face fewer formal constraints in setting committee structure, procedures, and agendas so that personalistic, idiosyncratic characteristics play a more important role in shaping their committees than is true in the House. This chapter explores the direct and indirect effects of procedural changes in setting new boundaries for committee chair behavior in the House, the influence of environmental change on leadership, and the relationship between member goals and leadership approaches.

Full Committee Chairs:
The Effects of Structural and Procedural Change

Changes in procedure have altered the base of power once controlled by committee chairs and directly constrained the extent to which chairs may shape their committees' activities. In addition, reforms have affected the congressional and public environments within which committee leaders must operate. Thus chairs have witnessed direct limits placed on the range of powers they exercise within their committees and indirect limits created in their political environment. Each of these is examined below.

Chairs and Committee Environments

In general, reform-induced environmental changes have challenged rather than reinforced the power of committee chairs. This, in turn, has forced chairs to adapt to their new, and more demanding, environments by altering their approaches to committee business. These environmental changes have come in several areas.

Perhaps the most significant change in the congressional environments of House chairs has been the Democratic Caucus's shift to secret ballot elections. In the first balloting in 1973, each of the seven ranking Democrats in line for elevation to a full committee chair was elected.[6] Incumbent chairs also were reelected easily, although four chairs received 40 or more opposition votes. Although no incumbents were defeated, committee chairs were put on notice that rank-and-file members would be scrutinizing their future activities. California's Philip Burton, chair of the Democratic Study Group, declared, "I'm wildly happy at what we've done. . . . We're finally getting somewhere."[7] Two years later, W. Robert Poage of Agriculture, Wright Patman of Banking, and F. Edward Hebert of Armed Services were unseated by the caucus. Since that time, no chair or heir apparent has been rejected, although a handful have survived significant challenges. For example, in 1977 Democrat Clement J. Zablocki of Wisconsin and in 1979 Democrat Jamie L. Whitten of Mississippi were elected as chairs of Foreign Affairs and Appropriations, respectively, by votes of 182 to 72 and 157 to 88.

Have elections forced a change in chairs' behavior? Systematic evidence is difficult to develop, but member reactions offer some clues. In each of the three cases where the chair had been defeated, differences between the unseated chair and the successor were expressed in procedural terms rather than in substantive terms. Democrat Thomas S. Foley of Washington, who was elected to replace Poage on Agriculture in 1975, noted:

> People think of me as chairman as if we were back in the days when chairmen ruled as well as reigned. . . . It isn't that way any more. The newcomers may pay a certain amount of respect to the leadership, but they're not going to defer to my judgment.[8]

Democrat George E. Brown, Jr., of California felt that Foley at least began his stint as chair of Agriculture in a conciliatory fashion:

> He's starting out very meticulous about observing the rules, respecting the rights of the members and following the lead of the members.[9]

This did not mean that Foley had to give up his central role on the committee, as seen in the previous chapter. Similarly, a member of Armed Services simply asserted that "Hebert's defeat means procedural fairness in the committee." [10] The emphasis on procedural fairness was consistent with the concerns of Democrats voting to depose the committee chairs. Political scientist Glenn Parker, using available vote tallies from the Democratic Caucus, information on chairs' ideological characteristics, committee records, and personal interviews, concluded that chairs' fairness on procedural matters affected the level of support among his or her committee colleagues more than policy views did.[11]

Now, House chairs also must pay more attention to the party rank-and-file when they consider specific legislation. Since 1969, when House Democrats rejuvenated the party caucus as a forum for policy discussion, the caucus has met several times a year to discuss major policy issues. Some Democrats have complained that these meetings are held too late to affect the direction of policy debates, but the meetings occasionally crystalized views on salient, divisive issues. As a result, chairs of major committees must be cognizant of the caucus as an alternative forum for policy discussion. In the Senate, chairs long have expected widespread discussion among noncommittee colleagues of major legislative issues before their committees. In fact, Senate Republicans hold weekly meetings where any member can voice concerns about matters before the Senate, including matters before committees.

Often, party leaders influence the way that committee leaders do their jobs. (This is discussed in greater detail in Chapter 8.) In the House, party leaders' ability to influence committee activity was consciously, if not always successfully, increased by the reforms of the 1970s. Multiple referral, an expanded whip system, closer ties to the Rules Committee, a strengthened party caucus, and the development of the Steering and Policy Committee have all put leaders in a stronger position to guide House activities. Party leaders are not always successful, but virtually all observers agree that current House majority party leaders have been more active in guiding legislation through the chamber than were their predecessors of the 1960s and early 1970s. The more individualistic Senate traditionally has afforded noncommittee members, particularly interested party leaders, the opportunity to monitor and to attempt to influence the progress of legislation. Thus, even without the formal tools of their House counterparts, Senate party leaders remain in a strong position to influence their party colleagues on committees.

The congressional budget process also has placed new constraints on committee chairs. The Congressional Budget and Impoundment Control Act of 1974 requires that by May 15 of each year all bills authorizing new budget authority be reported to the floor. In the first session of a Congress, when most committees do not get organized until late January or February, this means that committees have less than four months to set their priorities, hold hearings, and mark up legislation. Among the dozens of members and staff we interviewed, there was nearly unanimous agreement that the deadline provides too little time for committees to study policy problems fully and to write well-crafted legislation. For full committee chairs, who retain control over the full committees' schedules in most cases, the result is that their strategic options are severely limited. At the very least, delaying committee action to accommodate the demands of more members and to gain the last few votes necessary for majority support is less feasible. And the use of the reconciliation process has forced committees to make changes in programs to achieve budget cuts. Even without reconciliation, though, the budget process allows the full House and Senate to set targets in the first budget resolution that can severely constrain chairs' ability to set committee agendas and to pursue their own policy initiatives.

Chairs' public environments also have changed. Because committee chairs may be challenged for election or reelection to their positions, outside groups can attempt to influence the election outcome. For decades such interests have encouraged members to seek particular assignments or to lobby for or against members' assignments to particular committees. Where full committee chairs were concerned, however, no direct influence could be applied because members advanced through seniority. Today, seniority is still the primary determinant of accession to a committee or subcommittee leadership position, but the election process—required by House Democrats and allowed by both Senate parties—leaves room for increased outside influence.

In 1977, for example, Common Cause campaigned to have Louisiana's Russell Long deposed as chair of the Finance Committee.[12] Although the effort was unsuccessful, many negative votes were cast against Long. A similar incident occurred in the House in 1979 when a coalition of labor, consumer, environmental, and civil rights groups campaigned vigorously against the elevation of Mississippi's Jamie Whitten as chair of the House Appropriations Committee.[13] Given the overlap of committee memberships, a single change in committee or subcommittee chairs is likely to have a greater ripple effect in the Senate than in the House.[14] But in both chambers, outside interests will follow closely these potential changes—and not always as mere spectators—as they did when the Republicans were organizing the chamber for the first time in 25 years in 1981.

Committee chairs' environments thus have become more demanding, complex, and unpredictable. The result, as an experienced House committee staffer put it, is that

> being chairman isn't as fun as it used to be. I know of a chairman who's constantly looking over his shoulder and probably for good reason. You can't tell where problems are going to sprout these days.

While few chairs become this nervous, nearly all of them face rank-and-file members, party leaders, and interest groups that are more capable and willing to place demands on them. House chairs are less able merely to ignore these demands because they know that seniority shields them from challenges to their authority.

Chairs and Committee Operations

The ability of House chairs' to set their committees' subcommittee structure was given to each committee's Democratic caucus in the early 1970s. Democratic Caucus rules now guarantee members the right to bid for subcommittee seats in a meeting of the committee caucus, ensure that subcommittee chairs are allowed to hire at least one staff member, provide for written jurisdictions for each subcommittee, and place a ceiling on the number of subcommittees that most committees can create. Additionally, House rules force committees with more than 20 members to create at least four subcommittees and to guarantee the subcommittees a share of the committee's funds. These new rules have sharply reduced the discretion of committee chairs in shaping committee structure. As noted earlier, subcommittees were guaranteed independence from full committee chairs with further rules requiring referral of legislation to subcommittees and providing staff to subcommittees.[15]

The House Energy and Commerce Committee is a particularly good example of the significance of a chair's inability to determine the composition of subcommittees. Energy and Commerce's John Dingell, regarded as one of the shrewdest and most influential members of the House and a leader in the fight to expand the power of subcommittees, is in a much weaker position as chair of the committee than was his predecessor. At the beginning of each Congress, Dingell must preside over a meeting of the committee's Democrats as they organize for the coming sessions. Amendments to the committee's rules may be offered, changes in subcommittee jurisdictions may be proposed, and members may bid (in order of seniority) for their subcommittee assignments. Because Dingell does not control these assignments, members are actively lobbied by interest groups and their colleagues to choose certain subcommittees. Before the 98th Congress, for example, Henry A. Waxman of California worked long hours to "liberalize" the Subcommittee on Health and the Environment, which he chaired. The subcommittee has jurisdiction over the hotly contested Clean Air Act, the subject of pitched battles between the environmentally oriented Waxman and the auto-industry-oriented Dingell, who comes from a district near Detroit. Waxman's lobbying efforts, which included formation of his own political action committee to make campaign contributions to committee colleagues, apparently paid off.[16] The subcommittee became noticeably more liberal in the 98th Congress with the addition of Ohio's Dennis E. Eckart, New York's Richard L. Ottinger, Colorado's Timothy E. Wirth, and Minnesota's Gerry Sikorski to the Democratic side of the roster. These additions seemed to give Waxman a working majority on the committee on clean air legislation and considerably undermined Dingell's hopes to soften parts of the Clean Air Act opposed by major auto makers.

Changes in the Senate have been much more limited and subtle. No caucus or chamber rules exist that directly limit the control of committee chairs to organize their committees. Although frequently neglected, limits on the number of full and subcommittee positions that senators may hold suppress increases in the number of subcommittees. Chamber rules provide specific guidelines for committee meetings, hearings, and voting and require committees to publish additional rules governing committee procedure. But they do not specify internal committee organization in any detail. Most Senate committees' rules, in turn, continue to be very brief, often not even mentioning subcommittee structure and, when they do, often not specifying jurisdictions clearly. In most cases, the full committee chair is assumed to have great discretion, although even that is left unstated, and chairs usually consult committee colleagues. As in the House, senators may bid for their subcommittee assignments. Committees were encouraged by the 1977 reform resolution to adopt a procedure whereby each member is guaranteed a first choice before anyone receives a second choice (and each a second choice before anyone receives a third). While most Senate committees have not explicitly incorporated such a provision in their rules, the two parties appear to abide by it on all committees but Appropriations. Thus, except through informal efforts, Senate chairs are not in a position to singlehandedly "stack" subcommittees for political purposes. On balance, however, Senate chairs have more flexibility than their House counterparts in determining the structure of their committees, and Senate subcommittee chairs are formally less independent.[17]

On the procedural side, some full committee chairs resisted the implementation of new rules and had to be forced by their committees to give up privileges they once enjoyed. For example, less than a year after Commerce Committee Democrats adopted new rules limiting the chair's powers and just four months after the December 1975 reform caucus, Chairman Harley O. Staggers attempted to appoint New York's John M. Murphy to chair House Commerce's Subcommittee on Communications after Torbert H. Macdonald, a Massachusetts Democrat, became ill.[18] In his letter of resignation, Macdonald recommended that fellow liberal Lionel Van Deerlin of California be chosen by the committee caucus to succeed him. Van Deerlin had greater seniority than Murphy on the full committee but not on the subcommittee. Staggers ignored the request, appointed Murphy acting chair, and proceeded to schedule hearings for the subcommittee while Macdonald was recuperating. From his hospital bed, Macdonald exercised his right to call a caucus of committee Democrats by gaining the support of 11 committee members on a petition to Staggers. At that meeting, attended by Staggers, the committee's Democrats voted 21 to 0 to elect Van Deerlin the new chair.

Senate committee leaders are not nearly so constrained as House chairs. The referral of legislation to subcommittees, the discharge of legislation from subcommittees, and the distribution of majority party staff remain under the formal control of nearly all Senate full committee chairs. Where reforms limited chairs' discretion, many committees moved to minimize their effects. For example, as seen in the previous chapter, Finance members did not hold their chair, Russell Long, to his promise on the Senate floor to expand the legislative role of Finance subcommittees. Others have, in practice, given their chairs greater discretion in using proxy votes than Senate rules allow. In the extreme case of Governmental Affairs, the use of member polls to report legislation to the floor gives its chair far greater latitude than is intended by Senate Rule XXVI (7), which requires that "no measure or matter or recommendation shall be reported from any committee unless a majority of the committee were physically present." These examples are typical of the informal practices that continue to flourish in the Senate despite requirements that committees have and live by written rules. Unless someone objects, individual senators, including committee chairs, are given great leeway.

Agendas, Environments, and Committee Chairs

The three attributes of committee jurisdictions and environments examined in Chapter 3—fragmentation, salience, and conflict—directly affect options available to chairs in managing their committees. As committees vary considerably on these properties, so do the options available to chairs. In general, chairs facing highly fragmented, nationally salient, and divisive agendas confront greater challenges than do others. One response of such chairs is to create a large full committee staff so that the chair has at his or her immediate disposal the resources to gather and digest information about all topics under consideration and to monitor the work of subcommittees and their staff. With only a couple of exceptions, House chairs facing such agendas have done just that (see Chapter 7). Another response is to try to limit the committee's active agenda so that the chair can be involved in all issues taken up. This is no longer an option for House chairs. The most common response is for chairs to give way to the lead of other members on the committee who have a better grasp of certain aspects of the committee's jurisdiction. On committees such as Appropriations, Commerce, Education and Labor, Public Works, Judiciary, and Banking, full committee chairs frequently allow subcommittee chairs and their staff to take the lead even in full committee markup sessions. Full committee chairs choose their own, generally more narrow areas of concentration. Indeed, they are likely to have established areas of specialization as subcommittee chairs before taking over the full committee. Carl Perkins focused on school food and education programs on Education and Labor, John Dingell focused on air pollution and energy on Energy and Commerce, and Jamie Whitten focused on agriculture programs on Appropriations.

Pursuit of these interests often continues in their role as subcommittee chairs.

The problems of managing committees with large, fragmented agendas are compounded by the tendency for issues faced by the same committees to be highly salient and divisive (see Chapter 3). The intensity of outside demands on committee members and chairs, therefore, is especially great, making it difficult for chairs to avoid acting on those demands. In the face of contentious issues, chairs find it difficult to persuade some committee colleagues to move in particular directions because the intensity of the demands diminishes the political leeway perceived by members. The process of building winning coalitions is more time consuming, and the chances of stalemate are greater. It is no wonder that chairs of the energy, labor, and tax committees frequently give up on their potential roles as consensus builders.

As committee agendas and environments evolve, a result of either external events or jurisdictional reform, so do conditions shaping chairs' behavior. In some cases, chairs may only be reacting to related changes in member goals. More directly, agenda change may lead to changes in the composition of coalitions, to increases or decreases in the value of certain staff resources or organization, or to make more or less relevant the chair's experience and expertise as the committee agenda changes. For example, Wright Patman's concern for banking issues became much less relevant to his housing-oriented colleagues. Wayne Aspinall's interest in protecting western land interests came in conflict with new environmentalists on his committee. And even the Agriculture committees' traditional focus on commodity subsidies was complicated during the 1970s by new issues such as food stamps, family farms, and organized labor, undermining the advantages of expertise enjoyed by their senior chairs. On procedural matters, such chairs continued to be important to members, of course, but formal authority did not by itself engender the respect and influence that comes with expertise and helpful staff assistance.

House Chairs
and Member Goals

Drawing upon his observations in the 1960s, Richard F. Fenno argued that committee chairs' leadership must be understood in the context of individual members' goals. An effective chair, as he saw it, "articulates, extols, explains, rationalizes, exemplifies, and by any other means available, teaches" committee members the best way to achieve their individual goals.[19] Not surprisingly, few chairs have been completely successful in meeting the needs of committee colleagues, but successful chairs have used the prerogatives of their positions to further their common interests. In retrospect, the ability to use political tools to either enhance or diminish rank-and-file members' chances of goal attainment was the critical feature of committee leadership in the 1960s. Many were in a position to assume responsibility for their committees' decision-making processes and ultimate decisions for which they could rightly take credit or blame.

The most important difference in House committee leadership in the 1980s is that chairs are far less able to mold the decision-making processes of their committees to meet the collective needs of rank-and-file members. Indeed, the most common complaint we heard about committee leadership from committee members and staff was that chairs are no longer responsible for their committees' actions. Chairs can say, as they often do, that the decisions of their committees are solely the product of the will (or lack thereof) of the majority and that there is little that they can do about it. "What can he do," "he's helpless," and "he can't do anything to me," are the responses of participants when questioned about the ability of chairs to move their committees to action. The chairs' inability to mold and maintain a decision-making process consistent with member goals is a source of frustration and ambivalence for rank-and-file members, as was reflected in the responses of House members to a 1979 survey conducted by the House Select Committee on Committees.[20] While 42 percent of the respondents indicated they would give low priority to strengthening committee chairs' authority, 58 percent said they would give it high or medium priority.

House chairs are not completely helpless, of course. The same personal resources that were important in the 1960s are still important today. Subject matter expertise, knowledge of House procedure, friendship with party leaders, and associations with interest group representatives and other personal resources still give chairs an advantage over more junior members. Moreover, chairs still control large full committee staffs and can, within limits, manipulate the full committee schedule enough to gain some influence over committee activities. Thus a House committee chair is not yet merely one among equals, but in many cases he or she is no more than first among equals.[21]

Interestingly, the degree to which leadership appears to be a problem for members varies among committees and is conditioned by the balance of member goals. For example, most of our interviewees'complaints about the weakness of committee chairs came from members of constituency committees. It is on the constituency committees that chairs' ability to build and enforce a consensus is most crucial to members. Participants on policy committees, in contrast, identified few problems with their chairs, save for an occasional complaint that the chair did not share a point of view on an important issue. On prestige committees, members are most concerned about the chair's ability to maintain the committee's influence. Where complaints occur, as we heard about Appropriation's Jamie Whitten, Rules' Claude Pepper, and Ways and Means' former Chairman Al Ullman, they focus on the failure to build, maintain, or exercise this influence. Stronger chairs, such as Richard Bolling on Rules, George H. Mahon on Appropriations, and even Dan Rostenkowski on Ways and Means may have been more controversial, but they were often preferred by committee members. On the surface almost all House committee chairs appear to behave in ways consistent with members' goals, but a review of House committee leadership indicates that some underlying tensions exist.

Policy Committee Chairs

Policy committee chairs generally share their colleagues' basic goals. They would enjoy having enough power to push their own policy preferences through committee. But that is not always possible, partly because reforms have placed formal limits on what they can do and partly because members resist it. As one Government Operations Committee aide said of Chairman Jack Brooks of Texas: "Although he'd like to be an autocrat, he knows that House Democrats wouldn't tolerate a dictatorial chairman." [22] Policy-oriented members who have their own agendas and strongly held views are especially resistant, as noted in the previous chapter. Policy committee chairs, therefore, are policy combatants competing for committee endorsements of their own policy preferences rather than solitary leaders with the power simply to implement those preferences. The policy activism of these chairs is not begrudged them by rank-and-file members; it is expected of them. Policy committee chairs, therefore, are not viewed as consensus seekers but rather as coalition builders for their own causes.

The House policy committees most affected by the reforms of the 1970s, Banking and Commerce, stripped their chairs of special parliamentary prerogatives they had used to pursue their policy goals. That rank-and-file participation on Banking and Commerce lagged behind that of other policy committees in the early 1970s can be seen in the proportion of legislation managed on the floor by full committee chairs before and after the reforms (see Table A-9, Appendix). In the 92d Congress (1971-1972), the majority of legislation reported from Education and Labor, Government Operations, Foreign Affairs, and Judiciary was managed by someone other than the full committee chair—mostly by subcommittee chairs. But on Banking and Commerce, Chairmen Wright Patman and Harley Staggers retained personal control over legislation for their committees on the floor until they were forced to give it up. More recently, the policy committees, as a group, have exhibited the lowest percentages of legislation managed by full committee chairs. These findings are what one would expect of policy committees where active, policy-oriented members take advantage of new rules to expand their own participation.

Given the built-in procedural constraints facing policy committee chairs, leadership on these committees now demands a special aggressiveness and a willingness to exploit limited powers. Jack Brooks of Government Operations and John Dingell of Energy and Commerce are clearly the most aggressive of the six policy committee chairs. Peter W. Rodino, Jr., of Judiciary and Carl D. Perkins of Education and Labor are the least aggressive. Because member goals on these committees create demands for participation, the only hope that chairs have to influence the committee is to aggressively employ their remaining tools. In fact, rank-and-file members expect chairs to do so and are likely to criticize those who lack aggressiveness and praise those who display it. For example, Republican Edward R. Madigan of Illinois says of Dingell:

> Dingell is formidable not because he has more friends than anyone else, nor because he is more skilled—there are others as skilled as he is. His strength comes because he takes the skill he has and combines it with good staff work, a thorough knowledge of the issues, and a bulldog determination not to let go. He is the most tenacious member of Congress.[23]

And another Committee Republican, Tom Tauke of Iowa, adds:

> John Dingell feels about his committee much as Lyndon Johnson felt about his ranch. Johnson didn't want to own the whole world, he just wanted to own all the land surrounding his ranch. Dingell doesn't want his committee to have the whole world, just all the areas surrounding its jurisdiction.[24]

Contrast these observations with characterizations of Rodino and Perkins. One Judiciary member, who is close to Rodino on most policy questions, noted:

> Mr. Rodino may not be as activist as some chairmen, but he still is identified with a great many issues.... His stature during impeachment and his congeniality has enabled the committee to function smoothly, if somewhat short of expectations.[25]

A former Judiciary staffer adds that Rodino

prefers to administer almost goallessly. From the standpoint of legislation, on balance its bad. Usually good ideas don't become enacted just because they're good ideas. They need a champion.[26]

About Perkins one member asserts that

Carl Perkins doesn't control the Committee as tightly as he should. It's very loose. . . . The members don't respect his expertise or his political power.[27]

Majority party members of policy committees, especially ideological allies of the chairs, expect their chairs to be aggressive—and abrasive and partisan if need be—to achieve strongly held policy objectives.

Member expectations of committee chair activism have a limit of course. The limit is set at the point at which chairs begin to block others' efforts to openly compete for committee endorsements of their policy views. In the 97th Congress, for example, Democratic Banking Chairman Fernand St Germain of Rhode Island added provisions to a "clean" bill that was supposed to include only provisions reported by a Banking subcommittee to the full committee, or so the subcommittee chair thought. After the added provisions were discovered, members angrily claimed that St Germain was trying to "undermine the function of our subcommittees" and "he obviously doesn't care much for an open debate." Despite St Germain's insistence that he merely was "exercising the prerogatives of the chairman," the committee quickly dropped the provisions with the help of several members who claimed to support St Germain's additions on their merits, but who believed that he had "exceeded the bounds of fair play."

Policy committee chairs are on their most solid ground when they pursue their own interests as subcommittee chairs, and all of them do so. Clement Zablocki continued to chair the International Security and Scientific Affairs Subcommittee, which enabled him to pursue security assistance, arms control, and technology issues. But, as described in the last chapter, this did not guarantee that his position would win at the full committee level. Peter Rodino of Judiciary chairs the Monopolies and Commercial Law Subcommittee. Carl Perkins of Education and Labor chairs the Elementary, Secondary, and Vocational Education Subcommittee, as he did when Adam Clayton Powell was still full committee chair in the 89th Congress (1965-1966). He has used this position and his full committee power to stall cuts in social programs and to promote aid to education. St Germain, sometimes criticized as a secretive rather than an openly aggressive leader, has chaired the Financial Institutions Supervision, Regulation and Insurance Subcommittee on Banking since the 92d Congress. Jack Brooks chaired the Government Activities Subcommittee from his second year in office, 1954, until the 94th Congress when, having assumed the full committee chair, he instituted a subcommittee reorganization. He has chaired the Legislation and National Security Subcommittee—which handles nearly all committee legislation—since then. Only Dingell abandoned control of a subcommittee distinctly suited to his policy interests. Rather than continue to chair the Energy and Power Subcommittee, as he had done since it was created in the 94th Congress, he moved to chair the Oversight and Investigations Subcommittee. The new subcommittee would give Dingell broad oversight powers over all subject matter within the committee's jurisdiction. The Dingell and Brooks examples show how aggressive chairs, lacking great formal authority, can still shape their committees' work environment as committee and subcommittee chairs— often to the irritation of other subcommittee chairs.

Zablocki and St Germain have operated primarily through their subcommittees. Both have chaired important and active subcommittees and served on their full committees during periods of transition: Zablocki during the committee's transition from an executive support group to a frequent critic of executive policies and St Germain during a period when housing issues eclipsed the more esoteric banking issues favored by the deposed Wright Patman. Member goals on Foreign Affairs emphasize policy independence and require the freedom to explore alternatives to presidential policy initiatives—a change that Fenno was able to note at the end of his period of studying the committee. Zablocki, until his death in 1983, therefore, was forced to compete much like his fellow subcommittee chairs. Member goals for some of Banking's members are much like those of constituency committees: they require the efficient processing of housing legislation. But other policy-oriented committee members still actively compete with the chair in the other policy areas. Like Zablocki, St Germain has operated as a "super subcommittee chair."

Policy committees offer members an opportunity to actively pursue personal policy interests. These committees, except for Government Operations, have been characterized by active member participation, partisanship, and policy combativeness. Nothing in the member goals of these committees has changed that situation, and full committee chairs suppress these tendencies only at great risk. Within this context, committee leaders are free to pursue their own policy interests aggressively, especially in their roles as subcommittee chairs where they are less threatening to other committee members.

Constituency Committee Chairs

Constituency committee members appear to have more clearly defined expectations about committee leadership than do policy committee members. Unlike policy committee members, whose definition of a "good" leader varies somewhat from issue to issue and among committee factions, constituency committee members' interest in providing benefits for stable and predictable constituencies dictates consistent leadership support for such efforts. Thus constituency committee chairs are encouraged to build a committee consensus or a system of mutual noninterference, depending on the nature of the constituency interests served. Logrolling, comity, and specialization norms are stronger on constituency committees than on policy committees, and leaders are expected to reinforce these norms. Constituency committee members who want to compliment their chairs describe them as "consensus builders," "pragmatists," and "permissive" rather than as policy combatants. Indeed, a committee leader who pursued policies out of step with the committee consensus is likely to be viewed as disruptive.

Four constituency committee chairs were criticized by members. In sharp contrast to complaints about policy committee chairs, complaints about these chairs concerned their ability to "bring the committee together" and to "keep people in line." The most severely criticized leader was Armed Services Chairman Melvin Price of Illinois. His physical energy and intellectual capacity have been criticized by several committee members. But these problems were not the central issue; members also were concerned about his ability to control challenges to the preferences of the promilitary committee majority and to keep tabs on the quality of the proposals subcommittees sent to the full committee. It is here that Price's ineffectiveness threatened to undermine members' goals of serving their constitutencies.

Constituency committees can be separated into two groups based on their leadership context. One group of committees is comprised of clientele-oriented, narrow-jurisdiction committees—Veterans' Affairs, Small Business, Merchant Marine, and the undesired Post Office Committee. The other group is made up of committees with broader jurisdictions—Agriculture, Armed Services, Interior, Public Works and Transportation, and Science and Technology. This latter group is also distinguishable because committee leaders are more likely to deal with policy-oriented members. While both remain distinctly constituent-oriented, the two sets of committees place their chairs in different leadership contexts.

On the committees with narrower jurisdictions and environments, member participation rates are low. Members and staff report that it is often difficult to get a quorum for committee meetings and that subcommittee meetings are even more difficult to arrange. This is largely the result of the low salience of issues before the committees and their narrow clientele-oriented jurisdictions. Turnover rates are high and decidedly fewer members request positions for these committees—an average of only 16.5 requests per committee among Democrats for the entire 1971 to 1981 period. When the Democratic Steering and Policy Committee fills slots on these committees, it often does so by unanimous consent rather than by balloting because of the lack of competition.

These conditions leave a void that the full committee chair is expected to fill. The chair is expected to keep the committee operating smoothly, preserve the committee consensus by ensuring that clientele groups are represented adequately, and not burden members with unnecessary meetings. For example, participants applaud Merchant Marine and Fisheries Chairman Walter B. Jones of North Carolina for his "low profile" and his desire to "simply keep the committee moving." When the chair permits his or her personal policy interests to supersede the common interests of the committee, he or she is sharply criticized. Parren J. Mitchell of Maryland, chair of Small Business, has suffered such criticism for his activism on behalf of minority small businesses to the exclusion of more general problems of small business.

For several reasons, the chair's job is more difficult on the five constituency committees with broader jurisdictions and environments. First, these committees are more attractive to members than are the more narrowly focused group. They averaged 56.2 requests among Democrats during the same 1971 to 1981 period. As noted in Chapter 4, three of them, Armed Services, Agriculture, and Public Works, are treated as "major" committees by House Democrats; Interior and Science and Technology were top candidates for major committee status when Democrats formally categorized committees in 1971. Rates of participation are higher on these committees, and expectations for the chair's behavior are held more firmly. Second, almost without exception, life on these committees has been complicated by the addition of new issues and jurisdictions since the late 1960s. The food stamps issue on Agriculture, environmental and nuclear energy questions on Interior, transportation issues on Public Works, energy and technology issues on Science and Technology, and—somewhat less recently—new weapons and arms control issues on Armed Services, have challenged existing cohesion on these committees. And third, as noted, new issues sometimes undermine sources of the chair's personal influences.

The result has been that leaders on these constitutency committees face demands for greater participation, far more independent sub-committees, and a broadening of committee agendas. Initially, the few policy-oriented members were forced to bide their time. They could not oppose chairs who were supported by a committee consensus. For example, as Les Aspin, a liberal critic of the Pentagon, noted regarding former Chairman F. Edward Hebert of Armed Services:

> Its really hard to object to anything Hebert does on procedural grounds. He's very fair. Of course he can afford to be because he's got the votes. Only five of us oppose him on most things in committee.[28]

Over time, however, these committees and their chairs were forced to adapt to changes in member goals. The Interior Committee restructured its subcommittees to accommodate both policy-oriented members and constituent-oriented members, combining some subcommittees that had a parochial focus and creating new ones that focused on issues of interest to policy-oriented members. Public Works and Science and Technology have organized subcommittees along much the same lines. To put together a consensus in support of disparate aspects of agricultural policy, the Agriculture Committee has used a classic consensus-building strategy. It has put together an urban/rural coalition by joining the food stamp program and the biannual farm legislation in the same bill. These actions have allowed chairs to forge enough of a consensus in the areas where underlying agreement among members still exists while also managing to accommodate new rank-and-file demands. Only Armed Services has yet to fully accommodate its more policy-oriented members. As a result, that committee has a number of directly competing interests operating within its subcommittees.

Comments about the chairs of these committees bear out this observation. When Thomas Foley took over the Agriculture Committee he was described repeatedly as being pragmatic but also as being in touch with a broad range of issues. Fellow committee members and lobbyists described Foley as "consensus-oriented," "a hard-nosed compromiser," "pragmatic," and committed to the success of farm bills on the floor.[29] Armed Services' Melvin Price, a Democrat from Illinois, is described in much the same way. After Hebert was dismissed by the caucus, members anticipated greater latitude in holding hearings and employing staff. But they did not expect the committee's underlying consensus to be altered. Even so, the accession of several liberal members to subcommittee chairs increases pressure on the system to break down or be altered. After succeeding Aspinall as chair of the Interior Committee in 1973, Florida's James A. Haley said that he would give subcommittee chairs greater freedom than they had enjoyed previously. On his approach to his chairmanship, he added:

> The system is not without its faults.... I think many chairmen of committees have abused the power they have. After all, the chairman of the committee should be a presiding officer, that's all. He shouldn't take his own will and overpower his committee. Let the committee speak, that's the democratic process.[30]

Haley's successor, Democrat Morris K. Udall of Arizona, has viewed the chair's position as somewhat more powerful:

> ... you have more influence, you're listened to more closely, consulted by the leadership, by the White House. I find that things I believe in and want to do come easier now.[31]

Nonetheless, Udall is described as one of the most open and permissive chairs in the House. Democrats James J. Howard of New Jersey, chair of Public Works, and Don Fuqua of Florida, chair of Science and Technology, operate in much the same fashion.

Prestige Committee Chairs

Not surprisingly, leadership positions on prestige committees are regarded as positions of true distinction. The chairs of Appropriations, Rules, and Ways and Means are among the elite of the House. In fact, these positions confer upon members prestige tantamount to that of a party leadership position. At the beginning of the 97th Congress, for example, Illinois' Dan Rostenkowski had to choose between becoming party whip, the third-ranking position in the Democratic party hierarchy, and assuming the chair of Ways and Means. He took Ways and Means. At the beginning of the 98th Congress, 83-year-old Claude Pepper of Florida had to choose between finishing his career as chair of the Select Committee on Aging, where he had built a national constituency, and chairing the Rules Committee. As he put it at the time:

> I haven't decided. I would love to be chairman of Rules but I would have to give up the Aging Committee. The Rules Committee is a very powerful, great committee.[32]

Ultimately, there was really no choice and he took the Rules chair.

As with many committees, times have changed for these three influential panels. Their jurisdictions remain virtually untouched and their formal roles in the legislative process have changed little. But other largely procedural changes have placed new demands on these committee chairs—demands that reflect changing member goals, creating new challenges for the chairs of these panels.

185

Since Wilbur Mills' retirement as chair in 1975, Ways and Means chairs have played a role similar to that of activist chairs of policy committees. To a certain extent, the role fits the personalities of Al Ullman and Dan Rostenkowski, Mills' successors. But it also reflects changes in the committee that gave Ullman and Rostenkowski little choice but to shift away from a dependence on bargaining, compromise, and accommodation. Ways and Means now is simply too large, according to most observers, to operate in the fraternal pattern of Mills' era. The larger membership multiplies communications channels within the committee and between members and outsiders, making it more difficult for the chair to mold the decision-making processes to his personal needs. The presence of subcommittees distances the chair from some decisions, limiting his or her participation to stages after the basic shape of legislation has been set. Most importantly, the presence of many activist, policy-oriented liberals undermines chairs' ability to reach a consensus, even among majority party members. Some of the new Democrats have challenged the chairs in meetings of the Democratic Caucus and on the House floor. To be effective in such an environment, chairs have had to be more policy-oriented, more partisan, and more willing to alienate members. On the surface, the approaches of Ullman and Rostenkowski appear less successful than were Mills', but the changing opportunities and constraints they face have dictated both their leadership styles and success ratios.

Leadership of the House Appropriations Committee also has been affected by reforms. Under Mississippi's Jamie L. Whitten, as under his two predecessors, the full committee generally has rubber-stamped what the subcommittees have produced. Whitten has been constrained in his leadership. In part, this has been the result of a challenge to his election as chair in 1979. Because of that challenge, say some committee staff members, Whitten has been reluctant to play much of an activist role. Instead, he acts much like other subcommittee chairs on Appropriations—he heads the Agriculture Subcommittee—while offering whatever help he can to maintain a consensus at the full committee level. The consensus, however, has shifted away from fiscal conservatism to serving each others' parochial interests. As noted in Chapters 4 and 5, this is the product of subcommittee self-selection, open-meetings, larger subcommittees, and multiple subcommittee assignments. Under such circumstances, former Chairman George H. Mahon told us, it is difficult for members "to provide and maintain sufficient objectivity." Leadership, rather than drawing out the independent wisdom of members, must instead depend on the lowest common denominator to keep the committee moving. Critics argue that Appropriations has paid a high price in the form of a much diminished role in fiscal policy making. Instead of guarding the federal purse and gaining a reputation for power by selectively meeting constituent and colleague demands, the committee's subcommittees have become spending advocates. In any case, like the other constituent committees, member goals almost certainly dictate that any Appropriations chair interfere as little as possible with subcommittee operations.

The standard for Rules Committee leadership was set by Missouri's Richard Bolling. Bolling, a recognized authority on House history and procedures, assumed the chairmanship in 1979 and served only until the end of 1982. But both before and during his chairmanship he repeatedly made explicit his view of the appropriate role of a Rules chair. In 1981, for example, at a time when he opposed a parliamentary strategy supported by Speaker Tip O'Neill and most House Democrats, Bolling made clear his position:

> I have spent a couple of decades trying to change the committee I chair from a tyrannical committee which killed more good legislation and probably caused ... virtually every problem that society has had. ... Every program that mitigated the pains of the weak was held up in that committee forever. Too late—everything we did in the social field was too late. It was the ability of the reactionary coalition of Democrats and Republicans, from 1937 on, to bottle up any good legislation, until we broke that tyranny in 1961. And my dilemma is that I don't propose as an individual to reimpose that tyranny no matter how bad I consider your judgment.[33]

Bolling's position was not universally or completely appreciated by fellow Rules Democrats. While we heard no objection to Rules chairs doing the bidding of the party leadership, there was dissatisfaction with the fact that the same attitude had spilled over into the committee's attitude toward other Democrats' requests for Rules. One member said there was simply "too much consensus. Too much of an accommodation to the rank-and-file ... the committee could easily throw its weight around more." Bolling's successor, Democrat Claude Pepper of Florida, is unlikely to change this, although other Rules members may have greater influence over committee decisions than in the past.

As with other House committees, the leaders of prestige committees generally find their behavior shaped by member goals. On Ways and Means, leaders now are encouraged to behave more like policy-oriented committee chairs. On Appropriations, chairs are encouraged to behave much like chairs on constituent-oriented committees. On Rules, however, chairs respond more to the goals of party leaders than to their committee colleagues—a situation that has created some dissatisfaction within the committee in recent Congresses.

Senate Chairs
And Member Goals

Member goals have a much weaker relationship to the leadership styles of Senate committee chairs than they do in the House. Several factors contribute to this dampened effect. As noted in Chapter 4, members of Senate committees less frequently hold a nearly homogeneous set of goals, and they appear to hold those goals less intensely than their House counterparts. For the Senate committee chair, this means that committee members' goals do not as clearly dictate appropriate behavior as they often do in the House. Just as importantly, the lack of committee autonomy in the Senate means that Senate chairs must react more often to noncommittee members' preferences, preferences that are often based on goals other than the goal dominant among committee members. Effective Senate chairs must be as much Senate leaders as committee leaders, accommodating or overcoming the efforts of most senators to pursue their personal goals. Senate committee chairs thus face an environment that allows—in fact requires—great individualism among chairs, as it does for rank-and-file senators.

The individualistic nature of legislative leadership in the Senate is reflected in the distribution of responsibility for managing legislation on the floor. Data on bill management indicate that there has been a low level of bill management by committee chairs for several decades, that the tendency to manage more or less legislation is unrelated to member goals, and that few committees establish a consistent pattern of bill management over time (see Table A-10, Appendix). Few Senate chairs seem to dominate their committees. As a result, senators are less dependent on chairs to achieve their goals and are less demanding that chairs shape their leadership style to those goals.

Chair and rank-and-file individualism in the Senate do not mean that no norms govern chair behavior. To the contrary, strong norms of fair play, honesty, and informed participation apply, even to noncommittee members. James A. McClure, chair of the Energy and Natural Resources Committee, learned this in 1982. McClure stirred up trouble when he asked unanimous consent for several "technical" amendments to a nuclear waste disposal bill.[34] The amendments, which McClure professed were nonsubstantive, turned out to have the effect of overriding the laws of seven states that restricted construction of nuclear power plants. Several senators, including Patrick Leahy of Vermont, who has been keenly interested in nuclear power safety, were bitter about the maneuver. In response, Leahy refused to cooperate with any action requiring unanimous consent that had to do with Energy

Committee bills. For a state-oriented committee, which normally thrives on the ability to process legislation efficiently, this could be a serious problem—one for which the committee chair, in this instance, was to blame. Indeed, it caused one committee member to say about McClure:

> He plays games with the committee and tries to be Mr. Niceguy. But he's a little too slick. You can be the toughest kind of fighter in this place, but you better be honest.[35]

At about the same time another member of the committee, Dale Bumpers of Arkansas, became upset with McClure because he refused to schedule hearings on a bill important to Arkansas. In these cases, McClure was guilty of failing to protect committee member goals, which for Bumpers included hearings on a bill of interest to his home state, and of failing to observe norms vital to individualism and full participation on the Senate floor.

There are exceptions to the rule that member goals do not produce distinct expectations for the behavior of Senate committee chairs. These seem to occur when members' goals are particularly homogeneous and intensely held, making the committee similar to many House committees. For example, complaints about Jesse Helms, chair of the Senate Agriculture Committee since 1981, reflect dissatisfaction that is based on the strong constituency-oriented interests of rank-and-file members. According to some members and staff, Helms' pursuit of personal policy interests in areas outside the committees' jurisdiction has distracted him from committee business, sometimes making it difficult for the committee to process legislation efficiently and cohesively. Some assert that his strident advocacy of school prayer and his campaigns against abortion and school busing threatened the committee consensus on agricultural issues by "unnecessarily antagonizing committee members." And others, such as Sen. Robert Dole of Kansas, feel that Helms' leadership role in conservative causes on social and foreign policy issues invites a backlash from noncommittee members that will hurt agricultural programs of vital importance to the committee. The clarity of member goals on Agriculture, however, is not typical of Senate committees.

On Senate policy committees, Fenno has argued, members' goals discourage chairs from imposing their views on committee members and encourage majority rule and a relatively free rein for subcommittees.[36] The policy-oriented committees, particularly Judiciary, Labor, and Government Affairs, are among the most decentralized committees in the Senate. Nonetheless, styles of leadership differ widely. James Eastland, Edward Kennedy, and Strom Thurmond all brought different styles and political philosophies to the Judiciary Committee. Eastland opposed civil rights legislation and ran a fairly centralized committee until late in his career when committee members forced him to allow greater subcommittee freedom. Kennedy attempted to restructure and to restrict subcommittees, but he was only partly successful. He settled for a larger full committee staff and closer scrutiny of subcommittee activities. Thurmond has reduced staff overall but has continued to allow considerable subcommittee independence while pushing for his own personal policy interests such as the death penalty and limits on abortion. Each of these chairs has been successful, in part, because they have not stifled debate on the committee even if they actively pushed for policies not favored by all of their colleagues. As in the House, policy committee members require the freedom to pursue issues of personal interest even if they have no hope of success.

To reiterate, the behavior of Senate chairs is shaped by member goals. But the goals are less closely tied to particular committees or types of committees. There is a general expectation that chairs allow members to pursue their mix of personal goals in committee and on the floor.

Subcommittee Chairs

Early in 1983, allegations of mismanagement and wrongdoing by the Environmental Protection Agency (EPA) in handling the $1.6 billion superfund for toxic waste cleanup attracted national attention. It also attracted the attention of five House subcommittee chairs intent upon investigating various aspects of allegations made against EPA. Subpoenas were voted. Contempt-of-Congress proceedings were threatened. And deals were struck between Reagan administration officials and the various subcommittees seeking documents. In the midst of the flurry stood five subcommittee chairs on four different House committees: Democrats Elliott H. Levitas of Georgia of the Public Works Committee, James H. Scheuer of New York of the Science and Technology Committee, Mike Synar of Oklahoma of the Government Operations Committee, and James J. Florio of New Jersey and John D. Dingell of Michigan of the Energy and Commerce Committee. Each claimed jurisdiction over all or part of the problems facing EPA, and each opened an investigation. At one point, Speaker O'Neill even called them all into his office in an attempt to get them to coordinate their efforts. They refused. As Levitas put it at the time, "there are enough problems at EPA and superfund to go around." [37]

While unusual in its scope, this example is indicative of the shift toward more active subcommittee chairs. As noted in Chapter 2, the number of House and Senate members serving as committee or subcommittee chairs has expanded regularly since the mid-1960s. The expansion in the House during the early 1970s was accompanied by reforms that gave subcommittee chairs sufficient independence to be called committee leaders in their own right. In the Senate nearly all majority party members hold at least one subcommittee chair. Thus, in that chamber, everyone is a leader—a fact reflecting the individualism of the body. The characteristics of subcommittee chairs—their seniority, party support, activism, and autonomy—are the subject of this concluding section.

Seniority and Subcommittee Chairs

House subcommittee leaders are younger and less senior than they were before the reforms of the 1970s. Three factors contribute to this. First, the average age of all members has declined. Second, in the House, members may serve as chair on only one subcommittee. And, third, again in the House, the number of subcommittees has increased. As a result, more party members are now in a position to chair subcommittees than ever before, and they gain such positions earlier in their legislative careers than they did in the past. This is illustrated in Table 6-1 where the mean number of years a member must wait, on average, before

Table 6-1 Average Years of Service Prior to Gaining Subcommittee Chairs in the House, by Committee Type: 90th to 98th Congress*

Congress	Policy	Constituency	Prestige	Undesired	Average
90th	13.5(6) **	6.5(11)	12.6(6)	6.3(7)	8.7(27)
91st	12.6(6)	0.0(0)	16.0(1)	10.5(8)	11.7(15)
92d	11.0(9)	11.1(9)	14.0(1)	7.2(6)	10.3(28)
93d	9.3(7)	8.3(15)	14.0(1)	6.3(12)	8.0(35)
94th	12.4(14)	7.1(21)	14.9(8)	5.4(10)	9.4(47)
95th	6.9(15)	4.5(17)	12.8(6)	4.0(3)	6.3(39)
96th	6.4(11)	3.9(12)	8.8(6)	3.8(5)	5.6(32)
97th	6.6(14)	6.0(12)	9.5(8)	3.0(8)	6.3(20)
98th	5.5(6)	7.3(9)	9.0(2)	4.7(3)	6.6(20)
Average	9.4	7.3	11.9	6.4	

* Excludes Rules, Budget, and Standards of Official Conduct. Prestige category includes Ways and Means starting with the 94th Congress. Select and special subcommittees are not included.
** Numbers in parentheses are the absolute numbers of new chairs from the previous Congress.

gaining a subcommittee chair is provided for the 90th to 98th Congresses (1967-1984).[38] On average, members gaining chairs in the 90th through 94th Congresses had served 9.6 years or almost five terms. Since that time, members have served only 6.2 years on average, just more than three terms, before gaining such a position. Thus the real youth movement did not occur until three Congresses after the rule limiting members to a single chair and two Congresses after the subcommittee bill of rights was adopted by House Demo- crats.[39] The explanation for this, in part, is that a large number of moderately senior members, the reform activists, were the first to benefit from the rules changes. Subsequently, increased retirements and high turnover helped to advance the even less senior members more quickly.

Overall, this indicates that less experienced members are taking over as leaders of these newly influential House panels. But the pattern is far from uniform. Not surprisingly, members have waited consider- ably longer to gain a subcommittee chair on House Appropriations and Ways and Means (an average of 11.9 years during this entire period) than for a chair on Post Office, Veterans' Affairs, and District of Columbia (5.0 years).[40] Members of the more attractive policy commit- tees have waited longer to chair a subcommittee (9.4 years) than members of constituency committees (7.3 years). The only major excep- tion to this pattern is Armed Services, a constituency committee, which has the longest wait for any House committee, 13.6 years. Only 10 new members were elevated to subcommittee chairs on Armed Services between 1967 and 1983. More frequently than on any other major committee, Armed Services members take only one committee assign- ment, making it less likely that senior members will take subcommittee chairs elsewhere and lengthening the time junior members must wait. Nonetheless, the lower seniority of subcommittee chairs on the other constituency committees is not explained by the frequency of turnover. Turnover rates among subcommittee chairs are roughly equal on policy and constituency committees (with the exception of Agriculture among constituency committees, which has a very high rate of turnover among chairs.) In major part, the difference is due to members leaving chairs on some of the constituency committees—especially relatively minor pan- els such as Merchant Marine and Fisheries—when they have gained enough seniority to take a subcommittee chair on the more visible policy committees. (Two constituency committees in the House, Agriculture and Armed Services, are major assignments, of course, and members would not be able to serve on most of the policy-oriented committees at the same time.)

In contrast to the House, members of the Senate are virtually guaranteed a subcommittee chair upon their election. As noted in Chapter 2, even with the reduction in subcommittees after the 1977 reorganization, 98 percent of the majority party members hold at least one subcommittee chair. As in the House, some subcommittees are harder to come by than others. New York Sen. Alphonse D'Amato chaired the Legislative Appropriations Subcommittee during his first term in office. But Sen. John C. Stennis of Mississippi served 40 years in the Senate before gaining the chair of the Defense Appropriations Subcommittee. Even so, overall access to positions of leadership is much easier in the Senate than in the House.

Subcommittee Chairs and Party Support

As new leaders have taken over House and Senate committees and subcommittees, party support levels by members in these key positions also have changed. The most important change (demonstrated in Table 6-2) is that the numerous House subcommittee chairs have been more broadly representative of all House Democrats. Table 6-2 also shows an overall increase in the degree of party support by committee and subcommittee chairs in the House during the 1970s—from 47.2 to 71.3 percent and from 53.6 to 68.1 percent respectively. Liberals, of course, had been agitating for some time against a seniority system that locked conservative southern Democrats into power. In the 92d Congress, full committee chairs were much less supportive of party policy positions than was the average Democrat or northern Democrat. Subcommittee chairs were more supportive of the party's position than full committee chairs but still were less supportive of the party than the average Democrat. These patterns began to change in the 93d Congress. Subcommittee chairs came close to the average party support score during the rest of the period. Full committee chairs rose to a point slightly higher in support than the average Democrat and nearly as high as northern Democrats. Ironically, at the same time that subcommittee chairs have become more important relative to full committee chairs, subcommittee chairs have fallen slightly behind full committee chairs in terms of their overall support for the party.

In the Senate, separate scores for subcommittee chairs are not necessary because virtually all majority party members hold at least one chair. These scores indicate that party leaders, as in the House, lead their colleagues in party support. The figures also show that there is much less divergence among the various groups than in the House. Full committee chairs are less supportive of the party than are rank-and-file

193

Table 6-2 Selected House and Senate Party Unity Score: 92d to 97th Congresses (*in mean party unity score for the group*)

Group	Congress					
	92d	93d	94th	95th	96th	97th
House						
Leaders*	78.3	85.3	87.0	80.0	82.6	73.5
Full Committee Chairs	47.2	56.1	62.8	69.1	71.3	70.5
Subcommittee Chairs	53.6	65.5	64.1	64.2	68.1	68.9
All Democrats	65.6	57.7	67.7	65.4	68.6	70.5
Northern Democrats	74.9	71.2	77.2	72.8	74.6	77.5
Southern Democrats	47.5	37.5	46.6	48.4	56.3	54.3
Senate						
Leaders*	70.0	74.0	72.0	78.5	82.5	86.5**
Full Committee Chairs	47.6	55.1	60.7	64.7	63.0	76.3
All Democrats	60.0	66.0	65.0	64.5	66.0	78.5
Northern Democrats	69.5	76.0	74.0	73.5	71.5	76.5
Southern Democrats	43.0	39.5	42.0	44.5	55.0	59.5

* Leaders in the House include majority leader, whip, and chief deputy whip except for the 92d Congress, which includes the majority leader, whip, and two deputy whips. Leaders in the Senate include the majority leader and the whip.
** 97th Congress party unity scores are for Republicans in each category.

Source: *Congressional Quarterly Weekly Report.* Congressional Quarterly calculates party unity scores from roll-call votes on which a majority of voting Democrats opposed a majority of voting Republicans.

members, but they became more supportive during the 1970s. In the 97th Congress, the first full Congress in 25 years in which they controlled the Senate, Republicans were able to achieve very high levels of party support. Only a few northern moderate-to-liberal Republicans—Senators Lowell Weicker, Robert Stafford, Charles Mathias, and Mark Hatfield—failed to maintain high levels of support.

Subcommittee Chair Activism

In the previous chapter, the increased level of activity among House subcommittees and the stable or declining role for Senate subcommittees were described. As a measure of subcommittee chair activism, we have examined the floor management of legislation to see if similar House and Senate patterns emerge.[41] Bill management is important for both symbolic and substantive reasons. Symbolically, it represents control over the final stages of a bill's journey through the legislative process.

For some bills, especially the more controversial ones, it also may mean the difference between passage unamended, significant amendments, or defeat. Therefore, the skill of the bill manager may play an important role in determining the fate of a piece of legislation.

In the House, the Democratic Caucus has directed its committee chairs to allow subcommittee chairs to manage bills on the floor whenever possible.[42] For most full committee chairs, this rule change presented no problem. For example, upon taking over the Interior Committee in 1973, James A. Haley expressed his own willingness to have subcommittee chairs manage their own bills on the floor:

> I want the chairmen of the subcommittees who hear the testimony and ... have the responsibility of writing the bill to take it to the floor and explain it. I'll be glad to help them out when I can but I don't want to stand in the way of ... the man who has done the work [so] I take all the bows. ... If it's a good bill, fine, let him take the credit. If it's a bad bill, let him take that.[43]

There has been no need for such a rule change in the more open Senate where bill sponsors typically manage their own legislation on the floor.

Table 6-3 presents aggregate data on the management of bills in the House and Senate. As expected, House subcommittee chairs now manage most of the bills that reach the floor. Nevertheless, full committee

Table 6-3 House and Senate Bill Managers By Type For Selected Congresses (*by percent*)

Type	Congress						
	86th	*89th*	*91st*	*92d*	*93d*	*94th*	*95th*
House							
Full Committee Chairs	54.1	48.3	40.0	39.4	35.7	30.8	28.4
Subcommittee Chairs	30.3	41.8	49.0	49.4	53.1	63.3	66.9
Others	15.6	10.0	11.1	11.2	11.1	5.9	4.9
Total Bills	492	603	588	587	652	707	796
Senate							
Full Committee Chairs	15.3		14.3				13.6
Subcommittee Chairs	30.6		26.8				21.9
Majority Leader	12.7		23.2				45.2
Others	41.4		35.7				19.4
Total Bills	353		414				640

Source: *Congressional Record.*

chairs still manage legislation out of proportion to their numbers. In the 95th Congress, for example, 18 full committee chairs managed over 28 percent of the bills in the House. The remaining 72 percent were managed by 104 different members. When compared to what the average subcommittee chair manages, most full committee chairs remain very active participants. Nonetheless, House subcommittee chairs are much more active than they were before the reforms.

Most of the change in the overall pattern of House bill management is accounted for by seven largely policy-oriented committees. Armed Services, Banking, Commerce, Education and Labor, Interior, Judiciary, and Ways and Means all had significant drops in the number of bills managed by full committee chairs (see Table A-9, Appendix). The two constituency committees always have had broad participation by subcommittee chairs, even though they have evolved to even lower levels of full committee chair management. In contrast, three of the four policy committees and Ways and Means have all had periods of full committee chair dominance. There are few exceptions to this overall trend toward subcommittee management of bills. Activist Jack Brooks has markedly increased the management of bills by the full committee chair on Government Operations, although many of the bills originate in his Subcommittee on Legislation and National Security, and chairs of the Veterans' Affairs Committee generally manage most of that committee's reported legislation.

In the Senate, a large portion of the routine floor business is now managed by the majority leader. During the 86th Congress (1959-1961), the majority leader managed a healthy portion of the bills that reached the floor (12.7 percent). With the Senate's burgeoning workload, this responsibility has expanded dramatically. Majority Leader Robert C. Byrd "managed" 45.2 percent of the bills that reached the floor during the 95th Congress (1977-1979). Virtually all of these passed on a voice vote and without debate. Of the remaining bills managed on the floor, 21.9 percent were handled by subcommittee chairs, 19.4 percent by members who did not chair the subcommittee, and 13.6 percent by full committee chairs. The shift away from the "other" category and towards the routine handling of business by the majority leader is the major change. This has been an efficiency mechanism used to speed the handling of minor bills on the floor and to relieve Senate bill sponsors—who see little special prestige in speaking on the floor—from an additional burden.[44]

Unlike the House, Senate subcommittee chairs actually managed a smaller portion (but a larger absolute number) of the bills that reached the floor in the 95th Congress than in either the 91st or the 86th

Congresses. The explanation for this pattern lies in the fact that virtually all Senate bills are managed by the bill's sponsor (or by the majority leader in the sponsor's absence). Again, this means that participation in the Senate is tied more closely to individual initiative than to subcommittee government. In the 95th Congress, 75 different senators (including 19 minority party Republicans) managed at least one bill on the floor. In contrast, almost all of the 122 bill managers in the House held a related formal position and virtually no minority party Republicans managed legislation.

Subcommittee Chairs: Independence Versus Autonomy

In Chapter 1, full committee chairs of the 1950s and 1960s were described as sovereigns within a loose confederation of committees. Evolution in the House and Senate dates such a statement; it is clearly not an accurate description of the current network of committees and subcommittees. But is it accurate to describe subcommittee chairs as the sovereigns within a loose and fragmented system of subcommittees? The previous chapter indicated that this is certainly not the case in the Senate and that it overstates the situation in many House committees. Subcommittee chairs do not have a monopoly over staffs, cannot block legislation by refusing to report it to the floor, and even cannot manipulate their subcommittees' agendas as many full committee chairs did in the 1950s and 1960s. As with full committee chairs, the behavior of House subcommittee chairs is conditioned by member goals. On policy committees, chairs know that decisions made by their subcommittees will not necessarily go unchallenged at the full committee level. On constituency committees, chairs are mindful that a consensus is needed if their decisions are to hold up in full committee and on the floor. Under the circumstances, no subcommittee chair can afford to ignore the interests of committee colleagues.

The most effective reinforcements to this accountability are procedures for subcommittee chair selection and subcommittee selection by members. House Democratic Caucus rules provide for the selection of subcommittee chairs by seniority, with ratification by the Democratic caucus of each committee. Generally, committee seniority will determine the outcomes of these elections. But enough challenges occur to remind members that they hold their positions as a matter of privilege and not as a matter of right. Since the rules were changed, there have been at least a dozen publicly acknowledged challenges to members who, on the basis of seniority, should have been granted a preferred subcommittee

197

chair.[45] All but two of these challenges have occurred on policy committees—the exceptions being Ways and Means and Armed Services.

These challenges help to underscore the policy orientations of this set of committees—Banking, Commerce, Foreign Affairs, and Government Operations—and the willingness of policy-oriented members to challenge more senior members in order to advance their own policy preferences. In at least three cases, all in 1979, the member considered more liberal defeated a senior colleague. California's Henry A. Waxman was elected over North Carolina's Richardson Preyer for the Health Subcommittee of the Commerce Committee. Preyer said afterwards: "Members were voting on whether one candidate's views are closer to their [own] than the other's." [46] At the same time, Texas's Bob Eckhardt defeated New York's John M. Murphy to become chair of Commerce's Oversight Subcommittee and Connecticut's Toby Moffett was elected to chair Government Operation's Environment, Energy, and Natural Resources Subcommittee after three more senior colleagues had been rejected. Policy committee members have shown a decidedly greater willingness to exploit the new rules and procedures than have constituency committee members.

On House constituency committees, members' goals shape the behavior of subcommittee chairs through a somewhat different mechanism—but a mechanism that still reflects the new rules. Because members are allowed to choose their own subcommittee assignments, constituency committees tend to build subcommittees with like-minded members. As noted earlier, this tends to build a consensus on subcommittees that is ratified by the full committee. At the same time, the importance of the consensus at the subcommittee level works to constrain the actions of subcommittee chairs. Hence, if subcommittee government is at work, it is more likely to appear on district-oriented panels than on policy-oriented committees, and it will be as much a product of subcommittee consensus as of the inherent power of subcommittee chairs.

Evolution and reform have created a system of independent but not wholly autonomous subcommittees in the House. The leaders of these panels serve in positions of power and influence but they are answerable to numerous colleagues. These new leaders in Congress are less senior, more active, and generally more representative of their party colleagues than were their predecessors. But they hold positions of initiative rather than positions of ultimate authority.

Conclusion: The Changing
Context of Committee Leadership

As resources have become distributed more evenly and as the variety of goals of more members has been taken into account, the nature of committee leadership has been changed. Few chairs have ever been in the position of commanding their committees. Nonetheless, committee chairs before the 1970s were undeniably more powerful than they are today—especially in the House, but also in the Senate. Where these committee chairs once could lead by the skillful use of resources and personal persuasion they must now relate to the rank-and-file of their committees through bargaining. As noted earlier, they may not be simply one among equals, but in many cases they are no more than first among equals.

By and large, this shift is explained by contextual factors. There is every reason to believe that, on average, committee chairs are as talented, politically astute, and intelligent as they ever have been. Some, clearly, are still better than others at what they do because of the personal capabilities they bring to their positions. But changing political environments, new procedural requirements, and the continuing importance of other members' goals have greatly constrained committee chairs' latitude within committees. Thus even the most talented committee chairs cannot be, even if they were inclined to be, as powerful as their predecessors in the post-World War II period. Good leaders now must display an ability to work effectively in a more open, competitive, and egalitarian system.

On balance, but with perhaps one major exception, this has made committee leadership in the House more like that in the Senate. There are fewer barriers to participation in the House than there were two decades ago. As a result, full committee chairs in both chambers are forced to be conscious of the demands, not only of committee colleagues, but of their chamber colleagues as well. To be successful, therefore, House and Senate chairs must be effective in dealing with members beyond the confines of their respective committees.

The major exception to the convergence of House and Senate leaders lies in the subcommittees. In the Senate, broad participation, membership overlap, and the permeability of committees have prevented subcommittee chairs from gaining the intermediate level of status achieved by subcommittee chairs in the House. Subcommittee chairs in the House—though far from uniformly powerful—represent an influential new leadership category in that chamber. As should be clear from the previous two chapters, however, the power of subcommittee chairs should not be overemphasized. Like full committee chairs, their success or failure is affected by the environments in which they operate, the personal goals of their colleagues, and their own abilities.

NOTES

1. *New York Times,* February 13, 1983, E5.
2. *Washington Post,* November 8, 1980, A1.
3. Charles O. Jones, "House Leadership in An Age of Reform," in *Understanding Congressional Leadership,* ed. Frank H. Mackaman (Washington, D.C.: CQ Press, 1981), 117-134.
4. For an argument on context versus personality see Joseph Cooper and David W. Brady, "Institutional Context and Leadership Style: The House From Cannon to Rayburn," *American Political Science Review* 75 (June 1981): 411-425. For a different approach to studying the context of committee leadership, see Joseph K. Unekis and Leroy N. Rieselbach, "Congressional Committee Leadership, 1971-1978," *Legislative Studies Quarterly* 8 (May 1983): 251-270.
5. See Alexander George, "Some Uses of Dynamic Psychology in Political Biography," in *A Sourcebook For The Study of Personality and Politics,* ed. Fred I. Greenstein and Michael Lerner (Chicago: Markham Publishing, 1971).
6. "Seniority Rule: Change In Procedure Not in Practice," *Congressional Quarterly Weekly Report,* January 27, 1973, 136.
7. Ibid., 136.
8. "House Agriculture: New Faces, New Issues," *Congressional Quarterly Weekly Report,* February 22, 1975, 379.
9. Ibid., 380.
10. "A Change of Style on House Armed Services," *Congressional Quarterly Weekly Report,* February 15, 1975, 336.
11. Glenn R. Parker, "The Selection Of Committee Leaders In The House of Representatives," *American Politics Quarterly* 7 (January 1979): 71-93.
12. Thomas P. Southwick, "Senate Committee Changes: Major Impact," *Congressional Quarterly Weekly Report,* February 19, 1977, 330.
13. Ann Cooper, "Democratic Caucus To Vote on Whitten, New Rules," *Congressional Quarterly Weekly Report,* January 20, 1979, 78.
14. A good example of this occurred upon the death of Senator John McClellan. As chair of Appropriations, McClellan's replacement caused three other Senate chairs to switch positions. See "Three Key Senate Panels to Get New Heads," *Congressional Quarterly Weekly Report,* December 3, 1977, 2527-2528.
15. The rule was changed at the beginning of the 97th Congress from referral to the appropriate subcommittees to referral to all appropriate subcommittees. The change was offered by Representative Phillip Burton of California. See Rule 33(D) of the Democratic Caucus.
16. Andy Plattner, "Scrappy House Energy Panel Provides High Pressure Arena For Wrangling Over Regulations," *Congressional Quarterly Weekly Report,* March 12, 1983, 501.

17. As noted in Chapter 2, an amendment offered by Sen. Richard Clark of Iowa, which would have forced the creation of legislative subcommittees, was defeated on the Senate floor 63-20 on February 3, 1977. See Thomas P. Southwick, "Senate Approves Committee Changes," *Congressional Quarterly Weekly Report,* February 12, 1977, 282.

18. "Van Deerlin To Be Chairman of Communications Unit," *Congressional Quarterly Weekly Report,* May 1, 1976, 1030.

19. Fenno, *Congressmen,* 127.

20. U.S., Congress, House, Select Committee on Committees, *Final Report* (Washington, D.C.: Government Printing Office, 1979), 285-286.

21. Fenno, *Congressmen,* 173.

22. Harrison H. Donnelly, "House Chairman Brooks: A Tough Legislative Fighter," *Congressional Quarterly Weekly Report,* February 12, 1977, 266.

23. *Washington Post,* May 15, 1983, A14.

24. Ibid.

25. Nadine Cohodas, "Kennedy and Rodino: How Two Very Different Chairmen Run Their Panels," *Congressional Quarterly Weekly Report,* February 2, 1980, 270.

26. Ibid.

27. Fenno, *Congressmen,* 288.

28. "Profiles of Chairmen Deposed By Democratic Caucus," *Congressional Quarterly Weekly Report,* January 18, 1975, 165.

29. "House Agriculture," 379.

30. "New Chairman of House Interior Plans To Share Power," *Congressional Quarterly Weekly Report,* January 27, 1973, 135.

31. Bob Rankin, "Morris Udall Assesses Legislative Outlook, Recalls The Campaign," *Congressional Quarterly Weekly Report,* April 2, 1977, 603.

32. Andy Plattner, "New Rules Committee Head Expected to Carry Forward In Tradition of Rep. Bolling," *Congressional Quarterly Weekly Report,* November 6, 1982, 2804.

33. Taken from Democratic Caucus transcripts.

34. *Washington Post,* July 6, 1982, A3.

35. Ibid.

36. Fenno, *Congressmen,* 176.

37. Joseph A. Davis, "House Subcommittees Begin Reviewing EPA Documents: Two More Officials Are Fired," *Congressional Quarterly Weekly Report,* February 26, 1983, 411-413 and *Washington Post,* February 20, 1983, A1.

38. New chairs were determined by comparing the lists of chairs in the *Congressional Staff Directory* for each Congress. A chair was counted as new if he or she did not hold a position on a given committee in the previous Congress. Members who chaired a subcommittee in one Congress, gave it up, and returned to chair a subcommittee were counted only once on that committee. Chairs who left one subcommittee to take a chair on a subcommittee of a different committee were counted twice.

39. Using a different method, John E. Stanga, Jr., and David N. Farnsworth came up with roughly the same findings, although the break point in the 94th Congress is not revealed because their data ended too early. See Stanga and Farnsworth, "Seniority and Democratic Reforms in the House of Representatives: Committees and Subcommittees," in *Legislative Reform,* ed. Leroy N. Rieselbach (Lexington, Mass.: Lexington Books, 1978), 35-48.

40. It should be noted, however, that the Legislative Branch Subcommittee and the District of Columbia Subcommittee are not viewed as very attractive. Freshmen were given these chairs in the 96th Congress.
41. For a more complete discussion of bill management as an indicator of decentralization in the House and the method by which the data was collected (the same method was used for the Senate) see Christopher J. Deering, "Subcommittee Government in the U.S. House: An Analysis of Bill Management," *Legislative Studies Quarterly* 7 (November 1982): 533-546.
42. The rule is No. 39 in the House Democratic Caucus Rules. It reads: "The chairmen of full committees shall, insofar as practicable, permit subcommittee chairmen to handle on the floor legislation from their respective subcommittees."
43. "New Chairman Of House Interior Plans To Share Power," *Congressional Quarterly Weekly Report*, January 27, 1973, 134.
44. Robert L. Peabody explains that Byrd increased his management activities as a time-saving measure and because he enjoyed working on the floor. See "Senate Party Leadership: From the 1950s to the 1980s," in Mackaman, *Understanding Congressional Leadership*, 51-115.
45. In addition to those mentioned, John E. Moss of California beat Harley O. Staggers of West Virginia for a Commerce subcommittee in 1975; Frank Annunzio of Illinois beat Leonor K. Sullivan of Missouri for a subcommittee on Banking in 1975; Joe D. Waggonner, Jr., was sidestepped by Ways and Means members to prevent him from getting a chair in 1977; Michael E. Barnes of Maryland beat Gus Yatron of Pennsylvania for a subcommittee on Foreign Affairs in 1981; Jerry M. Patterson beat out Henry B. Gonzalez of Texas for a subcommittee on Banking in 1981; James H. Scheuer was deprived of a subcommittee by the Commerce Committee in 1981; and Samuel S. Stratton of New York was beaten by Charles E. Bennett of Florida for a subcommittee on Armed Services in 1983.
46. Ann Cooper, "New Setbacks For House Seniority System," *Congressional Quarterly Weekly Report*, February 3, 1979, 183.

The Role and Organization of Committee Staff

7

Committee staff are among the most controversial features of the congressional committee systems. For some, the expansion of committee staff has meant an increased capacity for members to cope with burgeoning workloads. For others, staff increases have overloaded the system with make-work while insulating members from each other. The popular press has characterized committee staff as "The New Power Elite," "The New Senate Barons," and as "Governors on the Hill." [1] Even members, who stand to benefit most, view staff with mixed emotions. As former Rules Committee Chairman Richard Bolling put it:

> Some staffing is disastrous, but the key is whether they do useful work. You can have a staff where 50 percent are stirring the pot and they're not putting anything in the pot. They're just stirring. On the other hand, you can have a staff that makes a committee function.[2]

Regardless of one's position, it is clear that committee staff have undergone rapid transformation during the last decade. By 1980 Congress employed more than 3,000 people on full committee, subcommittee, and minority staffs.

The primary purpose of this chapter is to examine staff as an aspect of committee organization and operations. The model of committee change outlined in the Introduction and subsequent analysis indicate that there are four major determinants of committee staff characteristics: (1) statutory, chamber, and caucus rules; (2) committee jurisdictions and agendas; (3) member goals; and (4) committee chair preferences. These factors are related hierarchically. Externally imposed rules, when present, place limits on committees' staffing options. The potential for variety in staffing patterns suggested by the other three factors is constrained within either chamber by these rules. Committee jurisdictions and agendas are comparatively objective conditions that influence committees' staffing decisions. It should be recalled, however, that jurisdictions and agendas also influence member goals and the role of committee chairs. Within committees, member goals help to shape demands placed on staff. Finally, committee chairs can play an important role in organizing committee staff and generally do so in the absence of strong influence by the other three factors. As will be seen, the House and Senate differ in the significance of these factors for changing staff patterns.

Formal Determinants of Committee Staff Structures

Large committee staff in Congress are a recent development even though committees in both the House and Senate have been authorized to hire assistants since the 1830s.[3] In 1856 the Ways and Means Committee and the Senate Finance Committee were authorized to hire several full-time clerks. Committee staff gradually increased after that point. In 1924 House committee staff had reached 120 and Senate committee staff 141. For many decades, as noted in Chapter 1, committees were the primary source of staff assistants, but these assistants were available only to committee chairs.

The formal determinants of the current staffing system for House and Senate committees originate in the Legislative Reorganization Act of 1946. The act provided that each committee could hire four professional and six clerical workers—except for the Appropriations committees, which were allowed to establish their own staffing levels. By 1947 committee staff levels in the House and Senate had expanded to 167 and 232, respectively, and they continued to increase during the next two decades (Figure 7-1).

Despite the staff increases allowed under the 1946 act and subsequent authorizations, better staffing remained a perennial reform issue throughout the post-World War II period. By the late 1960s and early 1970s a strong push was made in both the House and the Senate for increased staff. Many members believed that Congress was seriously disadvantaged in its competition with the executive branch because of inadequate staff support. For example, in 1975 Sen. Alan Cranston of California spoke of the gap between the branches:

> ... in the struggle of the Congress to hold its own with the executive branch and preserve the balance of powers and prevent one-man rule, we are overwhelmed and out-manned by the executive branch on staff and therefore on research to back up the positions, and on computerization and such elements.[4]

Figure 7-1 Congressional Committee Staff, 1947-1980 (selected years)

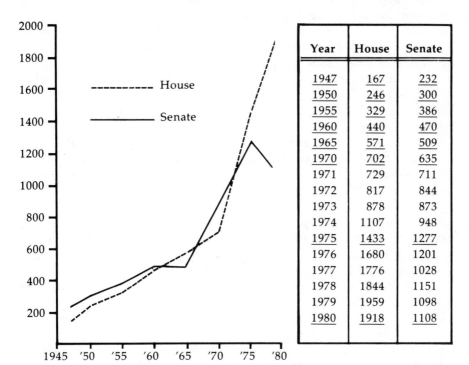

Year	House	Senate
1947	167	232
1950	246	300
1955	329	386
1960	440	470
1965	571	509
1970	702	635
1971	729	711
1972	817	844
1973	878	873
1974	1107	948
1975	1433	1277
1976	1680	1201
1977	1776	1028
1978	1844	1151
1979	1959	1098
1980	1918	1108

Source: House Select Committee on Committees, Final Report, House Report No. 96-866, 539; and Roger H. Davidson and Walter J. Oleszek, *Congress and It's Members* (Washington, D.C.: CQ Press, 1981), 238.

A year later in testimony before the Stevenson Committee in 1976, Sen. Robert Morgan of North Carolina argued that staff should rival executive personnel in every respect:

> I would say this: I think that the leading staff members of the Banking Committee staff should be equal to or exceed in ability and in experience the Comptroller of the Currency, members of the Board of Governors of the Federal Reserve Board, and leading committee members' staff should be equal to sub-Cabinet levels of Government. After all, they are the ones who write the legislation.[5]

Other members viewed staff as an important resource for furthering their own careers. In some of the more extreme cases they seemed to have become surrogate presidential campaign staff. Sen. Henry M. Jackson of Washington incurred the wrath of several of his colleagues in the early and mid-1970s by his use of committee staff. Sen. Lee Metcalf of Montana asserted: "This is an insidious thing that infects senators who are running for president. They just gather up every available thing and use it in their campaign." [6] Regardless of the motive, however, most members in both chambers (as well as outside observers) regarded staff increases as a desirable change.

The Legislative Reorganization Act of 1970 authorized another major boost in committee staff levels and also provided for minority staffing for the first time. The act raised the level of committee professionals from four to six, gave committees the power to hire consultants, allowed committees to provide their staff with specialized training, increased Senate staff salaries, and provided the minority one-third of staff funding while allowing them to appoint two of the six committee professionals.

The House took the process a step further in January 1971 when the Democratic Caucus adopted a rule guaranteeing the independent staffing of subcommittees. This change reduced full committee chairs' control over staff by providing greater access to committee staff for other members. Total House committee staff immediately increased by almost 100—from 729 in 1971 to 817 in 1972. Further increases were mandated by the Committee Reform Amendments of 1974 (the Hansen/Bolling reforms) and by additional Democratic Caucus action. The amendments also had included committee staffing for the minority party as a sweetener to attract Republican votes.[7] These new provisions tripled the professional staff (from six to eighteen) and doubled the clerical staff (from six to twelve) allocated automatically to each standing committee. As before, the House Appropriations Committee was allowed to set its own staff levels. The new Budget Committee in the House also was given this privilege.[8]

Despite the rules changes, not all committees responded quickly to either the minority staffing provisions or to the subcommittee staffing provisions. The Science and Technology Committee is a particularly good example of this reluctance.[9] Throughout the 1960s, successive ranking minority members pressured Democratic chairs of the committee for minority staff. In 1968 ranking minority member James G. Fulton of Pennsylvania was allowed to hire a single minority staff aide for the committee's Republican contingent. Fulton's successor, Charles A. Mosher of Ohio, was able to add a second professional in 1971, but even that gain was threatened in 1973 by Olin E. Teague of Texas and his new staff director, former astronaut Jack Swigert. Teague and Swigert wanted to implement a new, more centralized staff system that would seriously undercut the independence of the two minority staff professionals. This set off a round of negotiations between minority members and Teague that lasted more than a year and a half. By 1975 the House adopted a much clearer statement about minority staffing, but it took three years for the minority to overcome the foot-dragging tactics of Teague and Swigert to fill these slots. Not until 1978 did the minority gain separate office space for its staff.

A similar but less overt struggle occurred on the committee concerning subcommittee staff. Teague and Swigert both believed that provisions for subcommittee staff would undermine the chair's power and fragment committee staff work. By 1975 several subcommittee chairs tried to appoint staff aides but met with resistance from Teague and Swigert. Nominees were rejected as unqualified and characterized as political hacks rather than as professionals. Subcommittee chairs began to observe that the minority's rights to staff seemed better protected under the new system than were their rights. Ultimately, subcommittee chairs on the committee were allowed to hire their own staff, but even today the full committee staff retains considerable influence in guarding the staff's "professionalism" by screening all staff candidates. Thus, while Science is described below as having a decentralized staff organization, it retains some elements of centralized control, as do other constituency committees.

Staff increases took a distinctly different path in the Senate than in the House. In light of the presentation in previous chapters, it is not surprising that this path emphasized individual rather than committee-based resources. In 1975 an active bipartisan group of relatively junior members pushed successfully for a rule to allow each senator to hire up to three assistants to help him or her with committee responsibilities. These new staff assistants were not on committee payrolls (and therefore were not reflected in committee staff totals for that period), and they were not housed or controlled by committee chairs. Instead, office space and administration were provided directly by each senator's office. Thus, although they worked almost exclusively on committee business, this staff clearly "belonged" to an individual senator. An additional rule change was implemented as part of the Stevenson Committee reforms: Senate committees were allowed—at the request of the minority caucus on each committee—to adopt a two-thirds majority/one-third minority staffing policy. Almost all Senate committees subsequently formed separate minority staff. While these staff assistants were nominally associated with the committee, they too tended to be personalized rather than corporate in orientation. For example, when minority members of the Senate Foreign Relations Committee voted to establish a minority staff, the ranking minority member, Republican Jacob K. Javits of

New York, appointed a longtime personal assistant to direct the new group. Regardless of institutional origin, therefore, Senate staff remained much more personalized (and more extensively available) than in the House.

As a result of these formal changes, both House and Senate committee staff continued to grow—to 1,918 and 1,108, respectively, by 1980. Nonetheless, staffing reforms in the two chambers had different implications for full committee chairs and were carried out in different ways. In the House, chamber and caucus reforms placed limits on the discretion of full committee chairs. The purpose was to guarantee the dispersal of staff resources to more members of the majority party and to the minority party. In the Senate, reforms generally left untouched the existing discretion over committee staff by full committee chairs and focused instead on members' personal resources. Thus Senate full committee chairs retain greater formal control over committee staff than do their House counterparts, although senators have more personal staff to assist them with committee activities. The pattern of full committee and subcommittee staff growth observed in Chapter 2 reflects these differences.

Agendas, Jurisdictions, and Committee Staff Structures

Within the constraints set by statute, chamber, and caucus rules, committee jurisdictions and agendas also shape the size and organization of committee staff. Great jurisdictional fragmentation creates a need for large staff and provides a basis for differentiating staff responsibilities. Similarly, large committee agendas, regardless of fragmentation, also affect committee staff size and, to a lesser extent, staff organization. Unfortunately, because workload and fragmentation are so closely linked, separating the independent effects of these two factors is impossible. Table 7-1 demonstrates the relationship between fragmentation and staff size. In both the House and Senate there is a rough correspondence between the two rank orders, with committees such as Appropriations, Labor, and Commerce ranking near the top in total staff and fragmentation. Likewise, the least fragmented committees—Merchant Marine, House Administration, District of Columbia, the Veterans' Affairs committees, the Rules committees, the Small Business committees, and Post Office—have the smallest staffs.

Senate Foreign Relations, House Interior, and the tax committees are the major exceptions to this pattern. The staff sizes of the Foreign Relations and House Interior committees are below their fragmentation ranking. In the case of Foreign Relations, the need for staff has been reduced by a traditional dependence on the executive branch and its relatively light legislative burdens. As Chapter 3 indicated, the environment of this committee is highly focused on the executive branch; in fact, while less true than 15 years ago, the committee is unusually dependent on the executive branch for information. In the case of the tax committees, as seen in Chapter 3, the low fragmentation ranking obscures the complexity of tax issues and the related political environment, which are the responsibility of dozens of staffers on both committees. Finally, despite the fact that House Interior ranks quite high on the scale of fragmentation, it remains primarily a district-oriented

Table 7-1 Jurisdictional Fragmentation and Committee Staff Size: 1982

Rank By Fragmentation	Staff Size	Rank By Fragmentation	Staff Size
Senate		**House**	
Appropriations	81	Appropriations	137
Labor	85	Commerce	127
Commerce	79	Interior	66
Foreign Relations	36	Education and Labor	108
Governmental Affairs	107	Public Works	84
Judiciary	125	Foreign Affairs	84
Environment	51	Judiciary	74
Banking	38	Agriculture	56
Energy	26	Science and Technology	74
Agriculture	33	Government Operations	81
Finance	54	Merchant Marine	61
Armed Services	36	Banking	64
Rules and Administration	32	Armed Services	49
Veterans' Affairs	20	Ways and Means	84
Small Business	20	House Administration	36
		Small Business	54
		Post Office	60
		District of Columbia	39
		Veterans' Affairs	33
		Rules	42
Budget	73	Budget	94
(Spearman's r=.76; p<.001)		(Spearman's r=.81; p<.001)	

Source: Fragmentation rankings are from Tables 3-1 and 3-2. Committee staff sizes are from the *Congressional Staff Directory 1982* (Mount Vernon, Va.: Congressional Staff Directory, 1982), passim.

committee. The staff is decentralized in operating style, especially where its more policy-oriented subcommittees are concerned, but overall remains moderate in size.

In addition to size, the structure of committee staff is related to fragmentation, especially in the Senate where the rules have been less constraining. Generally, committees with more complex, fragmented jurisdictions have more differentiated staff structures. Well-developed subcommittee staff are the most visible manifestation of this differentiation. Senate committees with the narrowest jurisdictions and environments have the most centralized staff organizations: Agriculture, Armed Services, Small Business, and Veterans' Affairs all have relatively small and centralized staffs. At the opposite end of the spectrum, Appropriations, Governmental Affairs, Judiciary, and Labor have clearly differentiated subcommittee staffs. Senate Commerce has a large full committee staff to go along with its subcommittee staff. Even its full committee staff has been segmented into several workgroups in the management-by-objectives system established by Republican Bob Packwood of Oregon in the 97th Congress.

Less variety in staff organization exists among House committees. As noted, House Democratic Caucus rules now require that all committees with more than twenty members must have at least four subcommittees, and the subcommittees are allowed at least one professional assistant.[10] Nevertheless, those House committees with limited legislative jurisdictions—House Administration, District of Columbia, Rules, and Veterans' Affairs—have only small subcommittee staffs that work closely with each full committee staff. In at least one case, Veterans' Affairs, subcommittee staff slots budgeted by the committee have gone unfilled because the full committee staff does most of the work. Veterans' Affairs members exerted little pressure to fill these positions, at least as of the 97th Congress. Beyond this, House Agriculture and Armed Services, like their Senate counterparts, have small subcommittee staffs whose functions are not always clearly differentiated from those of the full committee staff. In contrast, Appropriations, Banking, Energy and Commerce, Judiciary, and Government Operations all have large, specialized, and independent subcommittee staffs.

While staff size reflects jurisdictional fragmentation, it also has an independent effect on staff specialization. Large staffs tend to require more clearcut organizational structures. Small staffs, such as that of the Senate Environment and Public Works Committee, permit less formally structured staff operations. But with very large staffs, such as those of the Senate Judiciary or House Energy and Commerce committees, informality would be virtually impossible. Indeed, the staff itself would almost certainly seek a relatively structured organization with well-defined responsibilities. This organizational differentiation is most likely to be reflected by the development of subcommittee staff, but also might lead to a more hierarchical full committee organization. Again, the Senate Commerce Committee—with modest subcommittee staff and a relatively complex full committee staff structure—is a prominent example. And it is hard to imagine a committee with a staff as large as the House Judiciary's without a well-developed staff organizational structure.

Member Goals and Committee Staff Structures _____

Member goals also shape the use of committee staff. Because both member goals and staffing patterns reflect differences in committee jurisdictions, it is not possible to conclude that staff are molded solely to serve members' goals. But interviews indicate that members' goals do have two significant independent effects.[11] First, member goals make an independent contribution to the size and centralization of committee staff. Second, and perhaps more importantly, member goals shape the role of staff. In both cases, the relationship is stronger in the House than in the Senate.

Size and Centralization

Three fairly distinct staffing patterns emerge in the House. Policy committees generally have large, decentralized staffs. Except for Education and Labor and Foreign Affairs, subcommittee staff outnumber full committee staff on each of these committees. Among the 22 committees, these six committees ranked second, third, fifth, eighth, ninth, and twelfth in total staff resources in 1982. No other set of committees in the House (or Senate) is so uniformly decentralized in terms of staff structure. Independent subcommittee staff were developing in each of these committees before the Democratic Caucus reforms of 1973. Member goals have encouraged such arrangements because of the desire to have sufficient resources to pursue personal policy interests and to explore new policy areas. And, of course, member goals reinforce the influence of these committees' broad jurisdictions on staff specialization and subcommittee staff autonomy.

Science and Technology, although a constituency committee, has staff characteristics similar to the policy-oriented panels. Categorized as an undesirable committee in the 92d Congress, the panel now attracts both policy-oriented and constituency-oriented members (see Chapter 4). Because of its jurisdiction over technology and energy research issues, its popularity increased noticeably during the 1970s. Not surprisingly, its staff is something of a hybrid. Separate subcommittee staffs have been developed, and they enjoy modest independence. But full committee aides carefully screen all professional subcommittee staff for their substantive expertise before appointment, a practice that helps to maintain a more unified staff identity.

In contrast to policy committees, the remaining constituency (and undesired) committees of the House have smaller, more centralized staffs—reflecting their more limited and less fragmented jurisdictions. Only Small Business and Interior have clearly decentralized staff structures, and only Merchant Marine has more staff at the subcommittee level than at the full committee level. Public Works has a large staff, the fifth largest in the House in 1982, reflecting its broad jurisdiction, but even it has more full committee staff than subcommittee staff.

These constituency-oriented committees also have been the slowest to change their staff patterns, even though they have moved in the direction of decentralized staffing. Five of the eight constituency committees had virtually no subcommittee staff in 1970 and a sixth, Armed Services, had staff for only one subcommittee. Today, only one of these committees, Armed Services, remains without distinct subcommittee staff, while a second, Agriculture, has a single "consultant" for each of its eight subcommittees. Despite these changes, constituency committees are still much less likely than policy committees to have a highly decentralized staffing pattern.

Agriculture provides a good example of these tendencies. While W.R. "Bob" Poage chaired the committee, staff resources were closely controlled. Subcommittee chairs could call on the full committee staff for assistance, but Poage reinforced his power by keeping the staff small and therefore busy with full committee duties. Since Poage left, neither Tom Foley of Washington nor Kika de la Garza of Texas has allowed expansion of subcommittee staff within the committee. Each subcommittee has only a single staff assistant, and even clerical support is provided at the full committee. Through the 98th Congress, subcommittee staff shared a single crowded office. Subcommittee chairs who need more assistance must request help from the full committee chair and staff, who may assign subcommittee duties to full committee aides for limited periods of time. The staff is certainly less centralized than in years past, but its structure is distinctly different from that of the policy committees.

Staffing patterns on the prestige committees of the House are less uniform and distinct. In each case, full committee staff outnumber subcommittee staff. But Appropriations has a clearly decentralized staff structure. And Rules, because of its narrow, intrachamber functions, has a small staff. (On each of these committees, the staff is supplemented by assistants appointed by each rank-and-file member to aid in his or her committee work.) Members' goals help to reinforce staffing patterns on the prestige committees because each produces an important intrachamber product. Staff expertise, important to ensuring the technical quality of committee legislation, continues to be a top priority on all three committees. Appropriations, which traditionally has had a decentralized staff organization but centralized hiring, has become more decentralized as it has become a more parochial panel. After the introduction of subcommittee self-selection, the practice of periodically rotating staff members to new subcommittees was discontinued. Subcommittee staff members therefore became more closely tied to subcommittee leaders, reinforcing the increased parochialism among members.

Despite reforms, especially the requirement to create subcommittees, Ways and Means continues to be a centrally staffed committee. In large part, this is because tax matters still are handled at the full committee level rather than at the subcommittee level. Chairs of Ways and Means since Wilbur Mills have increased staff expertise on the committee staff rather than depend as exclusively on the Joint Committee on Taxation's staff as Mills did. Typically, these new specialists have been kept tied to the full committee rather than distributed to Ways and Means' six subcommittees. The Rules and Budget Committees also remain centrally staffed.[12]

The relationship between rank-and-file members' goals and committee staff organization is weaker in the Senate than in the House. Two related factors appear to account for this difference. First, there is a greater dispersion of control over committee staff in the House as a result of the reforms of the 1970s. Consequently, the personal objectives of more members directly shape the functions of House staff. Senate committee staff, as we have seen, generally remain more firmly under the direct supervision of chairs, ranking minority members, and top full committee aides, while individual senators control considerable independent personal staff resources.

Before personal staff resources were expanded, this tendency towards centralization was the source of some friction among senators. Too often, it was argued, committee staff simply served the political interests of the committee chair by performing constituent services or, as noted earlier, by performing as a surrogate presidential campaign staff.

Sen. Mike Gravel, a Democrat from Alaska, asserted in 1975 that he and fellow Democrats Quentin N. Burdick of North Dakota, George S. McGovern of South Dakota, and Gaylord Nelson of Wisconsin all left the Interior Committee partly because of Henry Jackson's refusal to share the committee's staff. Said McGovern:

> I felt really frustrated ... I didn't feel we had the kind of dynamic, creative people there that we needed ... I did not feel that the committee was adequately staffed. And maybe if we had been I'd have been more reluctant to leave it.[13]

In the Senate, committees such as Judiciary, Labor, and Governmental Affairs still attract some members, independent of other criteria, because they have plentiful staff resources.

Second, rank-and-file senators have greater personal staff support to lean on for assistance in committee activities, reducing their interest in molding committee staff to meet their needs. Many Senate subcommittee chairs supplement their committee staffs with personal staff to assist them in preparing for hearings and other committee business. Indeed, personal staffs is often indistinguishable from committee staff for many senators, as responsibilities are shifted back and forth between the two groups. While this occurs occasionally in the House, it is far less common. Nevertheless, the most decentralized Senate staffs belong to policy-oriented committees (Judiciary and Governmental Affairs), and three other Senate committees, Appropriations, Budget, and Finance, have staffing patterns very similar to their House counterparts', while having similar but not identical balances of members goals.

Staff Roles

The informal roles played by committee staff also are influenced by member goals. David E. Price and later Michael J. Malbin described two primary roles in their research on committee staff.[14] Staff "professionals" view their roles as supportive of corporate committee goals rather than of a single member or a specific policy initiative. They tend to stay with the committee longer, seeking career advancement within the committee. Staff "entrepreneurs" tend to be linked to a single member and his or her legislative goals, to their own objectives, or both. They also tend to view their committee job as a steppingstone rather than as a career in itself. Thus turnover is higher among entrepreneurs than among professionals.

Not surprisingly, professionals are disproportionately attracted to constituency-oriented committees. Constituency committee members, whose immediate goal is to create a quality product for their constituents and whose attentiveness to committee activities often is limited to their own constituency-related concerns, seem to prefer a small, professional staff that can help control quality. They can be trusted to look out for members' interests. Such career-oriented staff tend to have more experience and contacts with related agencies and groups. The agriculture, armed services, and veterans committees, for example, all have staff members recruited from related departments and associations. Of course, the clarity and homogeneity of the legislative goals of constituency committees make it possible for committee staffers to develop a professional relationship with most members. Such a relationship helps a staff member survive member turnover.

In contrast, staff activists who constantly survey the political landscape for new ideas and issues and eagerly pursue hearings and investigations are well suited to policy-oriented members. They may be dangerous for the member more exclusively concerned about reelection. It is common for policy-oriented members to recruit energetic staff with strong views and ideological commitments so they can reap the benefits of staff activism. Recent graduates from professional and graduate schools are their common recruits. Nonetheless, such staffers have a high rate of turnover; they tend to "burn out" quickly and are often in a position to move to more lucrative jobs in law firms, associations, and executive branch offices after just a few years of "insider" experience in Congress.

An examination of data on committee staff turnover collected by Robert H. Salisbury and Kenneth A. Shepsle supports these observations (Table 7-2).[15] In the House, constituency-oriented committees display a much higher level of staff stability (measured by the amount of time it takes for half the staff to leave the committee) than do policy committees.[16] In the Senate, turnover is again higher on policy committees than on constituent or mixed constituency/policy committees. Overall, staff turnover is noticeably greater in the Senate, and the differences among the types of committees are less pronounced—a pattern that is consistent with the frequent observation that Senate staff are generally more entrepreneurial than House staff.[17]

Committee Chairs and Staff Structures

While committee leaders often share the goals of their committee colleagues, they also are in a position to influence independently the structure and role of committee staff. Full committee chairs are formally

Table 7-2 Average House and Senate Committee Staff Half-Lives, by Committee Orientation, 1962-1978 (*in years*)*

Senate	House
Mean Half-Life of Comm. Staff	Mean Half-Life of Comm. Staff
Policy = 3.75**	Policy = 4.23
Mixed = 4.46***	Constit. = 7.50
Constit. = 4.50	Prestige = 3.75
Undes. = 2.50	Undes. = 3.30

* Note: Salisbury and Shepsle calculated a committee's mean half-life by examining yearly staff cohorts, determining "how many years were required before half the cohort of the given year was no longer associated with the committee," and averaging over each of the years studied. See Robert H. Salisbury and Kenneth A. Shepsle, "Congressional Staff Turnover and the Ties-That-Bind," *American Political Science Review* 75 (June 1981): 393.
** Excludes Budget.
*** Excludes Small Business.

responsible for all staff employed by the committee; at a minimum, they must sign all the payroll paperwork. But in practice, control over staff usually is more widely shared. This is especially true in the House, where subcommittees are guaranteed adequate staffing. Also, the minority party in each chamber now has access to staff resources under its direct control. As a result, several members—committee chairs, subcommittee chairs, and ranking minority members at the full and subcommittee level—regularly influence the use of staff on most committees. Needless to say, this influence varies from committee to committee and is conditioned further by the chamber and caucus rules, agenda, and member goal variables already mentioned.

Most committees now have multiple, distinct staff operations. Some committees, those with distinct subcommittee staff operations, have a series of staff structures, and each is directed by a different member. Minority staffing has further complicated staffing patterns because minority and majority members often take different approaches to organizing and using their staff resources. For example, Democrats on the House Energy and Commerce Committee have a decentralized staff structure with strong, independent, and active subcommittee staff operations. Republicans have established a more centralized staff under the guidance of Rep. James T. Broyhill of North Carolina and his chief counsel. Moreover, the minority staff is made up almost exclusively of lawyers, while the majority staffs are made up of a variety of professionals—economists, lawyers, and engineers, for example. In general, minority staff operations are far more centralized than are majority staff operations. The lack of rules requiring the dispersion of staff, the inability of minority members to use staff to organize investigations or hearings without majority approval, and the political advantages of developing coherent opposition strategies all seem to contribute to the centralization of minority staff activities.

As indicated, the House and Senate differ in the extent to which full committee chairs can influence staff structure. The continuing significance of Senate full committee chairs in shaping staff use is illustrated by the shifting staffing practices of the Appropriations Committee. Under John McClellan of Arkansas and his full committee staff director, James Calloway, Senate Appropriations had a strong, centralized staff operation with little subcommittee staff autonomy. Most political matters were controlled by the full committee staff, while technical policy matters were handled by subcommittee staff. The transition to Sen. Warren Magnuson of Washington changed all this. Magnuson, more interested in home state and policy matters of personal interest, paid much less attention to the committee's intrachamber reputation and its crucial role in the budget process. The result, according to staff members who worked for the committee under both chairs, was a deterioration in the committee's ability to sustain its decisions on the floor. According to some, this was caused by Magnuson's laissez-faire approach and the weakening of the full committee staff. Instead of scrutinizing the work of subcommittees and preparing for floor debate, Appropriations' central staff became much more oriented toward Magnuson's personal interests, while drafting and floor preparation went to the subcommittee staff. Rather than produce legislation representing a collective full committee judgment, therefore, Appropriations increasingly developed a separate legislative product in each subcommittee. Subcommittee legislation was greatly affected by the uneven quality of separate subcommittee staffs and subcommittee leadership. On Appropriations, therefore, staff arrangements (and, in turn, staff influence) changed noticeably each time the chair changed.

The influence of Senate chairs remains far from absolute, however, and they often find it difficult to overcome the inertia of staffing practices. Sen. Frank Church of Idaho experienced this problem after Alabama Democrat John J. Sparkman's comparatively weak stewardship of the Foreign Relations Committee. And, more recently, Republican Mark Hatfield has had the same problem with Senate Appropriations in trying to recentralize committee staffing after taking over. Sen. William Proxmire of Wisconsin did not even attempt to centralize the minority staff on Appropriations during the 97th Congress when he assumed the ranking minority position and had only a single staff professional at the full committee level. In part, this was due to the decentralized structure he inherited from Magnuson; but it was also because Proxmire believed the minority staff on Appropriations had so few functions that fighting staff battles would have achieved little anyway. Apparently, not all of his Democratic colleagues agreed. At the beginning of the 98th Congress, John C. Stennis exercised his higher seniority ranking to take the ranking minority slot from Proxmire and moved his longtime Armed Services staff aide, Francis Sullivan, over to Appropriations. According to Senate staff members, this move, coupled with Henry Jackson's subsequent move up on Armed Services, was intended to provide greater conservative influence on defense spending policy than Proxmire was providing for the minority party Democrats.

Despite these counterexamples, a strong leader with clear ideas about how to organize a Senate committee staff can exert powerful influence on the size, organization, and role of that staff. New chairs often are aided by other breaks in the continuity of staffing practices. Staffing rules in the House allowed some minority leaders, such as James Broyhill on Energy and Commerce, to fashion new staffing operations. Committee leaders suddenly had larger staffs with more flexibility in organizing staff than was normally the case. In the Senate, the shift to Republican control allowed for some similar alterations but for slightly different reasons. Majority status bestowed on new Republican chairs much greater staff resources than they had enjoyed as the minority party. And party turnover, in itself, provided an unusual opportunity to mold new majority staffs. Thus, even with pressures to cut staff positions below previous levels, the new chairs were able to design essentially new staff organizations. The centralization and implementation of a management-by-objectives staffing procedure on Senate Commerce by Bob Packwood of Oregon and his chief counsel, William M. Diefenderfer, is a good example of such influence.

Once again, the Salisbury and Shepsle data are instructive (Table 7-3). For both the House and the Senate, committee staff turnover in years when there is a change in the full committee chair is higher than in years without the chair turnover. This difference is particularly noticeable on policy committees where closer ties between chairs and staff "entrepreneurs" are to be expected. Interestingly, chair turnover seems to have less effect on Senate constituency and mixed constituency/policy committees than it does on House constituency committees.

Table 7-3   The Effect of Chair Turnover on Average House and Senate Committee Staff Turnover, by Committee Orientation: 1962 to 1978.

Type	Base Change	Year of Change	Difference
House			
Policy	20.8	34.6	13.8
Prestige	16.3	41.3	25.1
Constituency	16.8	24.8	8.1
Undesired	22.8	50.3	27.5
Senate			
Policy	22.3*	38.6*	16.3
Mixed	16.3	27.0	7.7
Constituency	20.6	18.2	-1.4
Undesired	27.5	54.0	26.5

* Excludes Budget and Judiciary.

Source: Robert H. Salisbury and Kenneth A. Shepsle, "Congressional Staff Turnover and the Ties-That-Bind," *American Political Science Review* 75 (June 1981): 388-389.

In part, this is explained by the fact that there is greater staff turnover in the Senate than in the House; as a result, Senate chair turnover has less special effect. In any case, a new committee chair generally is afforded the opportunity to shape his or her committee by filling a number of staff vacancies.

The Consequences of Changing Staffing Patterns

In this study, staffing patterns are treated primarily as a product of reform, agendas, members' goals, and leadership. Staff are also an important causal agent in congressional and committee politics. "We see the committee staffs determining priorities," says House Republican James M. Collins of Texas. "We must put an end to this growth and return policymaking to the elected membership."[18] Democratic Sen. William Proxmire adds:

> Senators and staff are now stumbling all over themselves. Additional staff generates additional bills and additional work, much of it unneeded at a time when Congress has difficulty coping with its regular routine and oversight functions.[19]

219

Staff do much of the research, organizing, writing, and bill drafting that go on in committees. They influence and often expand committee agendas. They have authored and opposed major reforms. They have encouraged and supported member and leadership goals. And, while opinion is divided on the question of whether committee staff have been a help or a hindrance, they have expanded greatly Congress's institutional resources. The consequences of changing staffing patterns are examined here in three areas: deliberation among members of Congress, personal staff influences, and committee operations.

Deliberation

Malbin argues that staff have become far more than mere assistants to members of Congress.[20] They also have become agenda setters, policy initiators, negotiators, and Congress's chief investigators. That is, staff have become more activist and entrepreneurial. By doing so, Malbin complains, staff increase the legislative workload more than they help to manage it, assume functions members are more qualified to perform, and reduce the personal interaction between members that otherwise helps them to better understand political problems and to resolve conflict. Many senior committee aides agree. One Senate staff member observed: "The members gladly seize opportunities to lighten their workload," even if it means turning their own role into one of ratifying staff arrangements. He added that the process "might be good for the individual member, but probably is not good for representative government." Malbin correctly indicates that senators depend more on staff in these ways than do House members, but the House is becoming more like the Senate in this regard.

While Malbin's case studies of committee staff activities are convincing, he may overstate the significance of staff in the decline of the quality of congressional deliberation. Several additional contributing factors must be examined. The increasing demands of campaigns (especially in the Senate), the opening of committee hearings and markups, the decline of apprenticeship expectations, and the greater individualism of members also play a role in reducing the number of direct, serious discussions between members. To a large extent, the rise of entrepreneurial staff is only a symptom of underlying changes in the membership and in the decision-making process.

Moreover, as Malbin implies, the role of committee staff is not uniform across all committees. The more important the issue (and committee), the smaller the role of staff decisions. Thus for low priority committees, such as Veterans' Affairs, the staff's strategy is to minimize demands on members' time by writing legislation themselves and then having the committee members ratify the results. In this light, Malbin's account of a "phantom conference" between the two veterans' committee staffs is not so surprising. In contrast, Malbin's examples of staff work on the (then) Senate Government Operations Committee and the House Commerce Committee demonstrate the interaction of active, committed, and informed members and staff. On highly salient or controversial issues, staff do much of the leg-work but make fewer key decisions. But Malbin is certainly correct that as the number of issues of both great and little significance increases, dependence on staff also increases. Thus, if staff do increase the workload on committees, which is questionable on most constituency-oriented committees at least, then they truly are a major problem.

On many committees, particularly constituency committees such as the Armed Services and Agriculture committees, the influential role of staff has not really changed. Indeed, Malbin's analysis shows why. For constituency committees, a common, professional work product tailored for an ongoing and easily identified clientele must be crafted. These are not the type of committees where policy entrepreneurs are likely to thrive even though changing agendas may bring new clientele groups with new demands into a committee environment. Agriculture, for example, must now respond to clientele groups favoring food stamps. And Armed Services must occasionally deal with new contractors. But clientele committees' outside associations remain fairly static from year to year. Members seek to protect established relationships or to solidify new ones on an incremental basis, rather than to break new policy ground—a trend that would require altered behavior and a staff less oriented to pork-barrel legislative strategies. Nevertheless, these committees' staffs have been and remain influential participants in committee decision making.

In sum, it is not surprising, given Malbin's emphasis on policy committees, that some over generalizations about the effects of expanded staff have been offered. These are precisely the committees where all of the other factors discussed in this book are most conducive to member activism, staff entrepreneurship, and multi-staged decision making.

Personal Staff Influences

Like committee staff, personal staff in Congress have grown dramatically in the last 20 years: from 3,800 in 1960 to almost 13,000 in 1980.[21] Not surprisingly, these increases have allowed them to turn more and more to legislative—and thus committee—matters.[22] Committee staff frequently complained to us that personal staff involvement has made their jobs harder and has proven to be a general hindrance to the legislative process. They identify three related influences on member behavior.

First, committee staff in both the House and the Senate argue that personal staff have insulated members from each other and from the committee staff. A common lament is that rather than get a common "professional" briefing from committee staff on committee matters, members receive incomplete and sometimes incorrect information from their staff assistants. The information provided may be independently derived or it may be a condensed version obtained from the committee staff. In either case, the committee staff feels this buffer cuts down on their access to committee members and thus hinders the flow of information to them. Closely tied to this complaint is the belief that members also interact less with one another. Instead, their personal staff tend to interact in their places. In the view of committee aides, personal staff, not committee staff, are more responsible for the decline of deliberation.

Second, committee staff believe that many members are "programmed" by their personal staff. The scene of committee members shadowed by personal staff during committee hearings is a source of many complaints. Both committee chairs and staff believe this has cut down on the productivity of committee meetings, that it has encouraged absenteeism, and that members have been encouraged simply to parrot questions rather than digest issues personally and to engage in productive policy discussions. A few chairs have attempted, without much success, to limit personal staff attendence at committee meetings. And one disgruntled committee staff director claimed to have stopped attending committee hearings because they had deteriorated to such a degree that his presence made no difference.

A third consequence of the increasing dependence on personal staff is that members may be less well prepared. Members, always pressed for time, have added to their workloads but have delegated much of their work to their personal staffs. Some House members and staff believe that this has weakened the chamber's special strength, its norm of member specialization. Instead, most observers agree, many House members have become generalists with multiple responsibilities but reduced expertise. Because they are so dependent on staff, one staff director told us, individual members are less capable of defending House positions in conference, a traditional strength of the House.

These committee staff criticisms are consistent with Malbin's thesis, of course, although Malbin supported his argument by case studies of committee staff. The role of personal staff reflects and reinforces increasing individualism in Congress. But here, too, care must be taken not to overgeneralize. The role of personal staff in legislative decision making remains greater in the Senate than in the House. Moreover, interviews with committee staff suggest that there is an inverse relationship between the significance of committee staff and the significance of personal staff. It is on the committees where rank-and-file members are pursuing their individual policy interests that personal aides are most useful. As a result, personal assistants play a major role in developing significant amendments to legislation on committees such as House Energy and Commerce and Senate Labor. They play a much less significant role where their principals have less interest and where they have less incentive to take the initiative—such as on the more constituency-oriented committees where interests common to committee members can be adequately protected by committee staff. Unfortunately, more systematic and complete data are not available to substantiate this observation.

Committee Operations

Committee members and staff believe that enlarged staffs have had both adverse and beneficial effects on committee operations. Members feel that committee staff have strengthened the ability of Congress's work groups to compete with and oversee the executive branch. They also feel that Congress's committees are now in a better position to handle an expanded and more technically challenging workload in a reasonably effective and intelligent fashion. Finally, most members enjoy having added resources at their command. Indeed, several House and Senate staff aides argued that enlarged staffs had attracted members to their committees.

Staff effects on committee operations have not all been positive, though. In 1979, 62 percent of the member respondents to a survey by the House Select Committee on Committees (the Patterson Committee) felt that House committee staffs were generally too large.[23] Two things in particular drew fire from both members and staff in our interviews. First, as subcommittee staffs have expanded, some full committee staffs have lost an active role in many committee activities, especially in the House. In fact, some House full committee staffs have been thrown into the position of performing administrative duties and occasionally providing back-up support for subcommittee staff. On a few committees,

House Post Office and Civil Service for example, this has allowed the full committee staff to retain some influence. On balance though, full committee staffs have been forced into a more administrative role while subcommittee staff do most of the substantive work. In the Patterson survey, 62 percent of the House respondents also thought that subcommittee staff contributed to fragmentation and unmanageability in the House subcommittee system.[24]

As a result of this shift in staff responsibilities, it is more likely that prime staffing responsibility for a measure will be in the hands of less experienced, more transient, and more narrowly focused individuals. As one Senate staff director put it:

> They view their tenure as a short experience—perhaps three or four years. They see the job in terms of working on a specific task, getting it through the Senate, and then moving on to another job in Washington with a government agency, law firm, or private business.[25]

This has several consequences according to senior committee aides. One is that Congress's "institutional memory" is much shorter, making the odds of repeating past mistakes much higher. And substantive work is more likely to be in the hands of staff members who do not have a long-term commitment to the committee. As one full committee aide put it: "They don't have to live with the consequences of what they do." This reinforces the effect, noted in Chapter 5, of unstable subcommittee membership. Finally, and most importantly, critics argue that subcommittee staff are less likely to know or to be concerned about nonsubcommittee members. Thus they are less likely to be in a position to develop committee-wide support for a measure than are senior full committee aides.

A second major complaint is that separate subcommittee staffs have created an environment where interstaff disputes arise easily. If nothing else, subcommittee staff introduce additional career and other personal interests that may complicate committee decision making. Some full and subcommittee staff point with pride to their ability to "get along" with each other, while others (Labor in the Senate and Energy and Commerce in the House are prominently mentioned) suffer from frequent staff conflicts. With or without other barriers, staff infighting makes consensual, coherent decision making much more difficult.

Finally, minority staff have been viewed as something of a mixed blessing. Most minority party members and their staff praise the advent of minority staffing as a long overdue sharing of resources. Others claim that new minority staffs occasionally have encouraged and reinforced partisanship among members where none previously existed. Increased partisanship, it is said, slows down committee decision making, reduces floor success rates, and adversely affects personal relations among members. On some committees, such as House Post Office, House Veterans' Affairs, Senate Environment and Public Works, and even some subcommittees, such as the State-Justice and Energy and Water Subcommittees of the Senate Appropriations Committee, no real fallout has occurred. Even on these committees staff members seem to go out of their way to note that partisan staffing has not caused them any problems.

Conclusion: The Structure and Implications of Expanded Staffs

Congressional committee staff have evolved dramatically since 1970. Committee staff have evolved from small, centralized, support groups to relatively complex suborganizations of Congress. Statutes and chamber and caucus rules directly affect staff size and structure. In the House, these rules have allowed larger staffs and minority staffs and have ensured the virtually universal adoption of subcommittee staff. In the Senate, these rules have provided for larger staffs (though cutbacks were forced by Republicans in the 97th Congress) and some new or larger minority staffs, but did not mandate subcommittee staff. Thus House rules have limited variation in committee staffing patterns by circumscribing committee options to a greater extent than do Senate rules.

Chamber rules, committee agendas, member goals, and leadership preferences further shape the size, organization, and roles of committee staff. Because each works within the limits prescribed by the rules, each of these variables explains a proportionately smaller amount of the interchamber and intercommittee differences in staffing. Overall, it has been shown, Senate committee staff have been somewhat less affected by rules and member goals than House staff. Committees in both chambers have been shown to be affected by agendas and by committee leadership—with Senate full committee chairs more free to influence the organization or role of staff. Finally, it has been shown that committee staff have affected member behavior and committee operations in a significant fashion.

In sum, staff have significantly altered the behavior of members and the operations of committees. They have put the legislative branch on a more equal footing with the executive, but they also have distanced legislators from some aspects of legislative decision making. For many, the drawbacks have outweighed the benefits and there is considerable sentiment, even among staff, that committee staffs have become too large and too powerful.

NOTES

1. See, respectively, *Business Week*, March 27, 1978, 90; *Washington Post*, January 18, 1981, A1; and *Washington Post*, February 12, 1980, A1.
2. Irwin B. Arieff, "Growing Staff System on Hill Forcing Changes in Congress," *Congressional Quarterly Weekly Report*, November 24, 1979, 2631.
3. On the development of committee staffs see: Gladys M. Kammerer, *The Staffing of the Committees of Congress* (Lexington: The University of Kentucky Press, 1949); Kenneth T. Kofmehl, *Professional Staffs of Congress* (Lafayette, Indiana: Purdue Research Foundation, 1962); Harrison W. Fox, Jr., and Susan Webb Hammond, *Congressional Staffs: The Invisible Force in American Lawmaking* (New York: The Free Press, 1977); Michael J. Malbin, *Unelected Representatives: Congressional Staff and the Future of Representative Government* (New York: Basic Books, 1980); and U.S., Congress, House, Select Committee on Committees, "Congressional Staffing, 1947-1978," *Final Report*, 1979, 531 ff.
4. Cranston is quoted by Stephen Isaacs, *Washington Post*, February 16, 1975. Reprinted in U.S., Congress, Senate, Temporary Select Committee to Study the Senate Committee System, *Hearings*, July 20, 21, and 22, 1976, 273 ff.
5. *Hearings*, 106.
6. Stephen Isaacs, *Washington Post*, February 18, 1976. (Reprinted in *Hearings*, 283.)
7. See Roger H. Davidson and Walter J. Oleszek, *Congress against Itself* (Bloomington: Indiana University Press, 1977), 239-241.
8. For further information on the subject of committee personnel and committee office management, see David W. Brady, "Personnel Management in the House," and Susan Webb Hammond, "The Management of Legislative Offices," in *The House At Work* (Austin: University of Texas Press, 1981) ed. Joseph Cooper and G. Calvin Mackenzie, 164-177, 186-189.
9. This account is drawn from U.S., Congress, House, Committee on Science and Technology, *Toward The Endless Frontier: History of the Committee on Science and Technology, 1959-79* (Washington, D.C.: Government Printing Office, 1980).
10. The House Budget Committee is exempt from this rule.
11. David Brady in "Personnel Management in the House," suggests that committee personnel practices should be related to members' goals, but he does not test this hypothesis.
12. On Budget Committee staffing in the House and Senate see Allen Schick, *Congress and Money: Budgeting, Spending, and Taxing* (Washington, D.C.: The Urban Institute Press, 1980).
13. Stephen Isaacs, *Washington Post*, February 18, 1975. (Reprinted in *Hearings*, 283.)
14. The roles were first described by David E. Price in "Professionals and 'Entrepreneurs': Staff Orientations and Policy Making On Three Senate

Committees," *Journal of Politics* 33 (May 1971): 316-336. Malbin adopts the terms for his analysis in *Unelected Representatives*.

15. Robert H. Salisbury and Kenneth A. Shepsle, "Congressional Staff Turnover and the Ties-That-Bind," *American Political Science Review* 75 (June 1981): 381-396.

16. Prestige committees have even higher levels of turnover. But this low level of staff stability is accounted for primarily by the Appropriations Committee, which has a staff half-life of only 2.5 years, compared with Ways and Means, which has a half-life of 6.0 years. Rules lies roughly in the middle with a 4.3 year half-life.

17. See Malbin, *Unelected Representatives*, and Price, "Professionals and 'Entrepreneurs.' "

18. Arieff, "Growing Staff System," 2638.

19. Ibid., 2643.

20. See Malbin, *Unelected Representatives*, Chaps. 1 and 10.

21. Arieff, "Growing Staff System," 2631-2654. Figures for 1980 are from Roger H. Davidson and Walter J. Oleszek, *Congress and Its Members* (Washington, D.C.: CQ Press, 1981), 238.

22. See Steven H. Schiff and Steven S. Smith, "Generational Change and the Allocation of Congressional Staff," *Legislative Studies Quarterly* 8 (August 1983): 457-467.

23. U.S., Congress, House, Select Committee on Committees, *Final Report*, 1980, 285.

24. Ibid., 285.

25. Arieff, "Growing Staff System," 2634.

Party Leaders and Committees | 8

Party leaders play an important role in shaping, managing, and servicing their chambers' committee systems. Reformers have understood this point and frequently have sought to strengthen the role of party leaders to overcome the negative effects of independent committees with large resources and confusing jurisdictions. As recently as 1976, for example, several prominent political scientists writing for the Senate reform committee encouraged Senate parties to use their internal policy committees to provide policy analysis, develop party policy positions, and coordinate the work of committees. The hope was that through these party organs leaders could better focus the Senate's agendas and minimize duplication of effort, neglect of certain policy problems, and conflict among committees.[1] This chapter takes a step beyond the model of committee change to consider the interaction between committees and their organizational partners, party leaders.

Leaders' Goals

As it does in the case of rank-and-file members, understanding the motivations of party leaders helps us to explain their decisions and actions. Like other members, individual leaders are motivated by a blend of constituency, policy, and influence or prestige goals. But, as Barbara Sinclair has noted, leaders are charged with additional responsibilities that originate in the expectations of rank-and-file members.[2] The two responsibilities, translated into operational goals, are policy victory and party harmony.

The policy-victory goal applies to legislative efforts that are important to a large number of members; it seldom applies to matters of concern to only one or two committees. Concern about the collective reputation of a party is the usual stimulus for leadership action.[3] Policy victories require building majority coalitions at both the committee and floor stages in the legislative process. And at times they require large majorities to overcome filibusters and presidential vetoes or to push through constitutional amendments. Leaders' success in attaining policy victories is determined primarily by the size of the two parties and the cohesiveness of those parties on the issues at hand.[4] Within the constraints of party size and cohesiveness, leaders' success depends on the stock of political resources at their disposal and their use of those resources in moving their chambers to act as they wish.

Party harmony is largely a matter of "keeping peace in the family," explains Sinclair.[5] Leaders, especially elected ones and those seeking higher positions, seek to minimize conflicts between party colleagues out of self-interest. Conflicts between members often stem from their desire to get reelected, a desire that sometimes leads to competition for committee assignments or to differing policy objectives. Servicing these individual needs helps the party maintain or attain majority party status and, by doing so, assists members in achieving their policy and prestige goals. Thus "accommodation" is the operative rule party leaders mention when describing many of their duties, reflecting their conscious goal of meeting members' demands and thereby enhancing party harmony.

In most circumstances the two goals are mutually reinforcing.[6] Policy victories for the party help to reduce the number of complaints about dissenting factions within the party; good relations among party colleagues improve the chances that the necessary support can be developed on a significant policy matter. And yet there are times when the two goals pose difficult choices for leaders. Leadership support for a particular position on a divisive issue may alienate segments of the party, while acquiescing to a dissident faction's demands for access to key positions of power may reduce the chances of policy victory. Tension between the two goals is great when there are issues that divide the party, when members have many opportunities to pursue their separate interests, when jurisdictional ambiguities are present, or when the restraining norms of deference to senior members and intercommittee reciprocity are weak.

Our interviews with leaders and staff of the two parties in both chambers indicate that policy victory and party harmony are widely shared goals, although differences between parties and chambers provide varying and changing opportunities for and constraints on pursuing these goals. It is therefore important to distinguish among the four sets of leaders when considering leadership interaction with committees. Three components of committee-leadership interaction are considered: (1) committee size and assignment decisions, (2) leadership involvement in committee decision making, and (3) floor scheduling and strategy.

Committee Sizes and Assignments

Potentially, party leaders' most important involvement in their chambers' committee systems occurs at the beginning of every Congress when two related sets of decisions must be made: committee sizes and party ratios must be set, and, once the number of vacancies is determined for each committee, individuals must be assigned to particular committees. These size and assignment decisions create opportunities for party leaders to influence the long-term composition of committees. They also frequently require choices that directly affect leaders' policy victories and party harmony goals.

Committee Sizes

Committee sizes are set in each chamber's rules at the beginning of each Congress. Party ratios on committees are not set in chamber rules; ultimately, majority party leaders merely inform their minority counterparts how many seats will be allocated to the parties. In most cases, however, sizes and party ratios usually are set only after consultation between majority and minority party leaders. Majority party leaders, as an aide to Speaker Tip O'Neill explains,

> generally try to accommodate the minority's requests for seats when there's no apparent cost to us. After all, they can score political points against us if we cheat them out of too much.

The minority, especially in the Senate, can be irritatingly obstructionist if it believes it has been slighted by the majority.[7] Thus party ratios on most committees are close to the chamber-wide party ratio. The important exceptions are in the House, where Democrats have reserved extraordinary majorities on Appropriations, Rules, and Ways and Means.

The most dramatic feature of leaders' committee-size decisions is the tendency to increase the number of seats available. Although the number of standing committees remained remarkably stable between 1947 and 1982 (a net gain of three House committees and one Senate committee occurred), the total number of standing committee seats grew from 482 to 746 in the House and from 201 to 282 in the Senate. The increases in Senate committee seats in recent Congresses have required the repeated adoption of exemptions to the 1977 limits on the number of assignments senators may hold. In the 97th Congress, for example, 15 senators served on three or more of the 12 major committees for which a two-assignment limit had been set; at least 16 senators served on more than one minor committee, contrary to the 1977 rule.[8]

In addition to the minority's demands, party colleagues can put pressure on majority leaders to expand committees.[9] One set of pressures comes from members seeking assignments. To the degree that requests for a certain committee outnumber vacancies, requesters and their supporters are pitted against each other, sometimes creating intense conflicts within the party and producing many dissatisfied losers. Similarly, members become discontented when they must be bumped from a committee to reflect a loss of party seats in the chamber following an election. Leaders can minimize these threats to party harmony by increasing the number of seats available on affected committees. Because party leaders know of most vacancies immediately following an election and learn of members' requests by early December, they are in a position to create more seats where needed.

Other potential expansionist pressures are related to the policy-victories goal. Committee chairs, state delegations, and various factions often express concern about their ability to shape certain committees' decisions. In fact, party leaders themselves frequently take an interest in the policy views of prospective members of some committees. At times, ensuring control of a committee may require increasing the number of seats to create slots for allies. And leaders may believe that they can encourage or acquire some members' support by assigning them to coveted committees, a process that requires an adequate supply of seats on those committees. Louis Westefield asserts that congressional leaders

> accommodate member demands for committee positions in order to gain leverage with the members. To gain leverage leaders must guarantee a steady (increasing) supply of resources, i.e., party positions on committees.[10]

There also may be pressures to resist the temptation to expand committees. In terms of their policy interests, leaders may agree with committee chairs and other members who believe that their political causes would suffer if more members were added to certain committees. Sometimes this complaint is based on the observation that increasing the number of majority party seats would require a proportional increase in minority party seats. Moreover, leaders may wish to hoard their assignment resource so that assignments they do grant will retain special significance to recipients. Westefield argues that House leaders are most likely to take this attitude when considering the size of the most important committees, where loyalty is of great political significance to them.[11]

Party leaders also may face counterexpansionist pressure that affects their goal of maintaining party harmony. Leaders often hear pleas from committee chairs who do not want larger, less manageable committees. Other members may not want to share the influence of their committees with a large number of new members. Kenneth Shepsle argues that such a reaction is most likely to occur on the most prestigious or attractive House committees where members are likely to be the most protective of their monopoly over important policy decisions.[12] Leaders also recognize that unlimited expansion would make committees too large to function effectively and would produce chaos for members trying to manage a large number of committee duties. As an assistant to Senate Majority Leader Howard Baker pointed out, "We do have a sense of what's good for senators, even if they don't."

In practice, majority party leaders place far greater emphasis on party harmony than on policy victory when making committee-size decisions. Usually, ultimate policy outcomes are only remotely related to committee sizes; after all, who receives an assignment is more directly related to policy outcomes than is the number of assignments made. When policy concerns are considered, they often are closely associated with harmony concerns because disappointed requesters may be alienated from the leadership. This point was made by a Senate Republican leadership aide who responded tersely to a question about size decisions:

> We care more about angering a senator needlessly and exposing ourselves to his obstinacy on the floor or elsewhere than we do about buying somebody's support by creating another seat.

A House Democratic leadership aide gave an example from the 98th Congress:

> For some reason, the number of seats needed on minor committees was underestimated, and we had members fighting each other for the seats. Few Steering members seemed to know what the problem was, but they did go back and add seats to a couple of committees.

Only majority party leaders have the luxury of making such last-minute adjustments. None of the more than a dozen party leaders and leadership staff queried about committee sizes mentioned gaining leverage over members by expanding committees as Westefield originally suggested.

Several cases of committee chairs and other members expressing a desire to limit or reduce committee sizes for policy-related reasons were uncovered. For example, at the beginning of the 98th Congress, an assignment dispute on Senate Labor and Human Resources arose over the size of the committee. Republican Sen. John P. East of North Carolina, an ideologically conservative member, sought to retain a seat on the committee after requesting and receiving a transfer to another committee and after his Labor vacancy had been filled. Republicans who opposed East's efforts also opposed increasing the size of Labor to accommodate him. The issue was thrown into the lap of Majority Leader Howard H. Baker, Jr., who simply attempted to minimize the open conflict among fellow partisans. Baker eventually gave East his Labor seat by creating another Republican seat. The price paid was that Democrats were given another Labor seat to keep the party ratio in line with the chamber party ratio.

Strong evidence exists that recent House Democratic leaders have expanded committees in response to demands from their members. The first column in Table 8-1 indicates that members' expectations have risen dramatically during the past 25 years. In recent Congresses, freshmen

Table 8-1 Committee Requests and Seats for House Democrats, 1959-1982

Congress	Percent of Freshmen Requesting Two Assignments[1]	Percent of Democrats with Two Assignments[2]	Democratic Committee Seats Per Member	Total Democratic Committee Seats
86	38	32	1.28	364
87	58	37	1.34	352
88	56	43	1.36	352
89	56	43	1.38	407
90	54	50	1.44	355
91	n.a.	55	1.49	361
92	69	63	1.57	398
93	89	93	1.72	412
94	60	83	1.73	503
95	58	93	1.78	520
96	88	95	1.78	490
97	83	96	1.78	432

[1] Calculated from written requests to Democratic leaders. The authors would like to thank Kenneth Shepsle for request data for the 86th to 93d Congresses (91st Congress data were not available). Request data for the 94th to 97th Congresses were collected by one of the authors.
[2] Among the members eligible for two assignments.

seeking only one assignment have been a very small minority, with many of them seeking assignment to an exclusive committee. The second column indicates the percentage of Democrats actually receiving two assignments among those that were eligible for two (those assigned to exclusive committees are not eligible for two assignments). In the 1950s only about a third of all House Democrats had two assignments, but that number rose gradually in the 1960s under Speaker John McCormack and then shot upward in the early 1970s under Speaker Carl Albert. These changes also are reflected in the number of seats per member, which is provided in the third column. With Albert's help, reformers successfully pushed for caucus rules guaranteeing all Democrats two assignments, except for members of the three exclusive committees. Nearly all Democrats now take advantage of that right. The final column in Table 8-1 demonstrates that majority party leaders adjust the number of their own committee seats to electoral gains and losses. The large Democratic electoral gains in the 89th and 94th Congresses, for example, were accompanied by increases in the party's committee seat allocation, while losses in the 90th and 97th Congresses were accompanied by committee seat contraction.

Bruce Ray and Steven Smith have estimated the independent effects of party ratio change, the level of demand, and the countervailing pressure from prestigious committees on changes in committee sizes.[13] Their results are provided in Table 8-2. Pressure from intraparty competition played an insignificant role in the committee-size decisions of Speakers Rayburn and McCormack. Their decisions primarily reflected changes in chamber party ratios. In fact, according to a top assistant to McCormack and Albert, Rayburn and McCormack depended greatly on the Parliamentarian of the House, Lewis Deschler, to work out changes in committee sizes and party ratios at the beginning of each Congress. Deschler's recommendations represented a "fairly automatic process" of transforming committee ratios to the new chamber party ratio. Only for Rayburn did the counterexpansionist pressure associated with committee prestige have a significant effect, although the coefficients are generally in the expected direction.

In stark contrast to its significance for Rayburn and McCormack, competition for seats had a substantial effect on Albert's committee-size decisions, even once party ratio change was controlled. According to the McCormack and Albert aide, Albert deliberately and personally sought to accommodate the demands of new activist Democrats elected in the early 1970s. Under Speaker O'Neill, neither the level of competition nor changes in party ratios had so strong an effect on seat adjustments. O'Neill pays much less personal attention to committee-size decisions

Table 8-2 Determinants of Democratic Committee Seat Decisions, by Speaker (Regression Coefficients)

| Speaker | Chamber Party Ratio Change | Demand | Depressing Effects Associated with Committee Prestige | | R^2 |
			P1	P2	
Rayburn	.82*	.10	−.20	−1.90	.74
McCormack	1.03*	.03	.28	−.61	.91
Albert	.56*	.45*	−.34	−1.02	.49
O'Neill	1.24*	.40	−1.76	−1.78	.26

* $p < .05$

Dependent variable:	difference between the number of Democratic seats on a committee in a given Congress and the number of Democratic seats on that committee in the previous Congress.
Independent variables:	
Party ratio change:	the change in the number of Democratic seats on a committee that a direct translation of change in chamber party ratio would dictate
Demand:	ratio of the number of requests to the number of vacancies
P1:	Demand X committee prestige
P2:	Party ratio change X committee prestige

Note: Excludes Rules and Ways and Means because comparable data are unavailable.

than did Albert, and he places most of the responsibility in the hands of a staff assistant. As Table 8-3 demonstrates, O'Neill has faced substantially fewer requests per vacancy than his predecessors, leaving much less variance in competition to affect committee-size decisions. Clearly, House majority party leaders have changed their approach to setting committee sizes as the nature of demands from rank-and-file members has changed.

Senate committee expansion has not been so great as it has been in the House. The difference appears to be a product of less frequent demands and less vigorous pressure to increase the number of committee seats in the Senate. After the implementation of the Legislative Reorganization Act of 1946, most senators held two standing committee assignments, compared with just one in the House, a difference of one seat per member that remains in the 1980s. Moreover, as indicated in Chapter 4, senators generally are less intensely concerned about their

Table 8-3 Competition for Democratic Committee Seats by Speaker (*by percent*)*

Requests Per Vacated Seat	Rayburn	McCormack	Albert	O'Neill
0-1	40.6	45.3	43.6	71.7
1-2	18.8	26.4	20.0	13.3
2+	40.6	28.3	36.4	15.0
	100.0	100.0	100.0	100.0
(N)	(32)	(53)	(55)	(60)

* The unit of analysis in this table is the individual committee in each Congress during the period for which request data is available. The figures for Rayburn cover the 86th to 87th Congresses only; O'Neill's figures are for the 95th to 97th Congresses.

Source: Calculated from members' committee requests (see Table 8-1, note 1) and vacancies created by retirements, defeats, or committee transfers.

assignments. When expansionist pressure exists in the Senate, it is likely to involve the desire of an individual senator (and his supporters) to gain a seat on a particular committee, usually over and above the standard quota, rather than a more voluminous demand for popular committees that is common in the House. Thus Senate pressure is less frequently complicated by the potential of divisive conflict among requesters. Nevertheless, the number of Senate standing committee seats increased by more than 80 between 1947 and 1982, even though there had been an increase of only four senators and one standing committee during the period.

Committee Assignments

Once committee sizes and party ratios have been set, party leaders must make actual decisions on filling open committee seats. In this section the mechanism for making assignments, assignment criteria, and the effects of recent reforms are examined.

Service on the Committees on Committees. Committee assignments are the responsibility of each party in each chamber, and each has a committee on committees to perform this function (see box, p. 238). In each case, the party caucus and the full chamber must approve the committee lists prepared by the committee on committees. Only Senate Republicans' chief party leader does not chair the committee on committees, but the Republican leader does serve as a voting ex-officio member. House Democrats made the Speaker the chair of their commit-

---

Committees on Committees

The *Senate Democratic Steering Committee* is appointed and chaired by the Democratic floor leader and has about 25 members, as determined by the Democratic conference.

The *Senate Republican Committee on Committees* is appointed by the conference chair, except for top party leaders who sit as ex officio members, and has about 15 members.

The *House Democratic Steering and Policy Committee* is composed of 12 regionally elected members, 8 members appointed by the Speaker, and 10 top party and committee leaders who sit as ex officio members.

The *House Republican Committee on Committees* is composed of one member elected from each state with Republican representation in the House. Decisions usually are made by an executive committee of about 15 members made up of representatives of the largest states and others appointed by the floor leader to represent small states and other party groups. The floor leader chairs the full committee and the executive committee.

---

tee on committees in 1973 and strengthened his role in 1974 when the function was stripped from Ways and Means Democrats and given to the Steering and Policy Committee. In all four parties, other party leaders also now serve on the committee on committees, providing them with opportunities to directly influence committee assignments.

Party leaders also may indirectly influence committee assignment decisions by their role in appointing members to the committees on committees. This is especially true in the Senate where the Democratic leader has the authority to appoint all of the members of the Steering Committee, which makes Democratic appointments, and the Republican leader influences the choices of the party's caucus chair, who has the authority to name the committee on committees for Senate Republicans. Less control over committee on committees members is available to House leaders. For House Democrats, the Speaker appoints only eight of the thirty members of the Steering and Policy Committee; twelve of the members are elected by members from their region, and the remainder are other party leaders and major committee chairs. State delegations elect their representatives—one per state with Republican representation in the House—for the Republican committee on committees, but the Republican leader appoints three or four members to represent small delegations and junior members on the nineteen-member executive committee (98th Congress), which effectively makes assignment decisions for the party.

Although there are opportunities to do so, current party leaders do not attempt to exercise special influence over the vast majority of assignment decisions.[14] In most circumstances, the committees on committees attempt to grant the requests of members seeking assignments under the constraint of the number of vacancies. All four parties operate under the "property-right" norm, which provides that, except in the most unusual circumstances, members retain the assignments as long as they desire.[15] In addition, the parties have adopted formal and informal rules to help ensure that all members are given reasonably good assignments. House Democrats disperse choice seats widely by limiting the members of Appropriations, Rules, and Ways and Means to only one assignment (except Budget members) and by limiting other members to one major committee (see Chapter 4). House Republicans have similar but more informal practices. Senate rules provide that senators may serve on no more than one of the Appropriations, Armed Services, Finance, and Foreign Relations committees, although members of these committees may serve on other committees. Senate parties also guarantee each of their members a seat on one of the top committees before any member receives a second top assignment, a rule known as the Johnson Rule for Democrats (see Chapter 1).[16] Currently, the dominant emphasis is on party harmony and accommodating requests rather than on manipulating assignments for political advantage. Political scientist Charles Jones concludes that

> Such measures as the Johnson Rule, while laudable on other grounds, have made it even more difficult in recent years to employ the committee assignment process for party policy purposes. All Senators are guaranteed major committee assignments regardless of their policy stands.[17]

Nevertheless, party leaders do occasionally make a special effort to place a member on a committee, and they usually succeed. Consider these comments by assistants to House Republican, House Democratic, and Senate Democratic leaders, respectively:

> [Minority Leader Robert H. Michel] can get what he wants. He does the groundwork in advance. It's not a matter of making a special plea during the [Committee on Committee's] meeting.

> Tip [O'Neill] talks to the "boys" ahead of time and sometimes points out that he'd be embarrassed if he didn't get his way. He gets it.

> [Minority Leader Robert] Byrd can get what he wants. You know that he appoints all of the Steering Committee's members.

Party leaders do not make such an effort more than a few times in any Congress, recognizing that frequent demands on other committee on committees members "would wear thin quickly," as one aide put it.

In many of these cases, leaders are not acting in a leadership capacity, but rather they serve as advocates for home state members or close friends. Sometimes they regret such actions. House Majority Leader Jim Wright, for example, went out of his way in early 1981 to support fellow Texan Phil Gramm, who was then campaigning for a Budget Committee assignment. Wright wrote in his diary that Gramm is

> after all, one of "our own." He wants to be friendly and doesn't really understand how his playing to the gallery on proposed budget cuts, etc., can undermine my position. He is energetic, indefatigable, resourceful. He is genuinely interested in the budget process and deserves a chance to work at it. We certainly need people on the committee, particularly this year, who will work. There's one other possible consolation in Phil's being on the committee; as a party to its deliberations, he'll be less likely to undermine the final product of its deliberations on the House floor.

Despite objections from liberals, Speaker O'Neill deferred to Wright, and Gramm was placed on the Budget Committee. History proved Wright's assertions incorrect; Gramm used the assignment to conspire with Republicans against Democratic leaders.[18] In an unusual move, the Steering and Policy Committee did not reappoint Gramm to Budget at the beginning of the next Congress, and Gramm took the opportunity to switch to the Republican party.

Factors Shaping Assignment Decisions. The most obvious and important factor affecting a requester's chances of success is the level of competition for assignment to a particular committee. Statistically, the effect of no other measurable factor compares with the significance of the impersonal competitive situation in explaining assignment outcomes.[19] In large part, then, it is a matter of luck: the number of vacancies and competitors varies from committee to committee and over time. As Table 8-3 indicates, the competition has been less severe for House Democrats in recent Congresses; in fact, during the 95th to 97th Congresses, more than one-fourth of assignment decisions for Democratic freshmen were made by unanimous consent because there were fewer requesters than vacancies.[20] At the beginning of the 97th Congress, the House Democratic Steering and Policy Committee filled the vacancies on 12 of the 21 standing committees by unanimous consent.[21] Thus the assignment process increasingly has become a routine process of accommodating requests for House Democrats.[22]

Other personal and political factors come into play when there is competition, as there always is for the most important committees. In these situations, leaders and other committee on committees members must discriminate among requesters who actively campaign for their support. Many requesters write lengthy memos, which sometimes take the appearance of legal briefs, to convince party leaders of their personal qualifications or political need for certain assignments. The requesters also seek support from their state delegations, key interest group figures, and committee chairs. Party leaders and committee on committees members often serve as arbitrators between members from the same state, region, or faction, who risk dividing their support on the committee on committees. These campaign activities can be the decisive factor in assignment contests.

The range of factors taken into account by committee on committees members has changed little during the past 25 years.[23] Table 8-4 reports a tally of the comments House Democratic Steering and Policy members made in nominating requesters for assignments at the beginning of the 97th Congress.[24] Paralleling findings for the House in the late 1950s, the electoral needs of nominees were the most common argument made on

Table 8-4 Criteria Mentioned by House Democratic Steering and Policy Members Making Nominations to Standing Committees, 97th Congress*

Criterion	N
Electoral needs of member	19
State committee slot	13
Region committee slot (southern)	2
Team player (supports party or leadership)	7
Policy views	6
Seniority	6
Failure to receive another request	6
Responsible legislator	3
Policy expertise	3
General ability and maturity	3
Personal experiences	2
Ideology	2
Endorsements	2
Previous political experience	1
Personal interest	1
Acceptable to committee chairs	1
Served on committee as temporary assignee	1

* This count does not include Steering and Policy consideration of Appropriations and Ways and Means nominees.

their behalf, followed by claims that a particular state or region "deserved" a seat because it was underrepresented on the committee. A nominee's willingness to support the party and its leadership, policy views, seniority, and other personal characteristics also were mentioned. Interviews with House Republican and Senate Democratic members and leadership aides indicate that similar criteria are important in their parties' decisions.

Senate Republicans, however, apply seniority more strictly as a means for resolving competing demands. This helps reduce direct personal conflict among Republican senators, but it also reduces the number of opportunities Republican leaders have to influence assignments. Personal factors normally come into play only when senators of equal seniority are competing for the same seat. For the other three parties, seniority is usually "only weighed in the balance," as a Senate Democratic leadership aide explained. When seniority differences are a factor, it is often one member's previous effort to get an assignment, rather than seniority per se, that is critical.

The desire to accommodate as many members as possible does not apply equally to all committees. This is especially true in the House where the number of members assigned to the top committees is more limited. During the 95th to 97th Congresses, for example, fewer than half of the House Democratic nominees for prestige committees (including Budget) obtained the assignment, compared with three-quarters of constituency committee nominees and more than 60 percent of policy committee nominees. Speaker O'Neill provides "leadership support scores" to Steering and Policy Committee members for nonfreshmen seeking to transfer from one committee to another, nearly 60 percent of whom were seeking an assignment to Appropriations, Budget, or Ways and Means in the 95th to 97th Congresses (Table 8-5). It is impossible to determine how seriously Steering and Policy members take these scores, but in several cases where the scores were not mentioned by the Speaker, Steering and Policy members asked for them.

Majority Leader Wright made clear the significance of leadership support in September 1981 when he announced to the Democratic Caucus that members of the Appropriations, Budget, Rules, and Ways and Means committees would be held to a higher standard of support than other members.[25] Wright's announcement, which helped to prevent immediate disciplinary action against Gramm and other conservative supporters of the Reagan administration's budget and tax cuts of 1981, merely made explicit what generally had been the leadership's attitude about the top committees. Indeed, Ray and Smith have demonstrated that party support was an especially important factor for Demo-

Table 8-5 House Democratic Assignment Nominees by Seniority and Committee Type, 95th to 97th Congresses

Nominated to:	Freshmen	Nonfreshmen	Total
Prestige Committee	41	86	127
Policy Committee	105	26	131
Constituency Committee	147	38	185
	293	150	443

Note: Budget has been included as a prestige committee. Rules is not included because the Speaker makes Democratic Rules appointments. Many members are nominated for more than one committee and in more than one Congress.

cratic assignments to the prestige committees during the 95th to 97th Congresses.[26]

In the Senate, an additional factor is often significant for a Democratic requester: personal membership on the committee on committees. This is seldom a factor in the House, where the committees on committees are a small proportion of all party members. In contrast, the 22-member Democratic Steering Committee (98th Congress) is composed of nearly half of all Senate Democrats. Steering members tend to be fairly senior members who are not seeking new assignments, so there are fewer situations where there is a conflict of interest than there might be. But several participants mentioned instances in which membership on the committee on committees was decisive. In one reported case, a freshman senator had "done all the right things" and had gained the endorsement of a majority of the Steering Committee members. Later, a Steering Committee member decided he wanted an additional assignment—the one the freshman was seeking—and he won it "handily" when assignments to that committee came up.

Effects of the 1974 Democratic Reform. The current Steering and Policy Committee role was established by House Democrats before the 94th Congress.[27] The original 23-person committee included the Speaker (as chair), the majority leader, the caucus chair, eight members appointed by the Speaker, and one member elected from each of the twelve geographic regions. Since then, other party leaders and the chairs of the Appropriations, Budget, Rules, and Ways and Means committees have been added. The 30-member committee of the 98th Congress stands in sharp contrast to the 15-member Ways and Means committee on committees it replaced.

Despite party leaders' opportunities for direct participation, the size and composition of Steering and Policy's membership make it difficult for party leaders to control. The large size undercuts the credibility of individual Steering and Policy members when they attempt to claim responsibility for a requester's success or failure. As a result, the committee's members, including its leaders, gain less leverage over requesters by their actions than did Ways and Means Democrats. The membership of Steering and Policy also is far less permanent than the membership of Ways and Means. Ways and Means members hold their seats as long as they remain members of the House. In contrast, the Democratic Caucus requires that the elected and Speaker-appointed members of Steering and Policy serve for no more than two consecutive terms. When a member with more than 12 years of congressional service leaves, he or she must be replaced by a member with fewer than 12 years of service.

The reform also affected regional representatives' allegiances. Under Ways and Means, Democrats were divided into 15 zones, one per Ways and Means Democrat. Equality in numerical size was not always possible among zones, and zones were not always geographically contiguous. Under the current system the 12 regions (the term "region" replaced "zones") must be geographically contiguous and nearly equal in numerical size. Regional identities are preserved and reinforced by the election of these regional representatives. Thus the bonds between members and their committee on committees' representatives are stronger than before, serve as a potential obstacle to leadership control, and limit the credit that leaders garner in the assignment process.

Not surprisingly, Steering and Policy is not a cohesive group. One member observed, "We are all Democrats in there, but we differ on what that should mean, what the Steering Committee should be doing, and where the party should be heading." Nevertheless, the committee has not had the southern overrepresentation that was present on Ways and Means.[28] But like Ways and Means, Steering and Policy members have had above average support for the party and below average support for the conservative coalition when compared to all House Democrats.[29]

The assignment process has become much more open under Steering and Policy. This is due in part to the increased size of the committee, to the right of every member to either an exclusive or major assignment, and to greater participation by junior members in all party activities. Even more importantly, nomination is no longer a major barrier to appointment.[30] In general, every reasonable effort is made to give a requester an opportunity to compete for preferred assignments. Participants indicate that no requester has had to employ the caucus rule that permits his or her state delegation to force nomination. In fact, according to a senior assistant to Speaker O'Neill, only once has such an approach even been threatened. The monopoly power over nominations once held by Ways and Means zone representatives no longer exists.

The enthusiasm with which an applicant is nominated can vary widely, of course. In the 97th Congress, for example, Louisiana's Buddy Roemer, a freshman who had voted against a procedural motion leading to the adoption of the Democratic version of the House rules, was routinely nominated and routinely rejected for all of his preferred committee assignments. His disloyalty to the party infuriated many Steering and Policy members, but no one objected to his nomination.

The new Democratic assignment process has been accompanied by two changes in its working environment. First, freshmen's expectations about the quality and quantity of assignments to which they are entitled have risen. Second, nonfreshmen have sought and been given fewer committee transfers, largely because they receive better assignments as freshmen and move into positions of power more rapidly than in the past, making a transfer less attractive.[31] Thus under Steering and Policy the assignment duty increasingly focuses on providing seats for freshmen.

Openness and nominal control of the process by elected party leaders have helped to eliminate rumors of manipulation and conspiracy that frequently surrounded Ways and Means deliberations. But there is no strong evidence that the decisions of the committee on committees have changed in any systematic way.[32] The only exceptions are appointments to Rules, which came under the Speaker's direct control, and appointments to Ways and Means itself, which was expanded greatly in size. In many respects, Steering and Policy practices continue a trend, begun under Ways and Means, toward accommodating as many requests as possible.[33] Nor is there any strong evidence that members believe they "owe" their committee assignments to the top two or three party leaders, as some reformers had hoped.[34] Few members have a lasting feeling of gratitude to the Speaker for good assignments. Steering and Policy's size, composition, and environment have all pushed it in the direction of responsiveness to member demands.

The great emphasis placed on accommodating members' requests in size and assignment decisions reflects the significance of the party-harmony goal for party leaders. Not all members are happy with this leadership attitude. One senior House committee chair, for example, complained to us that Democratic leaders have been too accommodating. While he was disturbed by leaders' willingness to give their policy opponents good assignments, he was far more concerned about their tendency to place supporters on requested committees rather than where they were needed most. Indeed, for all four sets of leaders little conscious manipulation of seats for political advantage occurs; exceptions, while important individually, are few in number.

Leaders and Committee Decision Making

Both policy-victory and party-harmony goals dictate that party leaders take an interest in committee decision making. Nearly all of a majority party's policy proposals take shape in committee, even when party leaders take a personal interest in the product. Majority party leaders also are concerned about the timing of committee action on major legislation because they will be responsible for scheduling floor consideration of it. Even minority party leaders follow committee action closely and often encourage committee members to provide effective opposition to the majority; the minority party's best chance of obstructing or modifying the majority's legislation is often in committee. The significance of committee activity to policy making and to members' personal objectives makes intracommittee politics a frequent source of conflict among fellow partisans, which itself can threaten collective party success on policy matters.

Monitoring Committees

Leaders learn of committee activities in a number of ways. All party leaders depend heavily on personal, one-to-one opportunities to talk to committee members on the floor, in their offices, and on social occasions. In many cases, committee members call on leaders to help resolve intracommittee disputes. In other cases, leaders indirectly hear of a recalcitrant subcommittee chair or resistant committee faction that is holding up legislation or that might embarrass the party. All party leaders regularly consult with committee leaders handling legislation perceived to be important to the party. But the top leaders also have other, more regularized means of learning about committee activity.

In the smaller, more individualistic Senate, party leaders have depended on frequent meetings with committee leaders and other members. As majority leader, Democratic Sen. Robert C. Byrd of West Virginia held monthly meetings with committee chairs to keep informed about the progress of legislation, to learn of stumbling blocks that might be overcome with leadership assistance, and to encourage committee chairs to keep their panels moving on priority legislation.[35]

Under both Byrd and his predecessor, Mike Mansfield of Montana, the Democratic policy committee staff, which they controlled, gathered information on a weekly basis on the status and prospects of legislation important to the leadership.[36] Senate Republicans have retained a longstanding practice of holding weekly meetings with party leaders under the auspices of their policy committee.[37] Reports on significant committee activities usually are presented at these meetings and members are given an opportunity to voice concerns about any matter before the Senate, including matters under committee consideration.

In contrast, House Democratic and Republican leaders do not meet regularly with committee leaders as a group. When they do meet, it is seldom to hear reports from chairs; rather, party leaders ordinarily want to communicate directly with chairs about some matter of vital concern to all committees and party leaders. In the 97th Congress, for example, Speaker O'Neill discussed budget politics with committee chairs on several occasions. Leadership aides explained that the large number of chairs and ranking members makes such meetings an inefficient means for keeping leaders informed about matters they really care about. Moreover, a Republican aide explained, "the ranking members often cannot speak for the rest of the boys on the committee," a limitation that applies even more completely to majority party Democrats whose subcommittee chairs are more independent than most ranking Republicans on subcommittees. Furthermore, as one chair indicated, some chairs would resent the leadership's bringing in other chairs to discuss matters falling within their committees' jurisdictions. When House leaders want to involve more members, they often just call a meeting of the full party caucus because there are more than a hundred members in both parties who head subcommittee contingents, a number larger than the entire Senate.

House leaders therefore are more dependent on their staff for regular information about committee activities. Republican leadership aides meet weekly with senior staff from all committees and receive memos from them on committee activity. Republican committee staff believe this procedure gives their committees consistent access to party leaders and helps to keep up morale among committee aides who often find minority party status frustrating. Leadership aides, in turn, digest the committee reports and write a summary, with supplementary comments, for Minority Leader Robert Michel.

Democratic staff efforts to provide regular information to Speaker O'Neill about committee activity have failed in recent years. Under the previous Speaker, Carl Albert, and at times during the first two or three years of O'Neill's speakership, Steering and Policy staff provided weekly reports on committee activity to the Speaker. More recently, however, responsibility for overseeing major issues and committees has been assigned to or assumed by just two or three aides. Most committees' activities are not monitored or reported to the Speaker on a regular basis. Only a few meetings with senior committee staff have been held, and these have been seen as useless by many attending committee aides. Conflicting personalities and distrust of O'Neill's top aides have been part of the problem, but, more importantly, Speaker O'Neill generally has paid little attention to these staff efforts, providing little incentive for leadership or committee staff to take the effort seriously. O'Neill has preferred personal, ad hoc communications with chairs and rank-and-file members to these more formalized mechanisms. Generally, the initiative rests with the committees and their staff to keep the leadership informed about significant developments.

Coordination and Intervention

Monitoring committees is more of a defensive than an offensive activity for party leaders. Monitoring efforts do not constitute a survey of potential opportunities for leaders to intervene in committees. Rather, the information gathered signals leaders about what committees are doing and deciding. This is not surprising because committees place far more demands on leaders than leaders do on committees. In a 1980 survey of House Democratic subcommittee chairs, we discovered that, of the chairs communicating with party leaders about matters related to their subcommittees during the first three quarters of the 96th Congress, more than two-thirds reported that they were responsible for initiating the contact.[38] The content of the communication usually concerned scheduling requests for floor consideration of legislation. Less than 4 percent of the subcommittee chairs indicated that leaders initiated the communication, with the remainder indicating that both leaders and chairs initiated some of the contact.[39] Similarly, Senate Democratic Whip Alan Cranston of California indicates that a Senate leader's role "is just housekeeping now. . . . Occasionally you have an opportunity to provide leadership, but not that often." [40] The overall pattern is one of committee and subcommittee activism and leadership coordination of demands for floor action; it is not one of leadership intervention in committee decision making.

Nevertheless, there are occasions when leaders overtly or covertly intervene in intracommittee politics. For the vast majority of committees, where leaders do not regularly perceive vital party policy concerns, the leadership role is motivated entirely by an interest in party harmony.

Party harmony usually dictates that leaders give committee members room to act as they see fit. But sometimes leaders are called upon to help resolve intraparty disputes that threaten that harmony. The approach taken depends on leaders' personal relationship with the members involved, as House Majority Leader Jim Wright indicates in his explanation of how he deals with problem members:

> You deal with it by dealing with the individual, and the individuals vary. Some of them are capable of being fairly stubborn. If you try to hurry them, it slows down the process. Others are amenable to the kinds of persuasion that urges them on. Some you have to cajole, some you have to praise, some you have to flatter, some you have to threaten—though there is little you can use as a threat.

When leaders do get involved, they frequently prefer to seek the assistance of a friendly committee member to avoid the risk of a backlash against leadership intrusion into committee affairs. A House leadership aide explained that on those occasions when leaders intervene, they often seek "to identify friendly members—this is a political institution. There is a constant interchange going on every day between members and the leadership. We know who our allies are."

In 1981 Speaker O'Neill was called upon to support three members whose positions as subcommittee chairs were threatened. In one case, the full committee chair sought to eliminate a subcommittee; in another case, an incumbent subcommittee chair was challenged; in the third, a member in line to become a subcommittee chair was challenged.[41] O'Neill privately encouraged committee members to give the challenged members the chairs due them by seniority but was successful in only one case. Last-minute appeals to fellow Democrats in a closed session of the party caucus failed to save the other two.

Other instances of leadership intervention have involved scandals and jurisdictional disputes that threatened to disrupt relations within the party and tarnish the party's or institution's public image. For example, when committee "secretary" Elizabeth Ray claimed in 1976 that her main responsibility to House Administration Chairman Wayne L. Hays was to have sexual relations with him, Speaker Albert made it clear to Hays that he wanted him to resign as chair of the party's campaign committee. Albert moved quickly to start an investigation on charges of malfeasance.[42] Speaker O'Neill's inability to convince several House subcommittee chairs to coordinate their investigation of misfeasance at EPA in 1983 (see Chapter 6) exemplifies the problems created by overlapping jurisdictions. In this case, O'Neill was forced to intervene when the chairs' conflicting efforts to gather information and to hold hearings drew adminsitration criticism and threatened to embarass the party. Such interventions are usually unpleasant burdens for leaders. Committee members show little gratitude for most of these activities, even though rank-and-file members frequently demand that leaders step in to protect the party's reputation. And committee members' egos are easily bruised by being called into leaders' offices to explain their activities.

While accommodating demands and maintaining party harmony dominates leaders' relations with most committees, there are a few committees in each Congress that leaders follow closely in pursuing party policy objectives. Usually, leaders' involvement is grounded in a concern for the effect of certain issues on the party's electoral fate and thus is related closely to party harmony and rank-and-file expectations.[43] In recent years, the budget and tax committees have drawn the most leadership attention because of the significance of their jurisdictions on the national agenda. As noted in Chapter 3, other prestige- and policy-oriented committees also regularly attract leadership scrutiny.

Majority party leaders' primary concern, even for major committees on major issues, is the timing and pace of committee action. Political and practical pressures for either slow or swift action constantly concern majority party leaders. But even here, as Wright's statement suggests, leaders can seldom force committee action. Speaking in 1963, then Senate Majority Leader Mike Mansfield expressed a similar point of view:

> What powers do the leaders have to force these committees, to twist their arms, to wheel and deal, and so forth and so on, to get them to rush things up or to speed their procedures? The leaders in the Senate, at least, have no power delegated to them except on the basis of courtesy, accommodation, and a sense of responsibility.[44]

The current majority leader, Sen. Howard Baker, "believes in the committees doing their jobs, and he will push them to move expeditiously, but that's all he can do—push," an aide to Baker explained. The Speaker of the House can use his authority to set time limits on committee consideration of legislation from time to time, but the authority applies only to legislation that is referred sequentially to more than one committee.[45]

Leaders' limited ability to move committees to action (or, for that matter, to a particular action) is grounded in their limited ability to affect members' goals.[46] The most effective tool would be for leaders to hold members' committee assignments hostage, forcing them to risk losing valuable assignments by opposing or obstructing the leadership. Because leaders normally are not free to take assignments away from members, however, this source of leverage is not available. Gaining leverage over members is therefore a matter of affecting members' individual goals. Leaders usually cannot compete with the countervailing pressures of constituency demands on members and, outside of committee assignments, have control over resources that are of only marginal relevance to members' reelection efforts. In any case, reducing fellow partisans' reelection odds is hardly a wise move for leaders seeking to maintain or achieve majority party status. Committee members lose little power or prestige in conflicts with leaders. Conflict may even signal their importance in the House. And leaders do not have much control over these committees' decisions—such as project funding or minor tax code provisions—that make members important to chamber colleagues. Majority party leaders are in the best position to influence policy-oriented members who need the leadership's assistance for scheduling their pet legislation. But leaders are most likely to use their parliamentary tools discriminatingly when their party is not divided on the issue at hand and their help is not needed by party members. In short, because leaders lack the freedom to manipulate assignments, their tools typically are of peripheral significance to committee members.

Nevertheless, when a substantive party interest is seen as relevant, leaders will seek out and discuss policy with committee members. In 1981, for example, Speaker O'Neill convinced Ways and Means Chairman Dan Rostenkowski of Illinois to change his strategy in developing an alternative to the Reagan administration's tax cut proposals. O'Neill also has occasionally met with all Democrats of a committee. Senate leaders seldom call in an entire committee caucus but often will talk to groups of committee members on the floor or phone individual members to encourage them to support a particular policy position. Leaders also are aware that committee members pick up cues from them in their statements in press conferences, floor announcements, and by other means. But, except for House Budget and Rules, two committees where party leaders have a special role, leaders are perceived as outsiders attempting to influence the real decision makers.

Because they have few effective sanctions against committee members, leaders normally emphasize allegiance to the party and future rewards for "good" behavior. Emphasizing common party interests helps to reduce resentment to leadership intervention. When asked about the value of commission appointments, campaign assistance, and other enticements, one House subcommittee chair responded

> these are not important enough for most chairs to switch positions on a matter being considered by their subcommittees. If anything, they are the icing on the cake of some agreement which the leadership and the chairman come to without consideration of other goodies.

251

In fact, the "icing" may not be specified. Wright indicated that the leadership has relatively little to offer, "save the good will of the membership . . . and probably an unspoken measure of support for some objective members may want to pursue in the future." The subcommittee chair echoed this view: "I do my best to accommodate the leadership—not so much out of fear of reprisal or hope for immediate gain, but of the possibility of a favor later on." The future favor may be advantageous scheduling, willingness to do a whip count for the chair, or support for a committee transfer.

Effects of Reform on Leader-Committee Relations

House committee reforms during the 1970s made relations with the committees more difficult and frustrating for majority party leaders.[47] Most obviously, leaders now must deal with a much larger number of members, especially subcommittee chairs, than they did in the 1950s and 1960s. Majority Leader Wright explains:

> The full committee chairmen are not inviolable in their own precincts. They are not the great powers that they once were. They are dependent upon their own members for their election and for the support of their subcommittees for the program. And so, the leadership sometimes has to go beyond the committee chairmen and deal with the subcommittee chairmen. We always try to work with the person who will have responsibility of managing a bill on the floor. Increasingly, that is the subcommittee chair or some person who assumes that responsibility upon the subcommittee chair's appointment. . . . We have to deal with a great many more people than was the case in Mr. Rayburn's or Mr. McCormack's day.

On the controversial issues that involve the leadership, this means that leaders must deal with both subcommittee and full committee members, putting in great time and effort to create a successful coalition at each stage.

Leaders have difficulties beyond merely dealing with a greater number of people at more stages in the process, however. There also is greater uncertainty.[48] Wright continues:

> In Mr. Rayburn's day, about all a majority leader or Speaker needed to do in order to get his program adopted was to deal effectively with perhaps 12 very senior committee chairmen. They, in turn, could be expected to influence their committees and their subcommittee chairmen whom they, in those days, appointed. . . . Well, now that situation is quite considerably different.

Full committee chairs cannot "deliver" their committees for leaders as some committee chairs of the past could. Party leaders now must deal increasingly with subcommittee chairs who are younger and less familiar to party leaders. As a result, from the leaders' point of view, subcommittee chairs are less predictable than full committee chairs. The lack of long-term personal interaction also means that there is less likely to be a strong personal relationship between a leader and a chair that can serve as the basis for influencing the subcommittee chair. And because subcommittee jurisdictions are so narrow, leaders are less likely than they are in their dealings with powerful full committee chairs to be able to offer support on other legislation important to the chair in exchange for his or her assistance on a matter at hand. Even if their actions can be predicted or easily influenced, subcommittee chairs do not control their committee colleagues' decisions.

Leaders' tasks of monitoring and prodding committees have been further complicated by changes in the national agenda that have introduced issues that cut across committee jurisdictions. This has increased the number of committees, subcommittees, and members involved and has made the job of predicting demands on the floor schedule more difficult. It also multiplies intercommittee conflicts that the leadership often is asked to resolve. The House, of course, failed to adopt proposals to significantly realign committee jurisdictions to its new agenda. The 1975 reforms attacked the problem of committee jurisdictions by giving the Speaker the authority to refer legislation to more than one committee or, with the approval of the House, to create an ad hoc committee to handle the legislation. Multiple referral has been employed fruitfully by the Speaker in a few instances, but leadership and committee participants agree that it does not take the place of jurisdictional reform. A top assistant to Speaker O'Neill claimed that multiple referral

> lets us off the hook sometimes by letting us give a bill to everyone that wants it, but the number of times we can use it to manipulate outcomes is very small. It means we can get others involved, but we still cannot avoid some committees.

Committee members and staff also point out that they now expect multiple referral of legislation in areas in which they previously had only a minor jurisdictional claim. In fact, multiple referral has institutionalized the fragmented consideration of legislation in many policy areas and made expeditious House action even more difficult to achieve in some cases.[49] In the 95th Congress, for example, multiply-referred bills were only about half as likely to be reported to the floor and less than a third as likely to pass the House as were bills referred to a single committee.[50] Thus leaders' problems of moving the House to action and maintaining harmony among the competing committees are often more difficult to solve with multiple referral.

Ad hoc committees have not been used often because of committee members' jurisdictional jealousies. An ad hoc committee was used effectively in 1977 for consideration of the Carter administration's energy proposals, but another ad hoc committee on welfare reform failed to overcome conflicting demands from the concerned standing committees. The success of the committee on energy reform resulted from a combination of factors seldom present: a new Speaker desiring to demonstrate his leadership, a new Democratic administration with its reputation at stake, and widespread recognition that dramatic, swift action was needed in the wake of energy shortages and the threat of oil embargoes.[51] In most circumstances, though, ad hoc committees undermine rank-and-file members' efforts to achieve their personal goals through their permanent committee assignments, providing a motivation for strong opposition to leadership efforts to centralize consideration of legislation. Even in 1977, O'Neill found it necessary to sequentially refer the energy legislation to committees with jurisdictional claims before it was taken up by an ad hoc committee.

The role of both Senate and House leaders has been enhanced by the 1974 budget reform, although during the first few years, fiscal policy-making patterns changed little in Congress. The budget process potentially centralized chamber decision making by funneling major policy decisions through the budget resolutions and related legislation. As employed in the 97th Congress (1981-1983), for example, budget resolutions forced standing committees to report to the floor legislation that made major policy changes to reduce federal spending. Both policy-victory and party-harmony goals dictate that party leaders, especially majority leaders, take an active role in budget politics. Most obviously, the perceived significance of budget policy to party electoral fortunes places party leaders in the middle of budget politics.

In the first session of the 97th Congress, Senate Majority Leader Baker deliberately assumed the role of "point man for the administration," as one of his aides explained, pushing Senate committees to meet deadlines and adopt the Reagan administration's program. With a relatively cohesive party, Baker was able to focus on the policy-victory goal. In contrast, Speaker O'Neill faced a sharply divided party in 1981 when he saw that there was little chance of defeating the administration program. Committee members were livid about the budget-cutting instructions imposed on them by both majority and minority budget plans, and liberal Democrats were demanding retribution against party supporters of the Reagan administration's proposals. As a result, O'Neill was forced to place greater emphasis on party harmony than his Senate counterpart, in hopes that the party would regain its strength in the 1982 elections.[52] Baker was placed in a similar position in the spring of 1983 when Senate Republicans were deeply divided over the budget. Instead of serving as the president's representative in the Senate, Baker was forced to represent his divided party colleagues to the White House, hoping to persuade the president to support the necessary compromises to keep the budget process on track.

Overall, then, leaders take a somewhat more policy-oriented role in dealing with committee decision making than they do in committee size and assignment decisions. Given that committee decisions are more immediately relevant to party policy objectives, this is not surprising. Leaders, nevertheless, give most committees great room for action most of the time. This reflects not so much a lack of leadership interest in committee decisions as the fact that leaders and the party's committee members are likely to be in general agreement about the policy action to be taken. There is no need for leadership intervention. Thus, in most circumstances, both policy-victory and party-harmony goals are served by waiting for committees to act before leaders get actively involved.

Floor Scheduling and Strategy

Scheduling legislation for floor consideration is the majority party leaders' most direct and personal responsibility in dealing with committee decisions.[53] In contrast to intervening in committee decision making, which is often viewed as inappropriate for party leaders, exercising leadership discretion at the floor stage is perceived as completely legitimate. Committee members are highly dependent on leaders for timely floor scheduling. Consequently, leaders are most interested in and capable of pursuing party policy objectives at this late stage of the process.

Not coincidentally, the floor stage also provides party leaders with few opportunities to influence the content of legislation. For the most part, "the committee position is the leadership position," a House leadership aide explained, a point of view shared by recent majority party leaders of both chambers. Leaders can encourage their chambers to adopt certain amendments to committee bills, of course, but the difficulty and uncertainty of dealing with a large number of independent members usually is even greater at the floor stage than at the committee stage. Without a more significant role in committee decision making, leaders are not in a position to shape coherent party policy. Commenting on Senate practice, Charles Jones concluded that at present scheduling is designed primarily to accommodate the needs of the standing committees and is not employed as a means for achieving comprehensive policy review. It is questionable whether any such review is even possible to arrange at such a late point in the legislative process. If little or no direction is offered at earlier stages, then legislation arrives at the scheduling point as it will, not necessarily in a sequence facilitating cross-policy analysis or integrated policy development.[54]

The same is true of the House.

Nevertheless, leaders are in a position to enhance or damage committee members' prospects of floor success. Timing of floor debate, making endorsements, using whip polls to learn of support and opposition, assisting leadership staff, giving parliamentary advice, and, in the case of the House, getting a favorable rule for floor consideration can be very important to a bill manager; all are controlled or at least strongly influenced by majority party leaders. Wise committee members are aware that knowing leaders' views early in the bill process and keeping leaders apprised of a bill's progress helps to avoid unexpected delays or opposition at the floor-scheduling stage. An aide to Speaker O'Neill indicated that "the smart ones will be and are in contact with the leadership throughout the bill process."

Leaders' willingness to support a committee or bill manager is strongly affected by their attitude about the policy concerned. When the leadership disapproves of a bill's policy objectives but believes that token support must be given to a committee position, the leadership reaction is often very subtle. A House Democratic Whip assistant noted that leaders will

> let events take their course—by themselves ... hands off. You can be moderate or ardent in support of a position. There's a lot of distance— there's a wide range of enthusiasm with which you can support something.

A Senate leadership aide agreed, "The only real sanction leaders have at their disposal is noncooperation." Neglect is often all that is needed at the floor stage to obstruct a committee or bill manager. Care is taken not to appear too arbitrary, especially at the beginning of a Congress when there is not too much business on the floor. But a cold shoulder from the leadership can kill or delay legislation when reasons can be devised to schedule other legislation.

Leadership cooperation and assistance is more important in the larger House than in the Senate. House majority party leaders' influence over the Rules Committee and control of the whip system to count heads and enlist support are a vital part of House scheduling and floor strategy. Speaker O'Neill also created informal task forces of 25 to 30 members, often at the request of bill managers, to help the leadership and committee members gather support on the floor.[55] In the smaller Senate, bill managers operate far more independently of party leaders, even on major legislation. Under Democratic majority leaders Mansfield and Byrd, bill managers assumed most of the responsibility for polling their colleagues on their bills.[56] Democratic Whip Alan Cranston, who has a reputation among his Senate colleagues for highly accurate polls, assisted bill managers at his own discretion as a favor to friends and ideological allies. Senate Republican majority party leaders during the 97th Congress were more generous in their assistance and more assertive in dealing with legislation on the floor, but they still had less to offer than the House majority party leaders.

In both chambers, floor scheduling and strategy have become more difficult for majority party leaders. The problem in the House is the large number of individuals who make scheduling demands on the leadership as bill managers. A larger number of personalities to be accommodated and a larger number of bill managers with little floor experience have made the task more frustrating.[57] At one point in 1979, a leadership assistant reported, the majority leader's office was several days behind in returning phone calls of members seeking a place on the floor schedule, a highly unusual situation. Such demands give leaders an opportunity to be selective and to use their discretion to their own advantage, but the sheer volume of demands for scheduling often forces leaders to deal with requests in an efficient, administrative manner.

The problem for Senate leaders is that senators' parliamentary moves on the floor have become even less predictable than they were in the 1960s and early 1970s. One Senate aide complained that senators "have always been prima donnas, I guess, but in the 10 years I've been here they've become unpredictable prima donnas—a real danger." Democratic Sen. Joseph Biden, Jr., of Delaware asserted, using his maverick colleague William Proxmire of Wisconsin as an example, that "one Proxmire makes a real contribution. But all you need is 30 of them to guarantee that the place doesn't work."[58] Senators claim that increasing campaign demands, extraordinary demands on their time while in Washington, and the resulting breakdown of personal relations between members have undermined the civility and predictability of senators. Biden continues:

> There aren't as many nice people as there were before. It makes working in the Senate difficult. Ten years ago you didn't have people calling each other sons of bitches and vowing to get each other. The first few years, there was only one person who, when he gave me his word, I had to go back to the office to write it down. Now there's two

dozen of them. As you break down the social amenities one by one, it starts expanding geometrically. Eventually you don't have any social control.[62]

Senate leaders operating in such an environment find it increasingly difficult to predict trouble spots in the consideration of legislation, making their advice and assistance less valuable to bill managers.

Conclusion: Leaders and Changing Committee Politics

Two decades ago, Lewis Froman and Randall Ripley concluded that leadership activity is most likely to occur when it is least likely to be successful: when the issue is substantive rather than procedural, when issue salience is high, when the visibility of the action to be taken is high, and when constituency-related pressures are high.[60] The analysis here further indicates that leaders' policy-victory goal is given the greatest emphasis at the floor stage where leaders' resources are strongest and their intervention is perceived as most legitimate. Unfortunately for party leaders, the floor stage is also the stage at which the leadership is least likely to be able to shape the content of legislation in its effort to create a winning coalition. Leaders are handicapped severely by their inability to manipulate committee consideration of legislation, a problem exacerbated by the changes in committee politics since the late 1960s.

As noted at the beginning of the chapter, strengthening party leaders' tools for shaping and coordinating committee decision making is one of the most frequent themes of reformers both within and outside of Congress. Proposals to increase leaders' influences over the composition, agendas and priorities, schedules, and output of committees have been discussed throughout the twentieth century. Some proposals were adopted by the Senate in 1946, when party policy committees were established by the Legislative Reorganization Act, and by House Democrats in the 1970s. But these reforms have not led party leaders to assume a more assertive posture in their chambers for dealing with committees. In the few cases of leadership-initiated effort to develop distinct, coherent party policy proposals, the proposals have served only as input to standing committee deliberations; committees have rejected the proposals as often as they have accepted and reported them to the floor.[61]

A central problem for leaders is that the tools they have at their disposal must be employed to maintain party harmony as much as to pursue party policy interests. Improvements in leadership tools do not directly reduce conflicts between factions in fragmented parties. In fact, such improvements often increase expectations about leaders' abilities to reduce intraparty conflicts without giving them substantial advantage over other power centers in their chambers. For example, even some reformers have seen the Democratic Steering and Policy Committee, chaired by the Speaker, as a release valve for pressure from rank-and-file members who want the caucus to dictate policy actions to House committees, putting the leadership in a position of protecting standing committee prerogatives instead of molding policy for the committees to ratify.[62] While such a role might give leaders a source of leverage over committees, the fact is that leaders are just as fearful of regular caucus action as are individual committees, and they generally would prefer quiet, behind-the-scenes discussions with committee members to try to direct a caucus's actions. Leaders are not in a position, except in isolated cases, to direct either committees or their caucuses in a concerted action to develop coherent party policy.

NOTES

1. See papers by Charles O. Jones, Randall B. Ripley, Donald Allen Robinson, and Allen Schick in U.S., Senate, Commission on the Operation of the Senate, *Policymaking Role of Leadership in the Senate*, 94th Congress, 2d sess.
2. Barbara Sinclair, *Majority Leadership in the U.S. House* (Baltimore: The Johns Hopkins University Press, 1983), Chap. 1.
3. See the discussion in Chapter 3; also see Lewis A. Froman and Randall B. Ripley, "Conditions for Party Leadership," *American Political Science Review* 59 (1965): 52-63.
4. See Joseph Cooper and David W. Brady, "Institutional Context and Leadership Style: The House from Cannon to Rayburn," *American Political Science Review* 75 (June 1981): 411-425.
5. Sinclair, *Majority Leadership*, Chap. 1.
6. Ibid.
7. Kenneth A. Shepsle, *The Giant Jigsaw Puzzle* (Chicago: University of Chicago Press, 1978), 111.
8. See Judy Schneider, "Senate Rules and Practices on Committee, Subcommittee, and Chairmanship Assignment Limitations, as of April 20, 1982," Congressional Research Service, May 18, 1982.
9. This discussion is adapted from Shepsle, *The Giant Jigsaw Puzzle*, Chap. 6.
10. Louis P. Westefield, "Majority Party Leadership and the Committee System in the House of Representatives," *American Political Science Review* 69 (December 1974): 1593-1605.
11. Ibid., 1599.
12. Shepsle, *The Giant Jigsaw Puzzle*, 117-118.

13. Bruce A. Ray and Steven S. Smith, "Leverage, Reward, Accommodation, and Administration: Four Theories on the Growth of Congressional Committee Seats," paper presented at the annual meeting of the Southern Political Science Association, Atlanta, Georgia, October 27-30, 1982.
14. On the House, see Sidney Waldman, "Majority Leadership in the House of Representatives," *Political Science Quarterly* 95 (Fall 1980). On the Senate, see Robert L. Peabody, *Leadership in Congress* (Boston: Little, Brown & Co., 1976), 349-350.
15. On the House, see Shepsle, *the Giant Jigsaw Puzzle*, 29. On the Senate tradition, see Donald R. Matthews, *U.S. Senators and Their World* (New York: Vintage Books, 1960), 127.
16. Robert L. Peabody, "Senate Party Leadership: From the 1950s to the 1980s," in *Understanding Congressional Leadership*, ed. Frank H. Mackaman (Washington, D.C.: CQ Press, 1981), 82.
17. Charles O. Jones, "Senate Party Leadership in Public Policy," in *Policymaking Role*, 26.
18. Steven S. Smith, "The Budget Battles of 1981: The Role of the Majority Party Leadership," in *American Politics and Public Policy*, ed. Allan P. Sindler (Washington, D.C.: CQ Press, 1982).
19. Shepsle, *The Giant Jigsaw Puzzle*, Chap. 9; Steven S. Smith and Bruce A. Ray, "The Impact of Congressional Reform: House Democratic Committee Assignments," *Congress & The Presidency* 10 (Autumn, 1983): 219-240.
20. Smith and Ray, "The Impact of Congressional Reform."
21. Ray and Smith, "Theories on the Growth of Congressional Committee Seats."
22. See Irwin N. Gertzog, "Routinization of Committee Assignments in the U.S. House of Representatives," *American Journal of Political Science* 29 (November 1976): 693-713.
23. See Nicholas A. Masters, "Committee Assignments in the House of Representatives," *American Political Science Review* 55 (June 1961): 345-357; Matthews, *U.S. Senators*, 128, 135, 148-158.
24. These data were collected by one of the authors who attended the Steering and Policy committee on committees meetings at the beginning of the 97th Congress.
25. See Smith, "The Budget Battles."
26. Bruce A. Ray and Steven S. Smith, "Committee-Specific Patterns of Assignment and Growth in the U.S. House of Representatives," paper presented at the annual meeting of the Midwest Political Science Association, Chicago, Illinois, April 20-23, 1983.
27. This discussion draws from Smith and Ray, "The Impact of Congressional Reform," 28; George Goodwin, *The Little Legislatures* (Amherst: University of Massachusetts Press, 1970), 71.
28. Smith and Ray, "The Impact of Congressional Reform," provides the following table on southern overrepresentation on Steering and Policy during recent Congresses (southern percentage is reported):

Congress	94	95	96	97
Steering and Policy	30.4	29.2	25.0	37.9
All House Democrats	33.0	32.5	32.1	32.9
Southern Bias	−2.6	−3.3	−6.1	+5.0

South includes the 11 states of the Confederacy plus West Virginia, Kentucky, and Oklahoma.

29. See Shepsle, *The Giant Jigsaw Puzzle*, 146. Smith and Ray, "The Impact of Congressional Reform," provides the following table on party support and conservative coalition support among House Democrats and Steering and Policy members (calculated from Congressional Quarterly tallies):

Party and Conservative Coalition Support on Steering and Policy

	Party Support		Conservative Coalition Support	
Congress	Steering and Policy Mean	Caucus Mean	Steering and Policy Mean	Caucus Mean
94	63	42	−49	−18
95	56	46	−26	−21
96	54	41	−34	−20
97	50	48	−15	−16

Party support = party unity score—party opposition score.
Conservative coalition support = conservative coalition support score—conservative coalition opposition score.
Scores are taken from the previous Congress.

30. On prereform practices see Shepsle, *The Giant Jigsaw Puzzle*, 179-180, 199-200.
31. Bruce A. Ray, "Committee Attractiveness in the U.S. House, 1963-1981," *American Journal of Political Science* 26 (August 1982): 609-613.
32. See Smith and Ray, "The Impact of Congressional Reform."
33. See Gertzog, "Routinization of Committee Assignments."
34. See "Dec. 2 House Caucuses; Preparing for the 94th," *Congressional Quarterly Weekly Report*, November 16, 1974, 3118.
35. Peabody, "Senate Party Leadership," 74.
36. Donald Allen Robinson, "If the Senate Democrats Want Leadership: An Analysis of the History and Prospects of the Majority Policy Committee," in U.S., Senate, Commission on the Operation of the Senate, *Policymaking Role of Leadership in the Senate*, 94th Congress, 2d sess., 47.
37. Randall B. Ripley, *Power in the Senate* (New York: St. Martin's Press, 1969), 103.
38. Christopher J. Deering and Steven S. Smith, "Majority Party Leadership and the New House Subcommittee System," in *Understanding Congressional Leadership*, ed. Mackaman, 261-296.
39. This is similar to the pattern reported in the 1960s. See Charles L. Clapp, *The Congressman* (Washington, D.C.: Brookings Institution, 1963), 270-271. Also see Randall B. Ripley, *Party Leaders in the House of Representatives* (Washington, D.C.: Brookings Institution, 1967), Chap. 7.
40. Quoted in Alan Ehrenhalt, "Special Report: The Individualist Senate," *Congressional Quarterly Weekly Report*, September 4, 1982, 2181.
41. The committees referred to are Foreign Affairs, Banking, and Energy and Commerce. For background on the disputes see Irwin B. Arieff, "House Approves Committee Assignments; Ratios Disputed," *Congressional Quarterly Weekly Report*, January 31, 1981, 223; Richard Whittle, "House Liberals Retain Clout on Foreign Affairs Panel," *Congressional Quarterly Weekly Report*, February 7, 1981, 263; Nadine Cohodas, "Two Housing Subcommittees Take Shape After Settling Party, Personnel Disputes," *Congressional Quarterly Weekly Report*, February 7, 1981, 283.

Committees in Congress

42. "Democrats Fear Fallout From Hays Affair," *Congressional Quarterly Weekly Report*, May 29, 1976, 1331.
43. Richard F. Fenno, *Congressmen in Committees* (Boston: Little, Brown & Co., 1973), 24. Poor election results occasionally have played a role in the demise of incumbent party leaders; see Peabody, *Leadership in Congress*, 303-306.
44. Quoted in Peabody, *Leadership in Congress*, 33-40.
45. The Patterson reform committee suggested expanding the Speaker's authority to set time limits for committee consideration of all legislation that is multiply-referred, but the proposal was not adopted.
46. For a more complete development of this argument, see Sinclair, *Majority Leadership in the U.S. House*, Chap. 1.
47. Lawrence C. Dodd and Bruce I. Oppenheimer, "The House in Transition: Change and Consolidation," in *Congress Reconsidered*, 2d ed., ed. Lawrence C. Dodd and Bruce I. Oppenheimer (Washington, D.C.: CQ Press, 1981), 31-61; Barbara Sinclair, "Majority Party Leadership Strategies for Coping with the New U.S. House," in *Understanding Congressional Leadership*, 182-184; Norman J. Ornstein, "The House and the Senate in a New Congress," in *The New Congress*, ed. Thomas E. Mann and Norman J. Ornstein (Washington, D.C.: American Enterprise Institute for Public Policy Research, 1981), 363-383.
48. Sinclair, *Majority Leadership in the U.S. House*, Chap. 1.
49. Walter J. Oleszek, "Multiple Referral of Legislation in the House," paper presented at the annual meeting of the American Political Science Association, Washington, D.C., August 28-31, 1980.
50. U.S., House, Select Committee on Committees, *Final Report* 96th Congress, 2d sess., 474.
51. Bruce I. Oppenheimer, "Policy Effects of U.S. House Reform: Decentralization and the Capacity to Resolve Energy Issues," *Legislative Studies Quarterly* 5 (February 1980): 5-30.
52. On O'Neill's role, see Smith, "The Budget Battles of 1981"; on Baker's role, see James A. Miller and James D. Range, "Reconciling an Irreconcilable Budget: The New Politics of the Budget Process," *Harvard Journal on Legislation* 20 (Winter 1983).
53. Minority party leaders usually are consulted, especially in the Senate where unanimous consent agreements now structure most of that chamber's schedule.
54. Jones, "Senate Party Leadership," 25.
55. Barbara Sinclair, "The Speaker's Task Force in the Post-Reform House of Representatives," *American Political Science Review* 75 (June 1981): 397-410.
56. See Peabody, "Senate Party Leadership," 67.
57. Peabody's speculations on this point have proven accurate. See Robert L. Peabody, "Committees from the Leadership Perspective," *The Annals of the American Academy* 411 (1974): 140.
58. Ehrenhalt, "The Individualist Senate," 2177.
59. Ibid., 2176.
60. Lewis A. Froman, Jr., and Randall B. Ripley, "Conditions for Party Leadership," *American Political Science Review* 59 (1965): 52-63.
61. See Robinson; also see examples provided by James L. Sundquist, *The Decline and Resurgence of Congress* (Washington, D.C.: The Brookings Insititution, 1981), Chap. VIII.
62. Bruce F. Freed, "House Democrats: Dispute Over Caucus Role," *Congressional Quarterly Weekly Report*, May 3, 1975, 911-915.

Change in
Congressional Committees | 9

This study has examined the factors that shape Congress's committees. The emphasis has been on how individual committees differ and change. The analysis has shown that committees differ greatly in the fragmentation of their formal jurisdictions, the salience of their agendas, the conflict in their environments, and the goals pursued by their members. And each of these has been shown to be related to committee organization, activity, and attractiveness. More importantly, the study has shown that formal jurisdictions, agenda and environmental characteristics, and member goals change over time, providing an impetus for change in committee organization and activities. In this concluding chapter we make some summary comments about the direction and nature of change in committees during the last two decades.

Structure
and Participation in Committees

In Chapter 1 two distinct characteristics of congressional organization were identified: the number of individuals effectively participating in congressional decision making and the number of separate decision-making units that comprise the larger institution. Subsequent chapters have shown that change has occurred in both of these characteristics during the last 15 years. The direction of change since the late 1960s is indicated in Figure 9-1.

Change has not been uniform in the two chambers of Congress. In the House, subcommittees now are more numerous than they were in the 1960s, although the growth of subcommittees has been capped. The House has failed to reduce the number of standing committees. Through more independent subcommittees, better staffing, and other changes, rank-and-file members are more effective participants within and out-

Figure 9-1 Direction of Change in Structure and Participation in the House and Senate Since the Late 1960s

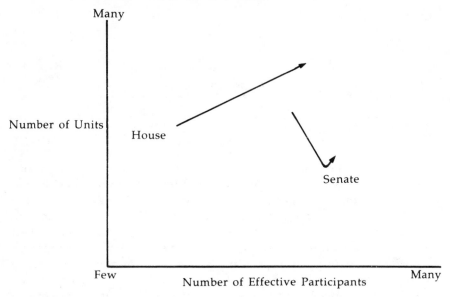

side of their committees. In the Senate, the growth in the number of subcommittees was reduced as a result of the 1977 limit on the number of subcommittee assignments a senator could hold. As noted in Chapter 5, though, several committees added subcommittees in the early 1980s and many senators acquired more subcommittee assignments than the 1977 limit allowed. Rank-and-file participation in committee and extracommittee decision making remains high in the Senate.

Subcommittee Orientation in Committees

The change represented in Figure 9-1 is far from uniform for all committees. Thus generalizations about decentralization or subcommittee government, even for the House, tend to obscure the *variety* of subcommittee orientations of committees. Committees exhibit multiple structural and participatory patterns. In some cases, decentralization means that subcommittee staff, rather than full committee staff, dominate decision making. In other cases, decentralization means that a subcommittee chair dominates his or her subcommittee. In yet other cases, decentralization only means that two battlefields exist for legislation: one in subcommittee and one at the full committee level.

To look at the direction and variety of change for individual committees, it is useful to create a composite measure of "subcommittee orientation." The measure used here is based on four properties examined in previous chapters: the percentage of reported legislation receiving subcommittee consideration (Chapter 5), the percentage of meetings held at the subcommittee level (Chapter 5), the percentage of bills managed by subcommittee chairs (Chapter 6), and the percentage of total committee staff employed by subcommittees (Chapter 7). The components of the index thus include four key aspects of committee decision making: committee procedure, activity, leadership, and resources. This composite index helps to summarize findings detailed in previous chapters, permitting an examination of the overall change in subcommittee orientation between the 91st Congress and the 96th Congress, changes by individual committees during that time, and the range of subcommittee orientations present among committees.

Change in Subcommittee Orientation

Table 9-1 provides a rank-ordering of House and Senate committees based on the mean of the four measures just noted. Two points are worth highlighting. First, while there is noticeably greater overlap among the House and Senate committees in the rank-ordering of the 91st Congress, House committees were clearly more subcommittee oriented in both periods. On average, House committees became noticeably more subcommittee oriented between these two Congresses. House committees had an average "subcommittee orientation" of 47 percent in the 91st Congress (1969-1971) and 62 percent in the 96th Congress (1979-1981). In contrast, Senate committees became (very marginally) more full committee oriented by the 96th Congress— dropping from 28 to 27 percent on average. Put slightly differently, 13 of the 17 House committees examined became more subcommittee oriented while 7 of the 13 Senate committees became more full committee oriented.

Second, the greater role of House subcommittees was at least partially related to member goals. In the 91st Congress, policy-oriented committees and constituency-oriented committees had almost identical averages—48.5 and 47.5 percent, respectively. But by the 96th Congress, the policy committees had become decidedly more subcommittee oriented (again on average) than their constituency-oriented counterparts—70.3 and 59.3, respectively. Thus within the House the policy

Table 9-1 Subcommittee Orientation by Committee: 91st and 96th Congresses*

91st (1969-1971)		96th (1979-1981)		
Committee	Average	Committee	Average	(Change)
H. Government Operations	77	H. Commerce	79	(+37)
H. Administration	66	H. Judiciary	78	(+16)
H. Judiciary	62	H. Banking	78	(+48)
H. Armed Services	60	H. Public Works	75	(+38)
S. Labor	60	H. Government Operations	70	(−7)
H. Merchant Marine	59	H. Science and Technology	68	(+18)
H. District of Columbia	57	H. Education and Labor	65	(+24)
H. Interior	53	H. Post Office	65	(+28)
H. Agriculture	51	H. Interior	63	(+10)
S. Judiciary	51	H. Administration	63	(−3)
S. Appropriations	51**	H. Merchant Marine	62	(+3)
H. Science and Astronomy	50	H. Armed Services	58	(−2)
S. Government Operations	46	H. Agriculture	57	(+6)
S. Interior	45	S. Appropriations	56**	(+5)
H. Commerce	42	H. Foreign Affairs	52	(+13)
H. Education and Labor	41	H. District of Columbia	51	(−6)
H. Foreign Affairs	39	S. Labor	50	(+10)
S. Commerce	38	S. Small Business	48**	(—)
H. Public Works	37	H. Ways and Means	44	(+44)
H. Post Office	37	S. Agriculture	43	(+18)
H. Veterans' Affairs	33	S. Governmental Affairs	43	(−3)
S. Banking	32	H. Veterans' Affairs	38	(+5)
H. Banking	30	S. Judiciary	37	(−14)
S. Armed Services	29	S. Energy and Natural Res.	36	(−9)
S. Agriculture	25	S. Armed Services	34	(+5)
S. District of Columbia	22	S. Commerce	32	(−6)
S. Public Works	19	S. Env. and Public Works	31	(+12)
S. Rules and Administration	16	S. Banking	20	(−12)
S. Post Office	9	S. Foreign Relations	10	(+1)
S. Foreign Relations	9	S. Finance	9	(+6)
S. Finance	3	S. Veterans' Affairs	0	(—)
H. Ways and Means	0	S. Rules and Administration	0	(−16)
S. Aerospace	0**	S. Budget	0**	(—)
Overall Average	38	Overall Average	46	(+8)
House Average	47	House Average	62	(+15)
Senate Average	28	Senate Average	27	(−1)

* Data for the second period for bill management are from the 95th Congress; for the other three indicators the data are from the 96th Congress.
** Committees for which only three indicators are available; others are excluded.
Note: On some committees in both Congresses, staff are listed under the full committee and under one or more subcommittee staffs. They are counted here as subcommittee staff (but only once if they appear under more than one subcommittee) and included in the overall committee figure for the purposes of arriving at committee averages.

committees accounted for the lion's share of the move toward greater subcommittee activity and resources.

This pattern can be partly explained by policy-oriented members' eagerness—especially on Banking, Commerce, Foreign Affairs, and Government Operations—to take advantage of new procedures and resources. The newly vitalized subcommittees provided an attractive vehicle for pursuing personal policy interests. In contrast, constituency committees, which depend more on consensus (or perhaps more accurately on mutual noninterference) in their operations, proved to be less intent on exploiting the new procedures and resources. The Post Office and Civil Service Committee (with major increases in subcommittee staff and bill management by subcommittee chairs) and the Public Works Committee (with major increases in hearings on reported legislation and bill management) are the most dramatic exceptions. Moreover, all of the committees faced constant, although uneven, changes in their political environments and agendas that may help to explain the overall shift toward greater emphasis on subcommittees.

No similar patterns appear in the Senate. In large part this is because senators—with larger numbers of committee assignments and a traditionally more open legislative process—are less dependent on committee assignments to pursue personal goals. Senators also have greater personal resources at their disposal than do members of the House. As a result, internal committee organization has been less vital to personal goal achievement in the Senate.

Patterns of Subcommittee Orientation

To examine variety in subcommittee orientations among committees after the reforms of the 1970s, committees have been placed into high and low categories for each of the four variables (50 percent and up as high, 49 percent and below as low). With 4 indicators there are 16 possible combinations of characteristics, or 16 possible types of committees. Of the 30 committees examined, 24 fall into just 5 of the 16 types (Table 9-2). Moreover, each of the 6 remaining committees exhibits a pattern similar to one of the 5 basic patterns; a shift from high to low (or vice versa) on one variable would have included each committee in one of the 5 types. These committees are listed in parentheses in the table.

The patterns indicate that the 50 percent mark for referral of reported legislation to subcommittee is the easiest threshold for committees to achieve—23 of the 30 committees fall into the high category on this indicator. Bill management follows with 20 of the 30 committees falling in the high category. Thus a majority of the committees—

Table 9-2 Typology of Subcommittee Orientation: 96th Congress

	Type				
	I	II	III	IV	V
Indicators:					
Reported Legislation	H	H	H	H	L
Bill Management	H	H	H	L	L
Meetings	H	H	L	L	L
Subcommittee Staff	H	L	L	L	L
Committees:	HIFC	HPWT	HPOCS	HVA	SBHUA
	HJ	HIIA	HIR	SAS	SFR
	HBFU	HAd	HWM	SENR	SF
	HST	HAS	SHR	SCST	SVA
	(HEL.)	HAg	SANF	(SGA)	SRA
	(HMMF)	HDC			(SEPW)
	(HGO)				(SJ)

Key to committees (some committee names have changed since the 96th Congress): House Administration (HAd); House Agriculture (HAg); House Armed Services (HAS); House Banking, Finance, and Urban Affairs (HBFUA); House District of Columbia (HDC); House Education and Labor (HEL); House Government Operations (HGO); House Interior and Insular Affairs (HIIA); House Interstate and Foreign Commerce (HIFC); House International Relations (HIR); House Judiciary (HJ); House Merchant Marine and Fisheries (HMMF); House Post Office and Civil Service (HPOCS); House Public Works and Transportation (HPWT); House Science and Technology (HST); House Veterans' Affairs (HVA); House Ways and Means (HWM); Senate Agriculture, Nutrition, and Forestry (SANF); Senate Armed Services (SAS); Senate Banking, Housing, and Urban Affairs (SBHUA); Senate Commerce, Science, and Transportation (SCST); Senate Environment and Public Works (SEPW); Senate Energy and Natural Resources (SENR); Senate Finance (SF); Senate Foreign Relations (SFR); Senate Governmental Affairs (SGA); Senate Human Resources (SHR); Senate Judiciary (SJ); Senate Rules and Administration (SRA); Senate Veterans' Affairs (SVA).

Note: Committees in parentheses are listed under closest type. Patterns for the six committees in parentheses for the four indicators, respectively, are as follows: House Education and Labor: high (H), high (H), low (L), high (H); House Government Operations and House Merchant Marine: H,L,H,H; Senate Governmental Affairs: H,L,L,H; Senate Environment and Public Works: L,L,H,L; and Senate Judiciary: L,L,L,H. The table excludes committees where data for only three of the indicators were available: House Appropriations, Senate Appropriations, House Budget, Senate Budget, House Small Business, and Senate Small Business.

although decidedly more in the House than in the Senate—achieve this minimal level of emphasis on subcommittees. In contrast, only 12 of the 30 committees have more meetings at the subcommittee level than at the full committee level and only 9 of the 30 have more staff at the subcommittee level. A scant four committees fall into the high category on all four indicators.

On the surface, Type I committees appear to be the most "decentralized." But appearances may be deceiving. More accurately, it could be said that Type I committees have the most *active* subcommittees. In general these committees feature independent, active, policy-oriented subcommittees. These are not necessarily the prototypes of autonomous subcommittees or "subcommittee government," however (see Chapter 5). Five of these seven committees are policy committees. Challenges to decisions made by Type I subcommittees occur frequently at the full committee level—especially on the five policy committees. Thus while the Type I subcommittees are active and independent, they are not necessarily autonomous.

Type II committees more closely approximate the idea of subcommittee government. Each of these committees falls into the high category on all categories except the staff indicator. Yet this (relative) lack of staff actually reveals an important characteristic about these committees. In contrast to Type I committees, four of the six Type II committees are constituency oriented. Subcommittees on these panels tend to be differentiated along clientele-related lines. Unlike policy committees, these constituency committees operate with an eye toward securing benefits for constituents rather than prosecuting policy interests. As noted earlier, this yields a decision-making process characterized by mutual noninterference. In such committees, independent subcommittee staff, used on policy committees to fight battles for the subcommittee chair at the full committee level and on the floor, become much less desirable. Indeed, the full committee seems much more likely to "rubber stamp" the actions of Type II subcommittees than of Type I subcommittees. Hence, despite the lack of staff, Type II committees are better examples of subcommittee government than are Type I committees.

Type III committees have subcommittees that are fairly active but less independent or autonomous than either Type I or II subcommittees. On at least four of these six committees—House Foreign Affairs, House Ways and Means, Senate Agriculture, and Senate Labor—the panel's most important bills are marked up (drafted in final form) by the full committee. Thus the percentage of subcommittee meetings (chiefly markups) on these committees is low, as is subcommittee staff—even though the percentage of subcommittee hearings tends to be high and subcommittee chairs tend to manage legislation referred to their subcommittees. These are clearly mixed cases, but certainly not examples of subcommittee government.

The remaining committees are essentially full committee oriented. Type IV subcommittees actively hold hearings, but virtually all markups are held in full committee. Type V committees are decidedly full committee oriented, and their subcommittees are used primarily for limited hearings. With a single exception, House Veterans' Affairs, all of the Type IV and V committees are from the Senate. Without exception, Type I and II committees are from the House.

These patterns indicate that differences among committees are not merely random. And they are not explained solely by the idiosyncratic characteristsics of committee or subcommittee chairs. Subcommittee orientations differ systematically from one committee to another. Institutional factors—namely, House and Senate characteristics—explain much of this pattern. Indeed, the committee-by-committee data summarized here reinforce interchamber differences described throughout the book. But formal rules, agendas, environments, and jurisdictions continue to explain a large portion of the variety that exists. Committees are not only the creatures of their respective chambers, they are also the creatures of the members who comprise them.

Future Changes in Committees

Committees have been and will remain a central if ever changing aspect of congressional decision making. Whenever change in Congress is contemplated, and that is an almost constant occurrence, committees will be the target for reform. The implications of this study for reform are numerous, but two deserve special attention.

First, reforms may well apply to committees equally, but they will never affect them equally. Whether organizational guidelines affecting committees are provided by statute or by chamber or party rules, the implementation of structural and procedural changes will depend on the political balance of power within the chamber and the personal goals of those who must put new structures and procedures into effect. Staff may need to be allocated; rules may need to be interpreted and followed in real rather than hypothetical circumstances; and new structures may need to be designed. Committees will respond differently to these situations. They may implement them at different rates. They may ignore them altogether. Member goals play an important role in this process. Liberal, policy-oriented Democrats were prominent in the reform movement of the 1970s, for example. Other, more constituency-oriented members, may have given lip-service (and votes) to reform, but they were in no rush to implement fully all of the reform provisions because their basic goals already were being met for the most part.

The second general lesson is that the House and Senate will continue to differ in the types of demands for change and in the approaches taken to change. In the Senate, approaches to institutional change are likely to continue to be chamber-oriented. That is to say, they are likely to focus on floor procedure and leadership problems rather than on committees. Committees are simply less crucial to the pursuit of personal goals in the Senate than in the House, and they are likely to remain so as long as the level of floor participation stays high. Nevertheless, reforms aimed at the flow of business on the floor may affect committees more than almost any other change. Restraints on floor participation, for example, would increase the importance of participation during committee deliberations. In turn, the permeability of Senate committees, the tolerance of committee chairs holding great discretion, and the full committee orientation of many Senate committees may be altered. In contrast, reforms in the House are likely to continue to be oriented toward formal structures, although strong opposition will persist whenever proposals run counter to member goals.

Conclusion:
The Importance of Committees _____

We approached this study cautiously because some observers have questioned the significance of subcommittees. House reforms of the 1970s had opened floor deliberations to more members and the majority party caucus had gained a greater role in the process, with standing committees losing some of their autonomy. Senate individualism continued unabated and Senate committees continued to face seemingly random, and often successful, challenges on the floor. All of this seemed to call into question the longstanding belief that committees mattered.

We have found that committees still matter. While member specialization has declined and committees are not so autonomous as they were in the 1960s, most members' legislative activity remains structured by their committee and subcommittee assignments. Committees remain crucial to their personal goals and members continue to calculate carefully the value of particular committee assignments to their personal goal pursuits. Members of both chambers still expect standing committees to commit the time and energy to write nearly all important legislation. And leaders on most legislative issues emerge from committees with appropriate jurisdictions. Floor battles, despite their increased importance, are still rearguard actions for the most part, a means of appeal for those who lose in committee. As long as committees remain valuable to large numbers of members, their role in the legislative process is assured.

Appendix

Table A-1 Changing Standing Subcommittee Structure in Congressional Standing Committees: 1949-1982*

	Congress																
	81	82	83	84	85	86	87	88	89	90	91	92	93	94	95	96	97
House																	
Reductions	−33	0	−7	−5	−8	−8	−4	−4	−3	−9	−3	−2	−1	0	−7	−3	
Additions	+4	+11	+15	+28	+2	+10	+4	+7	+9	+3	+5	+3	+11	+13	+4	+2	
Total Subcommittees	62	73	81	104	98	104	104	107	113	107	109	110	120	140	137	136	
Total Committees	19	19	19	19	19	20	20	20	20	21	21	21	22	22	22	22	22
Senate																	
Reductions	−12	−6	−9	−3	−2	−4	−5	−6	0	−1	−5	−3	0	−13	−23	−8	
Additions	+14	+10	+10	+24	0	+6	+6	+3	+7	+7	+8	+25	0	+8	+3	+2	
Total Subcommittees	63	65	66	87	85	87	88	85	92	98	101	115	127	122	96	90	101
Total Committees	15	15	15	15	16	16	16	16	16	16	16	17	18	18	15	15	16

* Reductions = total number of subcommittees dropped on committees with a net loss at the beginning of the new Congress; additions = total number of subcommittees added on committees with a net gain at the beginning of the new Congress. Change figures exclude losses and gains due to the creation or elimination of standing committees and thus do not always reflect the increases and decreases in the total standing subcommittee rows. The 94th-97th Congress House figures exclude Budget Committee task forces.

Source: Sula P. Richardson and Susan Schjelderup, "Standing Committee Structure and Assignments: House and Senate," Congressional Research Service, Report No. 82-42 GOV., March 12, 1982.

Committees in Congress

Table A-2 Jurisdictional Fragmentation Among House Committees

Committee	Number of Depts./Agencies Under Jurisdiction	Number of Areas of Legislative Jurisdiction in Chamber Rules	Average Rank
Appropriations	1	*	1
Commerce	3	4	3.5
Interior	6	5	5.5
Education & Labor	4	8	6
Public Works	4	9	6.5
Foreign Affairs	8	5	6.5
Judiciary	11	2	6.5
Agriculture	16	2	9
Science & Technology	8	10	9
Government Operations	1	18	9.5
Merchant Marine	11	10	10.5
Banking	8	15	11.5
Armed Services	13	12	12.5
Ways and Means	13	13	13
House Administration	19	7	13
Small Business	6	20	13
Post Office & Civil Service	13	15	14
District of Columbia	16	13	14.5
Veterans' Affairs	18	15	16.5
Rules	20	19	19.5
Stand. of Official Conduct	20	21	20.5
Budget	*	4	4

* Appropriations has jurisdiction over the funding of nearly all federal programs. Budget has no direct jurisdiction over any federal agency but nevertheless has jurisdiction over budget resolutions that may indirectly affect all federal programs.

Source: The number of departments was calculated from Judy Schneider, "House of Representatives Committee Jurisdiction Over Executive Branch Agencies," Congressional Research Service, September 28, 1979, with updates by the authors. 1981 chamber rules were used.

Table A-3   Jurisdictional Fragmentation Among Senate Committees

Committee	Ranked by:		Average Rank
	Number of Depts./Agencies Under Jurisdiction	Number of Areas of Legislative Jurisdiction in Chamber Rules	
Appropriations	1	*	1
Labor	3	2	2.5
Commerce	4	3	3.5
Foreign Relations	6	3	4.5
Govtl. Affairs	1	11	6
Judiciary	8	5	6.5
Environment & Public Works	7	6	6.5
Banking	5	9	7
Energy & Natural Resources	8	8	8
Agriculture	11	6	8.5
Finance	10	11	10.5
Armed Services	11	13	12
Rules & Administration	14	10	12
Veterans' Affairs	13	14	13.5
Small Business	14	16	15
Budget	*	15	15

* Appropriations has jurisdiction over the funding of nearly all federal programs. Budget has no direct jurisdiction over any federal agency but nevertheless has jurisdiction over budget resolutions that may indirectly affect all federal programs.

Source: The number of departments was calculated from Judy Schneider, "Senate Committee Jurisdiction Over Executive Branch Nominations," Congressional Research Service, October 31, 1979, with updates by the authors. 1981 chamber rules were used.

Table A-4 Types of Witnesses Before House Committees During the 91st and 96th Congresses, by Relationship to the Executive Branch

	Executive		Public		Congressional		Total	
	91	96	91	96	91	96	91	96
Administration-oriented:								
Foreign Affairs	54	168	46	77	12	19	113	276
Ways and Means	19	50	290	682	33	92	342	832
Budget	—	21	—	22	—	4	—	54
Agency-oriented, broad:								
Appropriations	741	927	266	700	93	105	1157	1749
Commerce	72	220	170	661	55	57	299	958
Science	25	137	33	242	1	8	61	391
Judiciary	14	66	41	169	31	23	89	287
Govt. Operations	83	51	51	85	14	14	156	158
Educ. & Labor	46	48	310	524	27	18	385	596
Banking	34	27	142	91	20	20	197	144
Public Works	21	22	82	321	38	40	148	361
Agency-oriented, narrow:								
Armed services	69	207	35	88	28	53	133	350
Merchant Marine	66	129	118	339	18	30	202	498
Post Office	22	49	70	155	16	13	109	221
Interior	16	39	178	121	17	10	213	171
Small Business	34	29	65	46	5	7	105	84
Agriculture	7	74	99	199	28	21	134	247
Veterans	8	17	30	80	13	4	51	102
Others:								
Dist. of Columbia	6	9	44	12	6	24	112	68
H. Administration	n.a.	7	n.a.	16	n.a.	16	n.a.	32
Rules	(see note)							

Note: The figures exclude witnesses that are not of one of the three listed types, including judicial branch witnesses. Thus there is a discrepancy between the sum of the three types and the total. The Rules Committee does not print hearings for special orders. Witnesses before both full committees and subcommittees are included.

Source: A one-fifth sample of printed committee hearings.

Table A-5 Types of Witnesses Before Senate Committees During the 91st and 96th Congresses, by Relationship to the Executive Branch

| | Type of Witness | | | | | | | |
| | Executive | | Public | | Congressional | | Total | |
	91	96	91	96	91	96	91	96
Administration- **oriented:**								
Foreign Relations	36	65	36	46	6	17	80	129
Finance	12	24	369	222	29	18	410	267
Budget	—	13	—	32	—	5	—	54
Agency-oriented, **broad:**								
Appropriations	291	226	183	165	15	26	494	434
Commerce	34	83	147	280	16	15	199	379
Judiciary	26	80	127	200	14	25	176	308
Govt'l. Affairs	95	77	95	148	10	7	138	242
Energy & Nat.Res.	28	69	184	361	44	28	256	463
Banking	21	61	130	185	23	25	176	276
Env. & Public Works	42	38	300	137	42	34	384	210
Agency-oriented, **narrow:**								
Armed Services	84	53	5	19	0	3	89	76
Agriculture	33	31	298	151	41	10	372	193
Sel. Small Bus.	—	24	—	103	—	11	—	143
Veterans	—	11	—	49	—	7	—	68
Others:								
Rules & Admin.	n.a.	2	n.a.	38	n.a.	8	n.a.	50

Note: The figures exclude witnesses that are not of one of the three listed types, including judicial branch witnesses. Thus there is a discrepancy between the sum of the three types and the total. Budget and Veterans did not exist in the 91st Congress. Small Business did not gain legislative jurisdiction until the 96th Congress. Aeronautics and Space, District of Columbia, and Post Office and Civil Service were abolished in 1977 and have been excluded. Rules and Administration printed no hearings in the 91st Congress. Witnesses before both full committees and subcommittees are included.

Source: A one-fifth sample of printed committee hearings.

Table A-6 Other Committee Requests of House Democrats Requesting Each Policy Committee, 86th to 90th and 92d to 97th Congresses (*number of requesters in parentheses*)

Banking		Education and Labor	
86-90 (53)	92-97 (48)	86-90 (35)	92-97 (42)
Commerce (17)	Commerce (18)	Banking (14)	Commerce (13)
Public Works (15)	Govt. Ops. (16)	For. Affairs (13)	Public Works (13)
Ed.&Labor (14)	Science (11)	Commerce (12)	Interior (12)
For. Affairs (11)	Interior (10)	Judiciary (9)	Govt. Ops. (11)
Science (9)	Ways & Means (9)	Interior (6)	Agriculture (10)
Judiciary (9)	Appropriations (8)	Post Office (6)	

Foreign Affairs		Commerce	
86-90 (44)	92-97 (30)	86-90 (67)	92-97 (91)
Ed. & Labor (13)	Interior (10)	Banking (17)	Govt. Ops. (28)
Banking (11)	Commerce (9)	Public Works (15)	Interior (28)
Commerce (11)	Science (8)	Interior (14)	Public Works (20)
Appropriations (8)	Ed. & Labor (7)	Judiciary (13)	Banking (18)
Judiciary (8)	Govt. Ops. (7)	Science (12)	Science (18)
Science (8)			

Government Operations		Judiciary	
86-90 (33)	92-97 (82)	86-90 (37)	92-97 (26)
Interior (11)	Commerce (28)	Commerce (13)	Commerce (14)
Agriculture (6)	Interior (22)	Armed Ser. (12)	Govt. Ops. (13)
Commerce (6)	Public Works (18)	Banking (9)	Interior (10)
Judiciary (6)	Banking (16)	Ed. & Labor (9)	Public Works (7)

Note: To the extent possible, other requested committees are excluded at natural break points. N's include total freshman and nonfreshman requesters for each period.

Source: Written assignment requests. See Chapter 4, footnote 55.

Table A-7 Other Committee Requests of House Democrats Requesting Each Constituency Committee, 86th to 90th and 92d to 97th Congresses (*Ns in parentheses*)

Agriculture 86-90(33)	92-97(52)	Armed Service 86-90(53)	92-97(44)
Commerce (11)	Interior (18)	Public Works (15)	Interior (10)
Banking (8)	Commerce (14)	Science (12)	Public Works (9)
Interior (8)	Govt. Ops. (13)	Judiciary (12)	Science (8)
Public Works (7)	Public Works (11)	Interior (8)	Govt. Ops. (7)
Govt. Ops. (6)	Ed. & Labor (10)	Commerce (8)	Merchant Marine (7)

Interior 86-90 (51)	92-97 (85)	Merchant Marine 86-90 (33)	92-97 (27)
Public Works (18)	Commerce (28)	Public Works (6)	Public Works (10)
Commerce (14)	Govt. Ops. (22)	Post Office (4)	Govt. Ops. (8)
Govt. Ops. (11)	Agriculture (18)	Interior (3)	Interior (7)
Post Office (10)	Science (15)		Commerce (7)
Agriculture (8)	Ed. & Labor (12)		Armed Services (6)
Armed Services (8)			

Post Office & Civil Service 86-90 (28)	92-97 (8)	Public Works 86-90 (58)	92-97 (58)
Interior (10)	Banking (4)	Interior (18)	Commerce (20)
Banking (8)	Commerce (4)	Armed Ser. (18)	Govt. Ops. (18)
Commerce (7)	Public Works (3)	Banking (15)	Interior (16)
		Commerce (15)	

Science and Technology 86-90 (45)	92-97 (42)	Veterans Affairs 86-90 (13)	92-97 (15)
Armed Ser. (12)	Commerce (18)	Public Works (7)	Commerce (6)
Commerce (12)	Interior (15)	Armed Ser. (7)	Ed.&Labor (5)
Banking (9)	Banking (11)	Interior (5)	Judiciary (4)
For. Affairs (8)	Public Works (9)	Commerce (5)	
Interior (7)	Armed Ser. (8)	Agriculture (4)	
	For. Affairs (8)		

Small Business 86-90 (-)	92-97 (26)
	Govt. Ops. (8)
	Commerce (8)
	Appropriations (7)
	Banking (6)

Note: To the extent possible, other requested committees are excluded at natural break points. N's include total freshman and nonfreshman requesters for each period.

Source, Written assignment requests. See Chapter 4, footnote 55.

Table A-8 Mean Size of House Subcommittees as a Percentage of Full Committee Size

	91st Congress	*97th Congress*
Constituency Committees:		
Agriculture	23	34
Armed Services	24	30
Interior	51	36
Merchant Marine	48	44
Post Office & Civil Service	31	32
Public Works	64	44
Science and Technology	32	29
Veterans' Affairs	46	39
Small Business	—	24
Policy Committees:		
Banking	38	41
Education and Labor	41	29
Commerce	24	40
Foreign Affairs	30	24
Judiciary	26	28
Government Operations	20	22
Prestige Committees:		
Appropriations	16	18
Budget	—	33*
Rules	no subcommittees	47
Ways and Means	no subcommittees	31
Others:		
District of Columbia	36	50
House Administration	28	28
Standards of Official Conduct	no subcommittees	

* Task forces only.

Table A-9   House Full Committee Chair Bill Management, by Committee (*in percent*)

Committee	Congress 86th	89th	91st	92d	93d	94th	95th
Constituency Committees							
Agriculture	59.3	36.0	26.1	18.5	37.5	38.6	46.4
Armed Services	33.3	30.0	27.7	30.0	16.0	11.5	23.1
Interior	35.9	52.2	30.0	31.6	00.0	00.0	12.9
Merchant Marine	25.0	50.0	10.0	11.5	18.4	68.8	63.3
Public Works	00.0	6.3	6.7	20.0	14.3	22.2	10.4
Policy Committees							
Banking	79.2	88.5	63.6	96.4	64.0	15.9	8.6
Education & Labor	33.3	62.5	79.4	46.7	21.1	9.5	9.1
Government Operations	00.0	00.0	00.0	40.0	57.9	52.4	57.5
Foreign Affairs	30.8	26.1	28.6	18.5	32.4	34.3	14.3
Commerce	78.1	89.5	86.9	100.0	100.0	7.6	6.2
Judiciary	12.0	20.9	11.7	12.0	2.4	00.0	4.2
Prestige Committees							
Appropriations	14.3	31.3	30.0	44.2	50.0	67.9	41.3
Ways and Means	91.1	96.2	57.4	90.5	40.5	64.5	48.4
Undesired Committees							
Post Office & Civil Service	60.0	00.0	68.8	26.7	22.2	19.1	2.1
Veterans' Affairs	88.9	100.0	95.5	100.0	57.1	96.9	80.7
House Administration	30.0	00.0	7.1	16.7	9.1	16.7	30.0
District of Columbia	70.7	29.9	16.7	20.4	41.1	50.0	43.8

Source: *Congressional Record*

Table A-10 Senate Full Committee Chair Bill Management, by Committee (*in percent*).

Committee	*Congress* 86th	91st	95th
Constituency Committees			
Agriculture	7.4	11.1	9.8
Appropriations	0.0	13.0	11.8
Commerce	14.7	5.7	11.3
Energy & Natural Resources (Interior)	2.7	8.9	12.7
Environment & Public Works	14.3	15.8	4.5
Mixed Constituency/Policy Committees			
Armed Services	8.0	18.2	22.2
Banking	0.0	12.5	40.0
Finance	29.7	57.9	38.9
Small Business	—	—	16.7
Policy Committees			
Foreign Relations	47.4	20.0	25.0
Government Affairs	23.1	0.0	8.1
Judiciary	0.0	18.8	2.7
Labor	0.0	8.6	4.0
Undesired Committees			
Rules	25.0	0.0	6.7
Veterans' Affairs	—	—	75.0
District of Columbia	50.0	6.3	—
Post Office	16.7	43.8	—

Source: *Congressional Record*

Index